EDWARD THOMAS: THE COLLECTED POEMS

D1421529

EDWARD THOMAS

The Collected Poems and War Diary, 1917

edited by R. GEORGE THOMAS
with an introduction by PETER SACKS

faber and faber

First published in 2004
by Faber and Faber Limited
3 Queen Square London WC1N 3AU

Photoset by RefineCatch Ltd, Bungay, Suffolk
Printed in England by T. J. International, Padstow, Cornwall

All rights reserved
Faber and Faber gratefully acknowledges its indebtedness to Myfanwy
Thomas for her gracious permission to reprint her father's verse

Editorial matter © The Estate of R. George Thomas, 1978, 1981
Introduction © Peter Sacks, 2004
Foreword by Walter de la Mare from the first edition (1920) of *Collected
Poems* © The Estate of Walter de la Mare, 1920

This book is sold subject to the condition that it shall not,
by way of trade or otherwise, be lent, resold, hired out
or otherwise circulated without the publisher's prior consent
in any form of binding or cover other than that
in which it is published and without a similar condition
including this condition being imposed on the subsequent purchaser

A CIP record for this book
is available from the British Library

ISBN 0-571-22260-9

10 9 8 7 6 5 4 3 2 1

Contents

Introduction

God bless us all, what a thing it is to be nearing 40 *& to know what one likes & know one makes mistakes & yet is right for oneself. How many things I have thought I ought to like & found reasons for liking. But now it is almost like eating apples. I don't pretend to know about pineapples and persimmons, but I know an apple when I smell it, when it makes me swallow my saliva before biting it . . .*
letter to Gordon Bottomley

Like the apple that Edward Thomas invokes in his typically understated yet immediately vivid – almost unconsciously so – rewriting or retasting of the tree of knowledge, his poems are instantly 'knowable' by their distinct savour. Indeed, many, such as 'Old Man', are partly about that intimate, yet uncanny, summoning pause in which we savour what we cannot know by any other means. For Thomas, savouring was the most reliable way of at once identifying the given gifts of life, and of celebrating the very ways in which distinctive objects and experiences resist our very arts of describing them. We inhale. The air is changed, scented with a material yet volatile presence that defies even as it attracts both language and consciousness. We swallow our saliva. The fruit itself remains suspended, not simply known but 'saved', for that instant, in a distilled mingling of memory and anticipation. The apple literally reexerts its own power on the poet, 'making' him do something involuntary. Glands, mouth, throat – not to be doubted, not to be embellished. Familiar, yet charged with something always in reserve, the apple becomes for the moment far more appetizing, even exotic, than the florid and more obviously strange pineapple or persimmon. Is it coincidental ('God bless us all') that the moment ushers in a

wordless, living rejoinder to the poet's preceding sense of
having made mistakes?

Apples included or aside, Edward Thomas is a poet of the
perennial. Not the swagger of 'make it new', but the humility,
attentiveness, and open clarity of perception to 'find' it so.
What 'it' might be – within the language and the art, within
the natural world as registered by the awakened senses, mem-
ory, imagination, and, above all, within the constantly reno-
vated affections of a human being who was neither immune
from depression nor less than acutely aware of his own mor-
tality – the following poems reveal. That they do so with such
crisp lucidity, with so little inflation, with such intrinsic grace
and shapeliness – this is their joy. That their clear-throated
celebrations increasingly (yet obliquely, and without rancour,
self-pity, or hysterical opinion) collide with an adverse histor-
ical world – the destruction of a beloved rural environment,
the carnage of mass warfare in which the poet himself would
be killed – this is one measure of their mature depth, their
grit, their surviving claim on our attention as we turn
between what might be two equally ruinous centuries.

As a poet of the perennial, Thomas formally channelled
and kept clean the flow of a distinctly English plain style
coursing from Chaucer to George Herbert, through early
Wordsworth, John Clare, and Richard Jefferies, to Thomas
Hardy – to name a few whose works he vigorously espoused
in books, introductions and reviews. Rejecting what he called
the stagnant 'pomp and sweetness' of late Victorian style on
the one hand, and the 'discord and fuss' of an overreaching,
interruptive avant-garde on the other, he favoured an appar-
ently natural diction and prosody whose worn-fresh *allées*
and fluencies have effortlessly kept pace with, if not out-
coursed, the more fashionable experiments alongside. And
his stylistic choices seem always to have been in service not of

the poet, nor perhaps even of 'poetry', but rather of those elements of a turning and returning world whose robust yet also delicate and destructible loveliness Thomas wished to witness in the deepest sense, as a communicant. Accordingly, his subjects were no more ambitious, no more intentionally (and hence obsolescently) world-historical, than his manner, as he sought out his own quietly ecstatic encounters with country lanes, birdsong, wind and rain, bright incipience of foliage, wildflowers, returning light, the various onsets of personal and historical darkness.

To bring the poems of Edward Thomas back into print, to read and especially to reread them, is therefore to pursue the poems' own primary action: the work of renewal, the uncovering of a way to perceive and to quicken the continuance of a world and of states of being that are thereby found to be not so much unprecedented – though of course his work was 'revolutionary', in the sense he accorded that of his friend and colleague Robert Frost – as rather, irrepressibly, and somehow forever resurrectively, alive. Like George Herbert, but rejecting Christianity (though what authentically English poet was not also a pagan at heart?), Thomas's impulse, as he defined it wonderingly in a poem titled 'Ambition', was to sing 'the loveliness of prime'.

From the opening 'Nu' of Caedmon's hymn, or the anonymous medieval 'Nu sing cuckoo', where 'nu' refinds itself as both now and new, to Chaucer's inceptive 'showres soote', or Clare's 'I heard from morn to morn a merry thrush/ Sing hymns to sunrise, and I drank the sound/With joy', or Thomas's own 'glory of the beauty of the morning, –/ The cuckoo crying over the untouched dew', English poets have instinctively relished what Hopkins called the 'strain of the earth's sweet being in the beginning'. When they recoil from a wasted world it is often either to Wordsworth's 'I'd rather be

a pagan', or to the Celtic mysticism that underlies the sensu-
ously radiant reconsecrations of Vaughan or Traherne.
Thomas himself, with his interest in Mabinogian tales and
rural lore, was not without Druidic traces of a near-animist
religion.

Admittedly, Vaughan and Traherne were Welsh, as was
Thomas, whose ancestry included a Traherne. But Thomas
claimed that his truest co-nationals were the birds, and his
distrust of competing patriotisms, especially that of the
British, included his sense that the anterior 'Briton', associated
with the badger of 'The Combe', derived from a trans-Breton-
Celtic-Gaelic stock too deep and too widely sourced for any
modern nationalisms. When asked why he had volunteered
for the army in July 1915, after the first crushing casualty
reports had dispelled any illusions, and at the otherwise
immune age of 38, he had bent down, scooped up a handful
of dirt, and said, 'Literally, for this.' A few months later, as a
soldier, he wrote, 'I hate not Germans, nor grow hot/ With
love of Englishmen . . . /Beside my hate for one fat patriot/
My hatred of the Kaiser is love true.' If part of our unease with
some of Thomas's more celebrated contemporaries rises in
part from the abstractive drag of nationalist or pan-European
ideologies, here again the waters of Thomas run clear. We
may drink easily from his work long after other reservoirs
have grown sour or in need of elaborate filtration.

On a loose slip of paper found inside the private diary
Thomas kept during the last three months of his life, and
which he was carrying in his pocket both on April 8, when he
was knocked down by a shell-blast near Arras, and again on
the next morning when he was killed by a shell while direct-
ing artillery fire from an exposed position, he had written
three unpunctuated lines:

Where any turn may lead to Heaven

Or any corner may hide Hell

Roads shining like river up hill after rain.

In this sequence, the roads seem to survive and outshine
both Heaven and Hell. They surpass either domain by sheer
vivacity – luminous, present, giving rise to figuration yet
doing what even the vehicle of the river cannot do (move up
hill). Perhaps purgatorial, certainly purifying in their new-
washed inclinations, roads themselves were among the most
recurrent objects (creatures, one might almost say) of
Thomas's observation and literal transport. He was an
ecstatic walker, a tramp in spirit. No other poet has written
such a large proportion of poems that take the literal road,
the path, the lane or track as both thematic and formal inspi-
ration. 'I love roads,' begins a poem entitled 'Roads', which
celebrates precisely their terrestrial endurance ('Roads go on/
While we forget, and are/ Forgotten like a star/ That shoots
and is gone') even as it marks how their lustre depends in part
on human acts of renewal ('The hill road wet with rain/ In the
sun would not gleam/ Like a winding stream/ If we trod it not
again'). When you read this alongside 'Words', which speaks
of a diction 'Worn new/ Again and again', you have a good
entrée to these interanimating passages of phrasing and far-
ing, 'winding' their way between the old and the brightly
recurrent.

So to read Thomas's poems is to tread a series of paths,
each one distinct, each bringing the reader some unforeseen
find, usually in or beyond the margin of the road, half-
hidden, like the dislodged objects of 'Birds' Nests', the
obscured country inn of his first poem, 'Up in the Wind', the
hill-shrouded yard and building of 'The Mountain Chapel',
the marker in 'The Signpost', the birdcalls, inaudible to all but

the pedestrian (or the unwontedly stopped passenger) in so many signature poems. Accompanying, or rather precipitating the inscapes of a subtly unfolding journey, these finds are everywhere once glimpsed – the 'white goose feathers' strewing the paths of 'The Green Roads', the innumerable appeals of wildflowers, gorse, individual trees, fugitive perspectives and encounters that occur along the *way* that is a Thomas poem.

> The peering sun
> Sees what has been done.
> The road under the trees has a border new
> Of purple hue
> Inside the border of bright thin grass.

Few poets match Thomas's effortless peripheral vision, essential to a sensibility so thoroughly drawn to what runs alongside our otherwise distracted linear movements. These lines from 'After Rain' tell literally of border within border, while the lines rhyme across their antiphonal lengths to complicate the formal analogue for those two margins. Here, too, Thomas's predilection for what is new finds its prize in and *as* the border, just as the displacement of personal by solar vision opens up the widest margin of perception – in this case of the ephemeral but now caught-oscillating contrast of reflective light and tree-shadow. In the mind, a vast, though simply phrased track and tract have opened up from sun to bright thin grass, the last two adjectives recapitulating the range even as they lend luster to the minutely seen. To walk on through the poem is to encounter torn November leaves of hazel and thorn, burnt-orange fern, 'leaflets out of the ash-tree shed/ . . . thinly spread/ In the road, like little black fish, inlaid', 'twelve yellow apples' (hanging, on the border between the literal and the legendary? 'on one crab-tree'), and finally, with characteristic delicacy and unquenched regard for termini that suspend within themselves further initiations, 'on each twig of every tree in the dell/ Uncountable/ Crystals both dark and bright of the rain/ That begins again.'

Thomas's peripheral 'peerings' were magically twinned with his uncommon auditory gifts. The phrase 'A gate banged in a fence and banged in my head' opens, not least by its internal time-lag and its framed threshold between world and mind, a complex field of reflection that summons further senses to the experience of memory: 'The past is the only dead thing that smells sweet,/ The only sweet thing that is not also fleet', in which the reverberation of the gate, sonically alive, however mutedly, in the pursuant repetition of sounds and words, swings between closure and a persistent, fleeing openness. Not by chance, the doubled word 'sweet' tunes back in to the sensations and findings that primed the speaker's way of hearing the gate: 'I heard the brook through the town gardens run./ O sweet was the mud turned to dust by the sun.'

Few of Thomas's poems fail to hearken especially after 'things/ That we know naught of'. 'Hark' is the imperative that ends his first poem; my sense is that part of his desire to keep his lines acoustically clean of rhetorical fuss or clamour stemmed from his need to keep listening, well into the act of writing. His poems search out and fine-tune the frequencies of a dispersed chorus, whether of 'short-lived happy-seeming things', or of enduring notes that counterpoint mere merriment. In what may be oblique acts of self-portraiture, his hearing is drawn, 'over and over', by the inhuman voice of marginal, else-neglected soundings. Sweet, yes, and often bright, but seldom without a vibrant undertone, or a modulation shaken, like the owl's cry, into darker keys. Amid the 'Sad songs of Autumn mirth', or the ever-farthering drift of bird-song across the shires, Thomas inevitably hears what seems to issue from a source that has an astringent power – sometimes to cheer, sometimes to edge and supplement the limits of the human will, often to chasten all self-centred human pretension or belief. Just to list the birdcalls 'wisely reiterating endlessly/ What no man learned yet, in or out of school' is to name a parliament, from owl to pewit, from cuckoo, thrush, chaffinch and robin, to gull, to blackbird and beyond, including 'The Unknown Bird'. This last resists all naturalists' classifications – reciprocal to solitude ('I alone could hear him . . . Oftenest when I heard him I was alone'), as much as to the poet's ingrained, and quite modern, philosophical distrust of all systems of generalization.

Similarly, to listen to the rinsing fall, trickle, plash, silence, or gush of water in Thomas's poems is to encounter particularized instances of liquidity while having one's ears and spirit deliciously asperged. Above and around all, there is the sound of the wind, tormenting and invigorating the setting of Thomas's first poem, 'Up in the Wind', preceding and outlasting the congregation's glassed-in hymns in 'The Mountain Chapel' ('When Gods were young / this wind was old'), and bringing ancient music out of the 'travelling air' in one of Thomas's last poems, 'The Sheiling'.

Acute radar or sonar may be a common attribute for lyric poets, especially those who are to be the 'antennae of the race'. But Thomas had a way not simply of repairing what T. S. Eliot, five years later, would follow the wartime neurologist Henry Head in calling a dissociation of sensibility (see Thomas's 'Old Man' – 'I, too, often shrivel the grey shreds, / Sniff them and think and sniff again and try/ Once more to think what it is I am remembering'; or 'Digging [1]' – 'Today I think/ Only with scents'), but also of mingling his senses in complex, self-interfering variants of synesthesia. 'The dim sea glints chill. The white sun is shy,/ And the skeleton weeds and the never-dry,/ Rough, long grasses keep white with frost'

('The Signpost'); 'A train that roared along raised after it/ And carried with it a motionless white bower/ Of purest cloud, from end to end close-knit,/ So fair it touched the roar with silence' ('Ambition'); 'The late year has grown fresh again and new/ As Spring, and to the touch it is not more cool/ Than it is warm to the gaze' ('October'). This poet walks and writes, in other words, with a variously awakened sensorium, none of whose tributary responses will be shortchanged or simplified for any dominant effect, any more than they will allow an iota of the given world to be conceptually abstracted without the telling measure of resistance that accrues and refines itself in the poem.

While a subtle receptiveness to all that lies at the margin of one's purview may be a crucial gift, Thomas's distinction was to suffer his gift's inseparability from a far-ranging, sensorially induced and felt compassion. Idiosyncratic and intellectually sceptical by nature, he was nonetheless instinctually quick to sense what others' sense-experience might be. This gave him an alert but quiet confidence that sets him off from many of his contemporaries' struggles with subjectivism. So, too, Thomas's intuitive empathy was as much a source of his freedom as it was the very nub of that deep-rooted, unrationalizing sense of accountability that would lead him to the trenches:

Then one evening the new moon made a difference . . . At one stroke, I thought, like many other people, what things that same new moon sees eastward about the Meuse in France. Of those who could see it there, not blinded by smoke, pain or excitement, how many saw it and heeded? . . . I was deluged, in a second stroke, by another thought, or something that overpowered thought. All I can tell is it seemed to me that either I had never loved England, or I had loved it foolishly, aesthetically, like a slave, not having realised that it was not mine unless I were willing and prepared to die for it rather than leave it as Belgian women and old men and children had left their country. Something I had omitted. Something, I felt, had to be done before I could look again so composedly at English landscape, at the elms and poplars about the houses, at the purple-headed wood-betony with two pairs of leaves on a stiff stem, who stood sentinel among the grasses and bracken by hedge-side or wood's edge. What he stood sentinel for I did not know, any more than what I had got to do. . . .' ('This England')

Complacency of any kind – even of an assumed knowledge – would have imprisoned, not protected him. Comfort, he knew, was inimical to genuine acts of rejoicing. 'The Owl' was written in late February 1915, three months before Thomas enlisted:

Downhill I came, hungry, and yet not starved;
Cold, yet had heat within me that was proof
Against the North wind; tired, yet so that rest
Had seemed the sweetest thing under a roof.

Then at the inn I had food, fire, and rest,
Knowing how hungry, cold, and tired was I.
All of the night was quite barred out except
An owl's cry, a most melancholy cry

Shaken out long and clear upon the hill,
No merry note, nor cause of merriment,
But one telling me plain what I escaped
And others could not, that night, as in I went.

And salted was my food, and my repose,
Salted and sobered, too, by the bird's voice
Speaking for all who lay under the stars,
Soldiers and poor, unable to rejoice.

As usual, the poet is on the road – typically aslope at that. It's hard not to take in the degree of immediate embodiment, tempered as it is by Thomas's resilient austerity and his scrupulous refusal to exaggerate. Such aspects of his bearing keep him open, in the midst of his relief, to the plain message he will hear in the owl's cry. Prolonging itself beyond the only stanza that is not end-stopped, rupturing the neat bars of the quatrains as it floats across the silent interval between words, the cry carries the poet's consciousness back outside the enclosure of the inn, and it takes over the primary act of utterance within the poem itself. Well-learned in myth and folklore though Thomas was, his actual sense-experience here enters and informs his conscience. An actual owl seems to outweigh any implicit knowledge of the bird's symbolic properties. To be moved away from what we have known towards what we sense and feel (wonderingly, suspensefully), and only thence to what we come to acknowledge; to be rescued from what comforts us to what discomfitingly claims us for the first time, or again as if for the first time – this is the reciprocal calling of 'The Owl'.

Few of Thomas's poems call in any other way, even when they refer to a call that is poignantly without sound. Take 'In Memoriam (Easter 1915)':

> The flowers left thick at nightfall in the wood
> This Eastertide call into mind the men,
> Now far from home, who, with their sweethearts, should
> Have gathered them and will do never again.

Beyond the title's inner war between resurrective ritual time and irrevocable historical time, beyond the heart-wrenching syntax and the semantic tension of the rhymes, beyond the standoff between organic renewal and human finality, or between an erotically tender calling/culling and a brutal though discreetly off-stage cutting-short, there is of course, for us, now, the gathered knowledge of Thomas's own death, on Easter morning two years later. He had written all of his approximately 140 poems in the space of less than two and a half years.

Edward Thomas lies buried in a cemetery not far from where he fell, near Agny, on the outskirts of Arras. His gravestone, embedded among flowers that climb and lean between more than four hundred similar stones, is uniquely marked less by his proper name than by the single word 'POET' engraved at its base. The plot is a field's breadth away from the road. At least in summer, birdsongs multiply in the surrounding trees. A visitors' book near the gate holds the names of many who have come specifically to visit this grave. Several have written out a line of his poetry, often in place of their own addresses, as if to indicate that this is where they, too, would like to be found. Several, including my immediate predecessor on the last day of June, 2002, have also recorded a sensation impossible to avoid: that of utter waste.

He was born in London on 3 March 1878. His parents had moved to the city as part of the great unmooring of rural populations during the preceding decades, but Thomas's regular visits to his grandparents, and his compulsive walking of country roads – throughout Wales and across many regions of England, especially Kent, Wiltshire, Herefordshire, Somerset, Sussex, Hampshire, Essex, and, yes, 'farther and farther', Oxfordshire and Gloucestershire – kept him intimately bound to a rural, historically prior world whose days and whose acreage he knew were already more than threatened. More than from his education at St Paul's and then at Oxford, he learned from his encounters on foot and from his precocious reading of such regional prose masters as George Borrow and Richard Jefferies. Under the mentorship of the editor James Noble, he began to write essays that would be collected in his first book, *The Woodland Life*, published when he was eighteen.

During the two decades that followed his graduation at Oxford, Thomas kept his wife and family barely afloat on his earnings as a freelance, grindingly productive author and editor of more than forty books of prose, as well as of more than a thousand reviews. The story of his astounding turn to poetry, in late 1914, has been dominated by the account of Robert Frost's injunction: to break his existing prose into lines, bringing his inherently musical cadence and his direct speaking voice into conversation with formal prosody. Thomas himself was already well primed, having made his own careful assessments of what was wrong with the enervated artificiality of a poetry that simply couldn't give life on the page to what he valued within and around him. He championed Frost's own early work:

These poems are revolutionary because they lack the exaggeration of rhetoric . . . Their language is free from the poetical words and forms that are the chief material of the secondary poets. The metre avoids not only old fashioned pomp and sweetness, but the later fashion also of discord and fuss. In fact the medium is common speech . . . Mr Frost has, in fact, gone back, as Whitman and as Wordsworth went back, through the paraphernalia of poetry into poetry once again.

But fifteen years before this, and well before even Pound's dicta regarding what modern poetry should learn from the rigour and accuracy of good prose, Thomas had arrived at a similar position, for example in an essay titled 'The Frontiers of English Prose' (1899). In an enthusiastic review of Yeats's work, he wrote, 'the best lyrics seem to be the poet's natural speech', and in *How I Began*, he remembered trying to 'make words of such spirit, and arrange them in such a manner, that they will *do* all that a speaker can do by innumerable gestures and their innumerable shades, by tone and pitch of voice, by speed, by pauses, by all that he was and all that he will become'. In mid-1914 Thomas told Frost that he wished to make a new start as a writer, beginning with the desire to 'wring the necks of my rhetoric – the geese'. If this matched the state-of-the-art French campaign (Verlaine's *'Prends l'eloquence et tords-lui son cou!'*), it would not have been like Thomas to flash his sophistication, but the opening line of his first poem reads, 'I could wring the old thing's neck that put it here!' – a fragment of actual speech, rather than a literary manifesto.

The poems came fast, sometimes at the rate of one a day. Within four months, Thomas had written more than fifty varied and accomplished lyrics, a pace that barely decelerated up to the last months of his life. These were not sloppy, form-less outpourings, nor were they lacking in the kinds of occa-sion that justify a turn to poetry in the first place. Sinuous, deft, wedding speech and song in their syntactic and prosodic mastery, the poems lightly mould themselves to a shape (and often a representation of self-shaping) which they seem to hold without clutching. They move as Thomas must have walked – lithely, observantly, not wishing to disrupt the stir or shieldings of life along the edges of his path. They preserve the momentum of the stride and the swaying aftershock of the encounter. If they enter a stillness – even a stillness that knows of death – they seek out the radiating energy of that stillness: 'long may it swing/ From the dead apple-bough,/ So glistening'.

Although they cover a mere twenty-seven months, the poems do show considerable development, both in manner and scope. To compare 'November Sky' with 'But These Things Also' (written less than four months later) and with 'October' (after a further seven months) is to see how much more nuanced and fluent the poems became, particularly in their ability to move between inner and outer promptings, as well as in their ways of refining what might have at first seemed obvious kinds of opposition. To these shifts we can add the larger tilting, as of the poet's internal axis, as he began to absorb the visceral knowledge of the war and of his own approaching engagement as a soldier. The poems open up to a more humanly populated world, marked by suffering and by a sense of violation that cuts across Thomas's disposition to trust in a continuous life. The small masterpiece, 'As the Team's Head-Brass', ends 'The horses started and for the last time/ I watched the clods crumble and topple over/ After the ploughshare and the stumbling team.' 'It Was Upon', one of Thomas's sonnets written soon after enlisting, turns from a stranger's confident forecast of a good harvest to the following sestet. As often in Thomas's work, the syntax (here painstakingly hesitant in its groping resistance to the very rupture or withering it fears) carries much of the lived meaning:

> And as an unaccomplished prophecy
> The stranger's words, after the interval
> Of a score of years, when those fields are by me
> Never to be recrossed, now I recall,
> This July eve, and question, wondering,
> What of the lattermath to this hoar Spring?

Given his age, Thomas could have honorably completed the war years as a map instructor in England. But his initial decision to enlist drove him to the further choice of volunteering for the front-line artillery. During the months in France, his almost eccentric blend of stoicism and his unquenchable attentiveness to the world around him moved him to the simplest notations. February 25, 1917: 'A dull morning turns sunny and warm. chaffinches and partridges, moles working on surface . . . Does a mole ever get hit by a shell?' March 18: 'Beautiful clear cloudless morning and no firing between daybreak and 8. Drew another panorama at 7. Linnets and chaffinches sing in waste trenched ground with trees and water tanks between us and Arras. Magpies over No Man's Land in pairs. The old green (grey) track crossing No Man's Land – once a country way to Arras. The water green and clear . . . with skeletons of whole trees lying there . . . I could hear a lark till the Archies drowned it. Fired 600 rounds and got tired eyes and ears.' March 21: '. . . a road between shell holes full of blood-stained water and beer bottles among barbed wire. Larks singing as they did when we went up in the dark and were shelled.'

On the last page of his diary, April 8, Thomas wrote:

> The light of the new moon and every star
> And no more singing for the bird . . .
> I never understood quite what was meant by God
> The morning chill and clear hurts my skin while it delights my
>   mind.
> Neuville in early morning with its flat straight crest with trees and
> houses – the beauty of this silent empty scene of no inhabitants
> and hid troops, but don't know why I could have cried and didn't.

The next morning, at 7:36, during the barrage against Arras, he was struck and killed by a shell.

The few poems published during Thomas's lifetime appeared under the pseudonym Edward Eastaway. He had not wanted to trade on his reputation as an established prose writer and reviewer, nor perhaps did he wish to damage it, having had numerous rejections. A collection appeared six months after his death and was followed by a sequence of editions, the most familiar of which included a moving introduction by Walter de la Mare, to whom we owe one of the most trenchant accounts of what it was like to be in Thomas's physical presence:

But how vivid are his features in remembrance! His face was fair, long and rather narrow, and in its customary gravity wore an expression rather distant and detached. There was a glint of gold in his sun-baked hair. The eyes, long-lashed and stooping a little beneath the full rounded lids, were of a clear dark blue . . . The lips were finely lined and wide, the chin square. His shoes were to his stature; the hands that had cradled so many wild birds' eggs, and were familiar with every flower in the Southern counties, were powerful and bony; the gestures few; the frame vigorous . . . His smile could be whimsical, stealthy, shy, ardent, mocking, or drily ironical; he seldom laughed. His voice was low and gentle, but musical, with a curious sweetness and hollowness when he sang his old Welsh songs to his children. I have never heard English used so fastidiously and yet so unaffectedly as in his talk.

Beyond the poems, Thomas is also vividly present in two books by his wife, Helen: *As It Was* (1926) and *World Without End* (1931). Their relationship was passionate, yet fraught by the poet's fierce, at times terrifyingly morose, fits of withdrawal. He would go off walking for days and nights. At times he feared his own coldness and anger. On at least one occasion, he turned against himself in an attempt at suicide. But the couple shared a remarkable candour, a capacity for instinctive delight, an almost preternatural manner of being rekindled by the beauty of the natural world. In one of the many letters exchanged between them, there is a passage that may serve to stand between this introduction and the poems. The letter is dated 9 October 1914, and was written during a long cycling trip that shortly preceded Thomas's turn to poetry:

I was first delayed by going back for my hat which I left when I was sitting. However by returning I made certain that a bird I had been hearing was the woodlark. It is a wild gentle timid song, not like a lark's so that you do not look for it up high but on trees or ground. But if you look up you see him 100 yards up making little flights and circling and hovering as if he lived there and never came down, not like the lark which soars up as high as he can get adventurously but

really belongs to the earth. He stayed as long as I listened, singing all
the time but with short intervals. The song is very sweet, wild and yet
homely, something like a pipit's, but with a slight yodel and a smack
of curlew too. As I sat there were several singing.

                                                        Peter Sacks

Note on the Text

This edition of *The Collected Poems of Edward Thomas* is an attempt to present the poems in chronological order, as closely as possibly to the form in which they would have appeared if Thomas had seen them through the press in 1917. He in fact saw few of his poems in print, and not all of those had the benefit of his well-trained proof-reader's eye. The detailed evidence of his notebooks, manuscripts and typescripts is fully documented in my textual edition of *The Collected Poems* (Clarendon Press, 1978), together with a selection of variant readings, early drafts and prose versions. The text of the 144 poems printed here is taken from that edition.

Manuscripts
LML (the Lockwood Memorial Library manuscript) (twenty leaves, 18 × 22 cm), an ordinary school exercise book, contains the first five poems, and prose versions of Poems 1 and 2; it illustrates Thomas's initial attempt to follow Robert Frost's suggestion that he should write verse because some of his prose was essentially poetry. Thomas's fidelity in following this advice is qualified in his letter to John Freeman on 8 March 1915, after he had composed the first thirty-eight poems: 'By the way what I have done so far have been like quintessences of the best parts of my prose-books – not much sharper or more intense, but I hope a little: since the first take off they haven't been Frosty very much or so I imagine and I have tried as often as possible to avoid the facilities offered by blank verse and I try not to be too long – I even have an ambition to keep under 12 lines (but rarely succeed).'[1]

1 *Moore*, p. 326.

Berg (the Berg Collection of manuscripts) (eight separate pages, 18 × 22 cm) in the New York Public Library[2] is a paper-covered Bedales School exercise book containing loose-leaf versions of Poems 27 (two drafts), 28, 29, 31, and 32. The poems have no titles and, except for the second draft of Poem 27, all are dated by the poet: the dates are identical with those in *BM* (see below), which contains the only other manuscript sources for these five poems.

M_1 (short for Merfyn Thomas, the poet's only son) (twenty-eight leaves, 10.5 × 15.5 cm) is a green cloth-covered notebook once used by Thomas for prose sketches, with a few leaves torn out and with 'Edward Thomas/Wick Green/Petersfield' on the flyleaf. The pages are unnumbered. The first page has a few lines of Poem 7: the remainder of the poems begin from the last page (with the first draft of Poem 7, dated 14 December 1914) and continue for twenty-six pages. The next date is on page 16 (17 April 1915). There are twenty-five poems, including the first draft of 'Lob' (Poem 56); the first draft of the last poem (Poem 74) is dated 23 May 1915. There are no titles.

BM (British Museum Add. MSS. 44990) (1–77 recto, 19.7 × 25.3 cm) is a large cloth-bound record book with poems on pages numbered 1 to 77. Some of these are fair copies; many more are working drafts. The first poem (Poem 11) is dated 24 December 1914 with the same pen and ink as the first dated poem in M_1. Poems are usually on the recto but quite a few are re-copied or partly reworked on the verso. All the poems are dated, and nineteen of them have titles; there is no place of composition (except for Poem 73), although the poet's letters

2 For a detailed description of the Edward Thomas material in this collection see 'New in the Berg Collection: 1959–61 (Part III)' by John D. Gordan, *Bulletin of the N.Y. Public Library*, vol. 68, no. 2, 1964.

confirm that the majority were written at Steep. The last poem (Poem 75) is a fair copy of the second draft of the same poem in M_1(II) and is dated 24 May 1915. There are sixty-three poems in all, counting the two versions of 'Sedge-Warblers' (Poems 74, 75) and two of 'A Tale' (Poems 52, 53), but only one version of 'Two Pewits' (Poem 48).

Bod (Bodley MS. Don. d. 28) (1–71 recto, 19.5 × 26.2 cm) is an old cloth-bound accounts book with ruled lines. On the fly-leaf is: 'Edward Thomas/Steep/Petersfield' and the date: 'vi.15 [June 1915].' Some pages have been torn out before the first poem (Poem 76) which is headed: '25 June 1915 Hucclecote.' Unlike *BM* this is principally a collection of fair copies (although a few of the poems are quite heavily worked), written at home during his frequent Army leaves and intended for Helen to preserve.[3] All the poems (except Poem 142) are dated (usually in figures which I have spelt out), and the place of composition is usually included. They are all written on the recto. Thomas has numbered the folios 1–28 (either in the centre at the top, or in the top right-hand corner): the Bodleian has continued the numbering from folios 29–71 (in the top right-hand corner). Poem 142 is on an inserted separate leaf (folio 70), with a footnote in Helen Thomas's hand – 'Sent from Codford'. Poem 143 which follows on the last folio is headed '24 December 1916 High Beech'. Another hand – Helen Thomas's, I think from the figuring – has also numbered each page with the corresponding page numbers in *Collected Poems* (1920). There are sixty-seven poems in *Bod*, ten of which are given titles by Thomas.

3 In an undated letter to her, probably in December 1916 just before his commissioning leave, Thomas writes 'I will copy out the verses if there is any time, and I feel sure there will be plenty'.

M_2 (forty-two leaves, 10.5 × 15.5 cm) is a blue-cloth companion to M_1. On the flyleaf is 'Edward Thomas/Wick Green/ Petersfield' and the date '26 December 1911'. Opposite is a list of contents, presumably of prose sketches: '(1) Evening Chapel (2) Sigmund (3) The Pilgrim (4) Dialogue (Jehovah etc.).' The pages are not numbered. The first eleven pages are torn out; page 12 contains the last lines of 'The Pilgrim'[4] and the next six pages have a dialogue between three speakers shown as P, T, and J. On page 7 is Poem 103, dated 4 March 1916; the poems end on page 40 with Poem 131, dated 1 and 5 July 1916. There are twenty-seven poems and two pages filled with trigonometrical sketches and calculations. All but three (105, 109, 111) of the poems are dated and I assume it was used as a working notebook in camp – and in the train. Like M_1 it gives an admirable example of Thomas's working method as a poet and, according to his letters to Frost, it contains many of the poems he adjudged to be his best. Nineteen of these poems were included in the sixty-four poems selected by Thomas for *EE*.

In addition there are a number of groups of manuscripts of single poems:

RF_1 (short for Robert Frost) Two poems (73, 77), were sent to Frost in letters from Thomas after Frost had returned to New Hampshire in January 1915. They are now in the Dartmouth College Library, Hanover, New Hampshire, U.S.A.

Helen Six poems (96,[5] 97, 106, 108, 130, and 144) were found among family papers after the death of Helen Thomas.

---

4 See *The Last Sheaf* (1928), pp. 51–8.

5 'Roads', with its accompanying letter to Helen, is in the Library of Lincoln College, Oxford.

*EF*₁ Fifteen significant valuable single manuscripts are the draft poems sent by Thomas to Eleanor Farjeon for typing and retained by her. Eight of them (Poems 65, 86, 90, 95, 106, 137, 139, and 143) were in (or with) letters from Thomas which were printed (not always accurately) in her *Edward Thomas: The Last Four Years* (*TLFY*); seven others (Poems 97, 98, 99, 107, 120, 121, and 134) were sent by her to the poet's family in 1965. The correspondence published in *TLFY* refers to numerous other poems which were sent to Eleanor Farjeon for typing, but none of these seems to have survived.

RLW Four single sheets (Poems 125, 126, 128, and 133) were given to Rowland L. Watson by Eleanor Farjeon some time after 1937 in recognition of his devoted work as Secretary of the Edward Thomas Memorial Fund. The titles (which follow *Collected Poems*) are added in Watson's hand.

*RGT*₁ The original pencil draft of Poem 141, given to the editor by Helen Thomas.

The few poems sent to Gordon Bottomley, and apparently retained by him, are not among Thomas's letters to Bottomley in the Cardiff University College Library.[6] Other single manuscripts may yet come to light, especially from the papers of Bottomley, Frost, James Guthrie, and, possibly, John Freeman, although it is more probable that Thomas circulated typescript copies to his various friends who were

6 Bottomley made his selection of eighteen poems for *AANP* from about forty typescripts; the remainder were returned. Among Helen Thomas's papers is a list of seventeen poems in Bottomley's hand, with the words 'Poems kept' at the top corner in Eleanor Farjeon's writing. Here is Bottomley's list: 'Old Man', 'Snow', 'The Cuckoo', 'The New House', 'Wind and Mist', 'The Unknown', 'The Word', 'The Glory', 'For These', 'Roads', 'Lovers', 'A Private', 'Beauty', 'The Brook', 'At Poet's Tears' ('Song [1]'), 'The Source', 'Sedge Warblers'.

attempting to get his poems published. Certainly J. W. Haines received such copies in Gloucester, copied them, and then returned them,[7] as did Harold Monro, Edward Garnett, and, I assume, Guthrie.[8]

Typescripts

Thomas had used a typewriter regularly since 1911, and I assume that he typed the earlier poems himself, although Eleanor Farjeon later provided typed copies for most of his verse.[9] Because most of her original copies are lost, the typescripts that have survived (mainly from the poet's parental home where he spent quite a time during his last three

7 See *Eckert Coll.*, Eng. lett. c. 282, a letter from Haines to Guthrie dated 10 April 1918.
8 Numerous copies sent to Frost during the intensive submarine warfare of 1916 never arrived in America.
9 See Eleanor Farjeon's letter to Gordon Bottomley on 18 April 1917: 'You know since he began to write poetry I have typed it nearly all for him, and with John Freeman have revised the proofs of this book [i.e. *EE*].' But compare Thomas's letter to her, dated 6 January 1915 (*TLFY*), when he sent his first batch of poems to her with a suggestion that she could make copies and keep them. At this time he was in bed or in a chair with an ankle injury and found 'typing at present too awkward'. He first thanked her for typescript copies in a letter dated 16 January 1915. She wrote to Myfanwy Thomas in February 1965: 'Now coming to the important point of the poems he chose with Ingpen or someone else, for the very first book that he left with Selwyn & Blount when he went to France. I had nothing to do with the choice and I don't know what typescript he was showing about at this time; I still think it must have been mine.' This is a complicated question and deserves extensive treatment elsewhere but, after a careful comparison of paper watermarks and typefaces of those typescripts that do survive, I think that many of the extant typed copies (i.e. RF_2, *MET*, and *JT*) were typed by Thomas and were certainly corrected in longhand by him. Most of Eleanor Farjeon's copies seem to have made up the original selection made by Thomas for Ingpen and the duplicate set which was sent to Frost in the autumn of 1916 and presumably lost at sea.

months in England) have been used as valuable sources for all the poems printed here, but especially for the poems that were published after 1917. The evidence of the manuscripts, of the poems which appeared before Thomas left for France, and of the typescripts, suggests that, in the last stages of his military training, Thomas took considerable care to leave his poems in their final form although it is only possible to conjecture what that final state would have been. There are four groups of typescripts:

RF_2 (Robert Frost group), now in Dartmouth College Library, New Hampshire, among Thomas's letters to Frost. Sixteen of them are included with a letter from Thomas at Petersfield to 'Robert Frost, Esq., Ryton, Dymock, Gloucester', in an envelope with the date stamp '16 December 1914'. They are Poems 2–13, 15–18, all written between 4 December 1914 and 5 January 1915. 'Up in the Wind' (Poem 1) and 'The Combe' (Poem 14) are missing. Probably a copy of the former had been sent to James Guthrie who later printed it in *In Memoriam*; the latter had been sent either to an editor or to Guthrie. (It has the only extant holograph signature of 'Edward Eastaway' and the surviving typescript has 'II' before the title, as though it were the second poem in a group.) Poem 74 was sent with a letter dated 23 May 1915. One assumes that Frost placed all the poems in one envelope when he left England for America in February 1915. This group gives the only independent source for 'The Other' (Poem 6) apart from *Last Poems* (1918): the remainder are often superseded by later, altered versions in manuscript, typescript, and print. Each poem has a title.

EF_2 (Eleanor Farjeon), in private hands. There are twelve typescripts of Poems 24, 47, 68, 89, 90, 99, 101, 107, 110, 114, 119, and 140; Poems 47 and 119 have manuscript alterations in

Eleanor Farjeon's hand. In February 1965 Miss Farjeon explained the hand-written alterations as follows: 'The great discrepancy between the version as it is always printed and the one I enclose, which contains the considerable changes he made after my first typing. When he made small changes they could be corrected in the first typescript; but sometimes, when I made fresh typescripts for him, I only corrected for my own keeping the copy I already had. And this is one of those cases. . . . But either all the second typings got mislaid, or he may have reverted to preferring the poem in its first form.' Only two of these copies (Poems 47 and 68) have titles and none is dated.

MET (the poet's mother, Mary Elizabeth), in private hands, contains twenty copies of seventeen poems discovered among the papers of Helen Thomas. They are all on quarto paper, with various water-marks and different coloured ribbons; the bundle was doubled over, tied with red tape, and labelled 'Mother' in Thomas's handwriting. Presumably they were preserved at his parents' home and given to Helen after her mother-in-law's death; most of the poems were composed at times when Thomas visited his parents at Balham or stayed with them while a soldier in training in and around London. The bundle contains Poems 1–5, 8, 9 (I and II), 15, 16, 52, 61, 67, 86, 87, 134 (two copies), 136 (two copies), and 137. Poems 1, 9 (II), 15, 16, 61, 67, 134, and 136 are carbons, the remainder are top copies. A few of the poems seem to be carbon copies of poems typed by Eleanor Farjeon; the remainder, particularly the early ones, were probably typed by Thomas. The last three poems have no titles. Seven of these poems were selected by Thomas for inclusion in *EE*..[10]

10 Poems 2, 5, 8, 9, 67, 134 and 137.

JT (the poet's brother, Julian Thomas), in private hands. In 1971 the poet's nephew, David, allowed me to consult a batch of typescripts – quarto size and stapled together – that had belonged to his father.[11] This group contains twenty-three poems: 1–5, 7–10, 14, 26, 30, 56 (two top copies, one headed 'unrevised' by Thomas), 76, 77 (two top copies, one headed 'unamended' by the poet), 79, 81–5, 87, and 88. The watermarks, ribbon colours, and typeface are similar to *MET*. Poems 3, 4, 5, 9, 14, 30, 79, and 81–5 are carbons; the remainder are top copies, but none of the twenty-five copies are exactly related to *MET*. A few were typed by Eleanor Farjeon and the remainder by the poet. These are clearly twenty-five working copies used by Thomas for revision during his final gathering of poems for Roger Ingpen to publish (*EE*). The early ones, presumably typed by Thomas, are closely linked to RF_2 and *MET*. All the poems have titles except Poems 76 and 77; many copies are altered in longhand, and a few have been pasted together. Poem 14 ('The Combe') is signed 'Edward Eastaway'. In all Thomas chose nine of these poems for *EE*.[12]

RGT_2 are copies of Poems 2 and 99 given to the editor by Helen Thomas; her daughters believe they originally belonged to Eleanor Farjeon.

I assume that *MET* and *JT* are the residual copies left at Thomas's parental home after he had made his selection of the poems in *EE* for Roger Ingpen and had sent off to Frost

---

11 Julian Thomas, Edward's youngest brother, who was most sympathetic to the poet's literary interests.

12 Poems 2, 5, 8, 9, 14, 26, 56, 77, and 88.

the duplicate set that never arrived in America.[13] As his letters indicate, Thomas was extremely busy during his final training as an Artillery Officer Cadet and he had little spare time to sort out his papers after he left Steep in August 1916. I have therefore given these typescripts the most careful consideration before arriving at the final text of the thirty-two separate poems they contain. In the case of three early poems I have adopted the title from *JT*: for Poem 2, and the *MET* versions of Poems 8 and 9. The hitherto preferred text of Poem 8 is a later version of the poem as printed in *RB* (and adopted for *EE*). Because the *EE* text of Poem 9 was subsequently emended in CP_1 I have decided to accept the *MET* text. The preference of the *JT*(II) text of Poem 56 over *EE* was made on two counts: first, Thomas had clearly revised this version in longhand and rejected *JT*(I), clearly marked 'unrevised' by him; secondly, the poet's punctuation of lines 78, 101, 103, 119, 128, and 140 in *JT*(II) is not followed in *EE*. I suspect that the latter follows the publishing house rules, and in the absence of any other manuscript intermediate between *JT*(II) and *EE*

13 Thomas's letters to Frost state quite specifically that Thomas arranged his selection at Balham after his family had left Steep. When his family settled at High Beech, near Loughton, Essex, a great many of his papers and books were left with his parents. See his letter to Frost, dated 19 October 1916, from High Beech: '. . . if he will publish I will do my best to hunt up the duplicates and send them on to you in good time for a possible American publisher.' The duplicates were posted on 27 November 1916 but, as Thomas's letters to Frost from France show, they never arrived. Ingpen was slow in reaching his decision, and the final agreement was signed by Thomas at the office of his solicitor friend J. W. Haines in Gloucester on 19 January 1917, and the manuscript left with Ingpen the next day. (See *Eckert Coll.* Eng. lett. c. 281, fo. 2, for a memo of the agreement with Selwyn & Blount, the publishers.) The long-drawn-out arrangements with Ingpen are charted in detail in letters from Thomas to Frost on 15 August, 19 October, 24 November, 27 November, 29 November, 16 December, 31 December (all in 1916), and on 12 and 19 January 1917.

– and despite *EE* reading of l. 119 – I have treated the *JT*(II) text as an example of a way the poet would have read the text.

Published Sources[14]

When Thomas died in April 1917, he had seen twenty-seven of his own poems in print and not all of these had the benefit of his final proof-reading.[15] Thomas began writing verse in November or December 1914 and, after many unsuccessful attempts to have his poems accepted anonymously by various editors, he relied on the good offices of his friends (James Guthrie, Robert Frost, Edward Garnett) to get them into print. When his lifelong acquaintance Roger Ingpen agreed to publish a selection of his poems, Thomas insisted that they appear under the pseudonym 'Edward Eastaway'. Eventually *Poems* by Edward Thomas (*EE*, 'Edward Eastaway') appeared posthumously on 10 October 1917, but Thomas never saw the proofs and the original typescript has been lost. In a letter of October 1934 Roger Ingpen stated[16] that he possessed

14 See Appendix I, p. 241.
15 He saw proofs of the eighteen poems in *AANP*, but he left the final reading to Gordon Bottomley. See *GB*, Letter 178, dated 11 December 1916: 'I sent the changes in to Constable [publishers of *AANP*] and I hope they will make them.' Thomas received his copy of *Six Poems* – four of which are included in *AANP* – on 21 March 1916, but there were some errors. (This corrected copy is used in notes to the present text.) See his letter to James Guthrie (*Eckert Coll.* Eng. lett. d. 281) and a letter from J. W. Haines to Eckert dated 11 July 1937 (*Eckert Coll.* Eng. lett. c. 281). There is no evidence that Thomas actually saw the proofs of the poems that appeared in *Poetry* (Chicago, 1917). Two of the poems in *Root and Branch* (vol. ii, no. 4) appeared after his death.
16 The most careful study of the state of *EE* is in *Eckert*; this evidence is extended in the correspondence of Judge Eckert with Ingpen and others in the Eckert Collection in the Bodleian. (See *Eckert Coll.* Eng. lett. c. 281.)

'what I believe to be the only proof copy' of *EE*, and at one time R. P. Eckert hoped to buy this proof copy which I have been unable to trace. Mr. Richard de la Mare, Ingpen's nephew, informed me that when he joined his uncle's office after the war there was no trace of a manuscript or typescript there. Consequently, except in the few cases already mentioned above, I have accepted *EE* as though it represented Thomas's own manuscript.

Last Poems (LP), by Edward Thomas, published in 1918, was based on the remaining manuscripts and on all the poems (not in *EE*) that existed then in print.[17] At about the same time a selection from *LP* was also published, but it has no independent status.[18]

In 1920 *Collected Poems* (CP_1) appeared (with 100 copies on Japon Vellum): with a slight rearrangement it followed the order of poems in *EE* and *LP*, with Poem 1 inserted between them. After the appearance of *Two Poems* in 1927, in a limited edition of eighty-five copies, Roger Ingpen offered to sell all 'our rights of publication in the Poems of Edward Thomas including stocks and stereotype plates of Collected Poems' to Jonathan Cape for £200.[19] Presumably the offer was not accepted: on 28 March 1928 a new edition of *Collected Poems* (CP_2) was published with four additional poems. This edition

17 I assume on the evidence of Eleanor Farjeon's letter to Gordon Bottomley in April 1917 (see *GB*, Letter 184) that John Freeman, Eleanor Farjeon, and (possibly) the poet's father were concerned with the preparation of this volume. Again, no typescript survives.

18 See a letter from Roger Ingpen to Eckert (*Eckert Coll.* Eng. lett. c. 281) dated 18 August 1934: 'This [*Twelve Poets*] was printed about the same time as Last Poems. I cannot remember which was actually printed first but I think *LP*.' For slight variations between *LP* and *TP*, see notes to individual poems.

19 See *Eckert Coll.* Eng. lett. c. 281.

was reset and first issued in the Faber Library in September 1936: it had the benefit of Walter de la Mare and Julian Thomas as proof-readers,[20] but there is no evidence of any collation with existing manuscripts. The subsequent history of *Collected Poems* – including the addition of Poem 99 – is given in the admirable publisher's note to *Collected Poems*, ninth impression, April 1965.

Titles of poems

Some of the titles in the text are new. Wherever possible I have used Thomas's own titles as they appear in manuscript or typescript, but occasionally I have used titles based on references in his letters. Thomas gave titles to most of his typescript versions, and all the poems that appeared during his lifetime were given titles; but many of the poems assembled in *Last Poems* adopt titles taken from the first lines of poems that were available only in manuscript form.[21] Generally, unless there is strong evidence to the contrary, I have accepted the titles in *EE* as Thomas's own, but I am less sure about titles used in *LP*,[22] and later in *CP*, except for those that

---

20 See letter from Julian Thomas to Eckert (*Eckert Coll.* Eng. lett. d. 282) dated 22 March 1938: 'I expect you have seen Faber's edition of Edward's Poems, the first to be free from misprints unless my vigilance and W. de la Mare's has been in vain.'

21 This practice was probably an extension of Thomas's occasional practice (in *Bod*) to use the first few words of the first line of a poem as a title (e.g. Poem 43). On the other hand, I doubt if Thomas was happy with the first-line title of Poem 121. See his letter to Eleanor Farjeon (*TLFY*, p. 144, wrongly dated 1915 for 1916): 'I don't know about a title for the blank verse. What about "The Last Team"?'

22 *EE* is the only source for the titles to Poems 22, 36, 46, 49, 50, 55, 59, 60, 63, 70, 90, 112, 113, 116 (first line), 117 (first line), 119 (first line), 121 (first line), 122 (first line), 125, 128, 129, 130, 132, 140, and the four 'Household Poems' 106–9 (all first lines). *LP* is the only source for titles to Poems 23, 29, 31, 32, 51, 57, 62, 64, 66, 93, 100, 115, 127, 131, 135–6 (first lines), 138, and 143.

appeared in print before his death. In the notes, the title is drawn from the same source as the text unless otherwise shown (i.e. in square brackets against the relevant source, or in a specific note about the choice of title).[23]

23 One title, 'Old Dick', is elusive. Thomas refers to it in a letter to Eleanor Farjeon dated 24 January 1915 (*TLFY*, p. 114): 'Still here they are. I haven't thrown away anything, even the worse version of "Old Dick"'. Only Poems 19 and 29 appear to be candidates for this title at this date. Poem 19 has two distinct versions in *BM*, but it is clearly called 'A Private' in *AANP*, which I accept as an unimpeachable Thomas source. Poem 29 does not exist in two distinct versions – bad or worse – but it seems the more likely candidate for 'Old Dick'.

Table of Dates

November Becomes a regular reviewer for *Daily Chronicle* on the death of Lionel Johnson.

1903 *February* First commissioned book, *Oxford*.

July Moves to cottage on Bearsted Green.

September Consults a specialist about ill health and exhaustion.

1904 *May* Moves to Elses Farm, The Weald, near Sevenoaks, Kent. Continues reviewing and works on *Beautiful Wales* (second commission).

1905 *Summer* Physically and mentally exhausted. Experiments with 'ejaculations in prose'.

October Invites W. H. Davies to share his small study cottage.

1906 Meets W. H. Hudson, Walter de la Mare.

April–July Walking tours; more reviewing; more commissioned books.

October Notice to quit Elses Farm. Stays in London.

November Regular reviewer for Hilaire Belloc with *Morning Post*.

December Moves to Berryfield Cottage, Ashford, Petersfield, near to Bedales School.

1907 *April* Visits a specialist about his 'melancholia'.

August Walking tour with Helen in 'Jefferies Country'.

1908 *January–February* First draft of *Richard Jefferies* completed at Minsmere, near Dunwich, Suffolk.

August–December Assistant Secretary to a Royal Commission on Welsh Monuments. Lives in London; continues to review and write books; resigns for health reasons.

1909 *January* Returns to Ashford where a new house is planned.

April Enters new study at top of Ashford Hanger; work begins on new house.

Autumn Merfyn and Bronwen attend Bedales; Helen teaches
   there in the Kindergarten.

Before Christmas Moves into new house, Wick Green,
   Petersfield, Hampshire.

1910   Continues to write books and to review for *Daily*
      Chronicle, Morning Post, Saturday Review, and
      The Bookman.

August Second daughter, Myfanwy, born.

September Cycling tour with Merfyn. Visits Conrad, Belloc,
   Ralph Hodgson, Rupert Brooke.

1911   *January* Follows a strict vegetarian diet.

March Low in health and spirit.

April–August At work on six books of various kinds.

September Severe breakdown caused by overwork and
   financial worry.

October–December In West Wales and Laugharne; writes
   George Borrow.

1912   *January* Begins fortnightly visits to London in search of
      literary work. Writes for H. Monro's *Poetry Review.*

April Stays with Clifford Bax in Somerset and is treated by
   Godwin Baynes (a nerve specialist).

May–June Near Bath. Treatment and writing continue.

July Begins reviewing for *The English Review* and *The*
   Nation.

August Cycles with Merfyn in Somerset and Kent.

November Leaves Wick Green; stays with Vivian Locke Ellis
   as a paying guest at Selsfield House, East Grinstead.
   Writes *Walter Pater.* Begins fiction, *The Happy-Go-Lucky*
   Morgans. Meets Eleanor Farjeon.

1913   *January–February* His health much worse. Travels in
      Wiltshire and Somerset, preparing *In Pursuit of Spring.*

March–May At work on various books, reviewing for
   monthlies, quarterlies, and *Daily Chronicle.*

July Sells books before moving to a small cottage (Yew-tree Cottage) in Steep village, near Petersfield.

August Moves to Steep village; retains hill-top study.

October Introduced to Robert Frost by Ralph Hodgson.

December Begins his autobiography at Selsfield House, East Grinstead, Sussex. Meets Frost again.

1914 *January–February* Chiefly in London; working on his autobiography.

March In Steep, reviewing, proof-reading, writing articles.

April Travels to Wales and then to see Frost in Herefordshire. *In Pursuit of Spring* published.

June At Cartmel with Bottomley, then Herefordshire with Frost.

July Reviews Frost's *North of Boston*. Helen and Edward visit Frost at Ledington.

August Thomases on holiday with Frosts at Ledington.

September Cycling tour in Midlands and the north of England, preparing articles for *The English Review*. Visits Frost and plans to leave with him for U.S.A.

October Monthly and quarterly reviewing. Cycling in Wales and then back to Ledington.

November–December At Steep, begins prose versions of earliest poems.

Earliest poems written and sent to Frost.

1915 *January* Confined to Steep with severely sprained ankle. Writing poetry. Eleanor Farjeon begins to type them.

February Unable to walk. Merfyn leaves with Frosts for U.S.A. Thomas sends poems to friends and, unsuccessfully, to some editors. Adopts pseudonym of 'Edward Eastaway' for his verse.

March–June Writing poetry and *The Life of the Duke of Marlborough*. Preparing anthology *This England* for the press.

July Enlists in the Artists' Rifles. Poems sent to Bottomley
for inclusion in *An Annual of New Poetry*.

August–September Billeted with his parents at Balham.

October In camp at High Beech, near Loughton, Essex.

November Moved to Hare Hall Camp, Gidea Park, Romford.
Promoted to Lance-Corporal. Acting as map-reading
instructor.

December Merfyn returns from U.S.A.

1916   *January* Still at Hare Hall Camp.

February A convalescent leave spent at Steep.

March Promoted to Corporal. Frequent leaves; continues to
write verse. *Keats* published.

June Awarded a £300 grant instead of a Civil List Pension.
Applies for a commission in the Royal Artillery. Asked to
leave his study at Steep.

July Granted £1 a week by the Civil Liability Commission
(to cease if he becomes an officer). Declines to stay on the
permanent staff at Hare Hall Camp.

August Roger Ingpen considers publication of a selection of
his verse.

September An officer cadet with the R.A. in London. Stays
often with his parents at Balham, begins to arrange the
typescripts of his poems. Moves his family to High Beech,
near Loughton, Essex.

October Moved to firing camp in Wiltshire, near Trowbridge.

November Commissioned 2nd Lieutenant; posted to 244
Siege Battery, R.G.A. Lydd, Kent. Visits Cartmel and
Gloucester before returning to High Beech.

December Volunteers for service overseas. Sees proofs of *An
Annual of New Poetry*. Sends duplicate set of poems [*EE*]
to Frost.

1917   *January* Embarkation leave, then final firing practice at
Codford, near Warminster, Wiltshire.

13 January 'Last poem' written in his diary.

29 January Embarkation from Southampton.

4 February Leaves Le Havre area for front line.

11 February Settles into positions near Arras.

9 March After a spell at Group H.Q. returns to his Battery. Begins duty at the Observation Post (Ronville).

26 March Positions moved up beyond Achicourt in preparation for forthcoming 'Battle of Arras'.

8 April Under constant artillery fire.

9 April On duty at the Observation Post. Killed by the blast of a shell at 7.36 a.m. during the first hour of the Arras 'offensive'.

POEMS 1914–1917

1] Up in the Wind

'I could wring the old thing's neck that put it there!
A public-house! it may be public for birds,
Squirrels and suchlike, ghosts of charcoal-burners
And highwaymen.' The wild girl laughed. 'But I
5 Hate it since I came back from Kennington.
I gave up a good place.' Her cockney accent
Made her and the house seem wilder by calling up –
Only to be subdued at once by wildness –
The idea of London there in that forest parlour,
10 Low and small among those towering beeches
And the one bulging butt that's like a font.

Her eyes flashed up; she shook her hair away
From eyes and mouth, as if to shriek again;
Then sighed back to her scrubbing. While I drank
15 I might have mused of coaches and highwaymen,
Charcoal-burners and life that loves the wild.
For who now used these roads except myself,
A market waggon every other Wednesday,
A solitary tramp, some very fresh one
20 Ignorant of these eleven houseless miles,
A motorist from a distance slowing down
To taste whatever luxury he can
In having North Downs clear behind, South clear before,
And being midway between two railway lines
25 Far out of sight or sound of them? There are
Some houses – down the by-lanes; and a few
Are visible – when their damsons are in bloom.
But the land is wild, and there's a spirit of wildness
Much older, crying when the stone-curlew yodels

30 His sea and mountain cry, high up in Spring.
He nests in fields where still the gorse is free as
When all was open and common. Common 'tis named
And calls itself, because the bracken and gorse
Still hold the hedge where plough and scythe have chased
   them.
35 Once on a time 'tis plain that the 'White Horse'
Stood merely on the border of a waste
Where horse or cart picked its own course afresh.
On all sides then, as now, paths ran to the inn;
And now a farm-track takes you from a gate.

40 Two roads cross, and not a house in sight
Except the 'White Horse' in this clump of beeches.
It hides from either road, a field's breadth back;
And it's the trees you see, and not the house,
Both near and far, when the clump's the highest thing
45 And homely too upon a far horizon
To one who knows there is an inn within.

   ' 'Twould have been different' the wild girl shrieked,
      'suppose
   That widow had married another blacksmith and
   Kept on the business. This parlour was the smithy.
50 If she had done, there might never have been an inn:
And I, in that case, might never have been born.
Years ago, when this was all a wood
And the smith had charcoal-burners for company,
A man from a beech-country in the shires
55 Came with an engine and a little boy
(To feed the engine) to cut up timber here.
It all happened years ago. The smith
Had died, his widow had set up an alehouse –
I could wring the old thing's neck for thinking of it.

60 Well, I suppose they fell in love, the widow
    And my great-uncle that sawed up the timber:
    Leastways they married. The little boy stayed on.
    He was my father.' She thought she'd scrub again,
    – 'I draw the ale, and he grows fat' she muttered—
65 But only studied the hollows in the bricks
    And chose among her thoughts in stirring silence.
    The clock ticked, and the big saucepan lid
    Heaved as the cabbage bubbled, and the girl
    Questioned the fire and spoke: 'My father, he
70 Took to the land. A mile of it is worth
    A guinea; for by that time all the trees
    Except those few about the house were gone.
    That's all that's left of the forest unless you count
    The bottoms of the charcoal-burners' fires –
75 We plough one up at times. Did you ever see
    Our signboard?' No. The post and empty frame
    I knew. Without them I could not have guessed
    The low grey house and its one stack under trees
    Was not a hermitage but a public-house.
80 'But can that empty frame be any use?
    Now I should like to see a good white horse
    Swing there, a really beautiful white horse,
    Galloping one side, being painted on the other.'
    'But would you like to hear it swing all night
85 And all day? All I ever had to thank
    The wind for was for blowing the sign down.
    Time after time it blew down and I could sleep.
    At last they fixed it, and it took a thief
    To move it, and we've never had another:
90 It's lying at the bottom of our pond.
    But no one's moved the wood from off the hill
    There at the back, although it makes a noise

When the wind blows, as if a train was running
The other side, a train that never stops

95 Or ends. And the linen crackles on the line
Like a woodfire rising.' 'But if you had the sign
You might draw company. What about Kennington?'
She bent down to her scrubbing with 'Not me.
Not back to Kennington. Here I was born,

100 And I've a notion on these windy nights
Here I shall die. Perhaps I want to die here.
I reckon I shall stay. But I do wish
The road was nearer and the wind farther off,
Or once now and then quite still, though when I die

105 I'd have it blowing that I might go with it
Somewhere far off, where there are trees no more
And I could wake and not know where I was
Nor even wonder if they would roar again.
Look at those calves.'

                                    Between the open door
110 And the trees two calves were wading in the pond,
Grazing the water here and there and thinking,
Sipping and thinking, both happily, neither long.
The water wrinkled, but they sipped and thought,
As careless of the wind as it of us.

115 'Look at those calves. Hark at the trees again.'

2] November Sky

November's days are thirty:
November's earth is dirty,
Those thirty days, from first to last;
And the prettiest things on ground are the paths

5 With morning and evening hobnails dinted,
   With foot and wing-tip overprinted
   Or separately charactered,
   Of little beast and little bird.
   The fields are mashed by sheep, the roads
10 Make the worst going, the best the woods
   Where dead leaves upward and downward scatter.
   Few care for the mixture of earth and water,
   Twig, leaf, flint, thorn,
   Straw, feather, all that men scorn,
15 Pounded up and sodden by flood,
   Condemned as mud.

   But of all the months when earth is greener
   Not one has clean skies that are cleaner.
   Clean and clear and sweet and cold,
20 They shine above the earth so old,
   While the after-tempest cloud
   Sails over in silence though winds are loud,
   Till the full moon in the east
   Looks at the planet in the west
25 And earth is silent as it is black,
   Yet not unhappy for its lack.
   Up from the dirty earth men stare:
   One imagines a refuge there
   Above the mud, in the pure bright
30 Of the cloudless heavenly light:
   Another loves earth and November more dearly
   Because without them, he sees clearly,
   The sky would be nothing more to his eye
   Than he, in any case, is to the sky;
35 He loves even the mud whose dyes
   Renounce all brightness to the skies.

3] March

Now I know that Spring will come again,
Perhaps tomorrow: however late I've patience
After this night following on such a day.

While still my temples ached from the cold burning
5 Of hail and wind, and still the primroses
Torn by the hail were covered up in it,
The sun filled earth and heaven with a great light
And a tenderness, almost warmth, where the hail dripped,
As if the mighty sun wept tears of joy.
10 But 'twas too late for warmth. The sunset piled
Mountains on mountains of snow and ice in the west:
Somewhere among their folds the wind was lost,
And yet 'twas cold, and though I knew that Spring
Would come again, I knew it had not come,
15 That it was lost, too, in those mountains cold.
What did the thrushes know? Rain, snow, sleet, hail,
Had kept them quiet as the primroses.
They had but an hour to sing. On boughs they sang,
On gates, on ground; they sang while they changed perches
20 And while they fought, if they remembered to fight:
So earnest were they to pack into that hour
Their unwilling hoard of song before the moon
Grew brighter than the clouds. Then 'twas no time
For singing merely. So they could keep off silence
25 And night, they cared not what they sang or screamed,
Whether 'twas hoarse or sweet or fierce or soft,
And to me all was sweet: they could do no wrong.
Something they knew – I also, while they sang
And after. Not till night had half its stars

30 And never a cloud, was I aware of silence
   Rich with all that riot of songs, a silence
   Saying that Spring returns, perhaps tomorrow.

4] Old Man

Old Man, or Lad's-love, – in the name there's nothing
To one that knows not Lad's-love, or Old Man,
The hoar-green feathery herb, almost a tree,
Growing with rosemary and lavender.
5 Even to one that knows it well, the names
Half decorate, half perplex, the thing it is:
At least, what that is clings not to the names
In spite of time. And yet I like the names.

The herb itself I like not, but for certain
10 I love it, as some day the child will love it
Who plucks a feather from the door-side bush
Whenever she goes in or out of the house.
Often she waits there, snipping the tips and shrivelling
The shreds at last on to the path, perhaps
15 Thinking, perhaps of nothing, till she sniffs
Her fingers and runs off. The bush is still
But half as tall as she, though it is as old;
So well she clips it. Not a word she says;
And I can only wonder how much hereafter
20 She will remember, with that bitter scent,
Of garden rows, and ancient damson-trees
Topping a hedge, a bent path to a door,
A low thick bush beside the door, and me
Forbidding her to pick.

                                        As for myself,
25 Where first I met the bitter scent is lost.
    I, too, often shrivel the grey shreds,
    Sniff them and think and sniff again and try
    Once more to think what it is I am remembering,
    Always in vain. I cannot like the scent,
30 Yet I would rather give up others more sweet,
    With no meaning, than this bitter one.

    I have mislaid the key. I sniff the spray
    And think of nothing; I see and I hear nothing;
    Yet seem, too, to be listening, lying in wait
35 For what I should, yet never can, remember:
    No garden appears, no path, no hoar-green bush
    Of Lad's-love, or Old Man, no child beside,
    Neither father nor mother, nor any playmate;
    Only an avenue, dark, nameless, without end.

5] The Signpost

    The dim sea glints chill. The white sun is shy,
    And the skeleton weeds and the never-dry,
    Rough, long grasses keep white with frost
    At the hilltop by the finger-post;
5   The smoke of traveller's-joy is puffed
    Over hawthorn berry and hazel tuft.

    I read the sign. Which way shall I go?
    A voice says: You would not have doubted so
    At twenty. Another voice gentle with scorn
10 Says: At twenty you wished you had never been born.

One hazel lost a leaf of gold
From a tuft at the tip, when the first voice told
The other he wished to know what 'twould be
To be sixty by this same post. 'You shall see'
15 He laughed – and I had to join his laughter –
'You shall see; but either before or after,
Whatever happens, it must befall,
A mouthful of earth to remedy all
Regrets and wishes shall freely be given;
20 And if there be a flaw in that heaven
'Twill be freedom to wish, and your wish may be
To be here or anywhere talking to me,
No matter what the weather, on earth,
At any age between death and birth,
25 To see what day or night can be,
The sun and the frost, the land and the sea,
Summer, Autumn, Winter, Spring,
With a poor man of any sort, down to a king,
Standing upright out in the air
30 Wondering where he shall journey, O where?'

6] The Other

The forest ended. Glad I was
To feel the light, and hear the hum
Of bees, and smell the drying grass
And the sweet mint, because I had come
5 To an end of forest, and because
Here was both road and inn, the sum
Of what's not forest. But 'twas here
They asked me if I did not pass
Yesterday this way? 'Not you? Queer.'
10 'Who then? and slept here?' I felt fear.

I learnt his road and, ere they were
Sure I was I, left the dark wood
Behind, kestrel and woodpecker,
The inn in the sun, the happy mood
15 When first I tasted sunlight there.
I travelled fast, in hopes I should
Outrun that other. What to do
When caught, I planned not. I pursued
To prove the likeness, and, if true,
20 To watch until myself I knew.

I tried the inns that evening
Of a long gabled high-street grey,
Of courts and outskirts, travelling
An eager but a weary way,
25 In vain. He was not there. Nothing
Told me that ever till that day
Had one like me entered those doors,
Save once. That time I dared: 'You may
Recall' – but never-foamless shores
30 Make better friends than those dull boors.

Many and many a day like this
Aimed at the unseen moving goal
And nothing found but remedies
For all desire. These made not whole;
35 They sowed a new desire, to kiss
Desire's self beyond control,
Desire of desire. And yet
Life stayed on within my soul.
One night in sheltering from the wet
40 I quite forgot I could forget.

A customer, then the landlady
Stared at me. With a kind of smile

They hesitated awkwardly:
Their silence gave me time for guile.
45 Had anyone called there like me,
I asked. It was quite plain the wile
Succeeded. For they poured out all.
And that was naught. Less than a mile
Beyond the inn, I could recall
50 He was like me in general.

He had pleased them, but I less.
I was more eager than before
To find him out and to confess,
To bore him and to let him bore.
55 I could not wait: children might guess
I had a purpose, something more
That made an answer indiscreet.
One girl's caution made me sore,
Too indignant even to greet
60 That other had we chanced to meet.

I sought then in solitude.
The wind had fallen with the night; as still
The roads lay as the ploughland rude,
Dark and naked, on the hill.
65 Had there been ever any feud
'Twixt earth and sky, a mighty will
Closed it: the crocketed dark trees,
A dark house, dark impossible
Cloud-towers, one star, one lamp, one peace
70 Held on an everlasting lease:

And all was earth's, or all was sky's;
No difference endured between
The two. A dog barked on a hidden rise;
A marshbird whistled high unseen;

75 The latest waking blackbird's cries
Perished upon the silence keen.
The last light filled a narrow firth
Among the clouds. I stood serene,
And with a solemn quiet mirth,
80 An old inhabitant of earth.

Once the name I gave to hours
Like this was melancholy, when
It was not happiness and powers
Coming like exiles home again,
85 And weakness quitting their bowers,
Smiled and enjoyed, far off from men,
Moments of everlastingness.
And fortunate my search was then
While what I sought, nevertheless,
90 That I was seeking, I did not guess.

That time was brief: once more at inn
And upon road I sought my man
Till once amid a tap-room's din
Loudly he asked for me, began
95 To speak, as if it had been a sin,
Of how I thought and dreamed and ran
After him thus, day after day:
He lived as one under a ban
For this: what had I got to say?
100 I said nothing. I slipped away.

And now I dare not follow after
Too close. I try to keep in sight,
Dreading his frown and worse his laughter.
I steal out of the wood to light;
105 I see the swift shoot from the rafter

By the inn door: ere I alight
I wait and hear the starlings wheeze
And nibble like ducks: I wait his flight.
He goes: I follow: no release
110 Until he ceases. Then I also shall cease.

7] After Rain

The rain of a night and a day and a night
Stops at the light
Of this pale choked day. The peering sun
Sees what has been done.
5 The road under the trees has a border new
Of purple hue
Inside the border of bright thin grass:
For all that has
Been left by November of leaves is torn
10 From hazel and thorn
And the greater trees. Throughout the copse
No dead leaf drops
On grey grass, green moss, burnt-orange fern,
At the wind's return:
15 The leaflets out of the ash-tree shed
Are thinly spread
In the road, like little black fish, inlaid,
As if they played.
What hangs from the myriad branches down there
20 So hard and bare
Is twelve yellow apples lovely to see
On one crab-tree,
And on each twig of every tree in the dell
Uncountable

25 Crystals both dark and bright of the rain
    That begins again.

8] Interval

    Gone the wild day.
    A wilder night
    Coming makes way
    For brief twilight.

5   Where the firm soaked road
    Mounts beneath pines
    To the high beech wood
    It almost shines.

    The beeches keep
10 A stormy rest,
    Breathing deep
    Of wind from the west.

    The wood is black,
    With a misty steam.
15 Above it the rack
    Breaks for one gleam.

    But the woodman's cot
    By the ivied trees
    Awakens not
20 To light or breeze.

    It smokes aloft
    Unwavering:
    It hunches soft
    Under storm's wing.

25 It has no care
   For gleam or gloom:
   It stays there
   While I shall roam,

   Die and forget
30 The hill of trees,
   The gleam, the wet,
   This roaring peace.

9] Birds' Nests

The summer nests uncovered by autumn wind,
Some torn, others dislodged, all dark,
Everyone sees them: low or high in tree,
Or hedge, or single bush, they hang like a mark.

5 Since there's no need of eyes to see them with
   I cannot help a little shame
   That I missed most, even at eye's level, till
   The leaves blew off and made the seeing no game.

   'Tis a light pang. I like to see the nests
10 Still in their places, now first known,
   At home and by far roads. Boys never found them,
   Whatever jays or squirrels may have done.

   And most I like the winter nest deep-hid
   That leaves and berries fell into;
15 Once a dormouse dined there on hazel nuts;
   And grass and goose-grass seeds found soil and
      grew.

10] The Mountain Chapel

Chapel and gravestones, old and few,
Are shrouded by a mountain fold
From sound and view
Of life. The loss of the brook's voice
5   Falls like a shadow. All they hear is
The eternal noise
Of wind whistling in grass more shrill
Than aught as human as a sword,
And saying still:
10   ' 'Tis but a moment since man's birth,
And in another moment more
Man lies in earth
For ever; but I am the same
Now, and shall be, even as I was
15   Before he came:
Till there is nothing I shall be.'

Yet there the sun shines after noon
So cheerfully
The place almost seems peopled, nor
20   Lacks cottage chimney, cottage hearth:
It is not more
In size than is a cottage, less
Than any other empty home
In homeliness.
25   It has a garden of wild flowers
And finest grass and gravestones warm
In sunshine hours
The year through. Men behind the glass
Stand once a week, singing, and drown

30 The whistling grass
    Their ponies munch. And yet somewhere
    Near or far off there's some man could
    Live happy here,
    Or one of the gods perhaps, were they
35 Not of inhuman stature dire
    As poets say
    Who have not seen them clearly, if
    At sound of any wind of the world
    In grass-blades stiff
40 They would not startle and shudder cold
    Under the sun. When Gods were young
    This wind was old.

11] The Manor Farm

    The rock-like mud unfroze a little and rills
    Ran and sparkled down each side of the road
    Under the catkins wagging in the hedge.
    But earth would have her sleep out, spite of the sun;
5   Nor did I value that thin gilding beam
    More than a pretty February thing
    Till I came down to the old Manor Farm,
    And church and yew-tree opposite, in age
    Its equals and in size. Small church, great yew,
10 And farmhouse slept in a Sunday silentness.
    The air raised not a straw. The steep farm roof,
    With tiles duskily glowing, entertained
    The midday sun; and up and down the roof
    White pigeons nestled. There was no sound but one.
15 Three cart-horses were looking over a gate
    Drowsily through their forelocks, swishing their tails
    Against a fly, a solitary fly.

The Winter's cheek flushed as if he had drained
Spring, Summer, and Autumn at a draught
20   And smiled quietly. But 'twas not Winter –
Rather a season of bliss unchangeable
Awakened from farm and church where it had lain
Safe under tile and thatch for ages since
This England, Old already, was called Merry.

12]   An Old Song [1]

I was not apprenticed nor ever dwelt in famous
          Lincolnshire;
I've served one master ill and well much more than seven
          year;
And never took up to poaching as you shall quickly find;
    But 'tis my delight of a shiny night in the season of the
          year.

5   I roamed where nobody had a right but keepers and squires,
          and there
    I sought for nests, wild flowers, oak sticks, and moles, both
          far and near,
    And had to run from farmers, and learnt the Lincolnshire
          song:
      'Oh, 'tis my delight of a shiny night in the season of the
          year.'

I took those walks years after, talking with friend or dear,
10   Or solitary musing; but when the moon shone clear
    I had no joy or sorrow that could not be expressed
      By ' 'Tis my delight of a shiny night in the season of the
          year.'

Since then I've thrown away a chance to fight a gamekeeper;
And I less often trespass, and what I see or hear
15 Is mostly from the road or path by day: yet still I sing:
     'Oh, 'tis my delight of a shiny night in the season of the
        year.'

For if I am contented, at home or anywhere,
Or if I sigh for I know not what, or my heart beats with
        some fear,
It is a strange kind of delight to sing or whistle just:
20 'Oh, 'tis my delight of a shiny night in the season of the
        year.'

And with this melody on my lips and no one by to care,
Indoors, or out on shiny nights or dark in open air,
I am for a moment made a man that sings out of his heart:
     'Oh, 'tis my delight of a shiny night in the season of the
        year.'

13] An Old Song [2]

The sun set, the wind fell, the sea
Was like a mirror shaking:
The one small wave that clapped the land
A mile-long snake of foam was making
5 Where tide had smoothed and wind had dried
The vacant sand.

A light divided the swollen clouds
And lay most perfectly
Like a straight narrow footbridge bright
10 That crossed over the sea to me;
And no one else in the whole world
Saw that same sight.

I walked elate, my bridge always
Just one step from my feet:
15   A robin sang, a shade in shade:
And all I did was to repeat:
    'I'll go no more a-roving
    With you, fair maid.'

The sailors' song of merry loving
20   With dusk and sea-gull's mewing
Mixed sweet, the lewdness far outweighed
By the wild charm the chorus played:
    'I'll go no more a-roving
    With you, fair maid:
25   A-roving, a-roving, since roving's been my ruin,
I'll go no more a-roving with you, fair maid.'

In Amsterdam there dwelt a maid –
Mark well what I do say –
In Amsterdam there dwelt a maid
30   *And she was a mistress of her trade:*
I'll go no more a-roving
With you, fair maid:
A-roving, a-roving, since roving's been my ruin,
I'll go no more a-roving with you, fair maid.

14] The Combe

The Combe was ever dark, ancient and dark.
Its mouth is stopped with bramble, thorn, and briar;
And no one scrambles over the sliding chalk
By beech and yew and perishing juniper
5   Down the half precipices of its sides, with roots
And rabbit holes for steps. The sun of Winter,

The moon of Summer, and all the singing birds
Except the missel-thrush that loves juniper,
Are quite shut out. But far more ancient and dark
10 The Combe looks since they killed the badger there,
Dug him out and gave him to the hounds,
That most ancient Briton of English beasts.

15] The Hollow Wood

Out in the sun the goldfinch flits
Along the thistle-tops, flits and twits
Above the hollow wood
Where birds swim like fish –
5 Fish that laugh and shriek –
To and fro, far below
In the pale hollow wood.

Lichen, ivy, and moss
Keep evergreen the trees
10 That stand half-flayed and dying,
And the dead trees on their knees
In dog's-mercury, ivy, and moss:
And the bright twit of the goldfinch drops
Down there as he flits on thistle-tops.

16] The New Year

He was the one man I met up in the woods
That stormy New Year's morning; and at first sight,
Fifty yards off, I could not tell how much
Of the strange tripod was a man. His body,
5   Bowed horizontal, was supported equally
By legs at one end, by a rake at the other:
Thus he rested, far less like a man than
His wheel-barrow in profile was like a pig.
But when I saw it was an old man bent,
10 At the same moment came into my mind
The games at which boys bend thus, *High-cockolorum*,
Or *Fly-the-garter*, and *Leap-frog*. At the sound
Of footsteps he began to straighten himself;
His head rolled under his cape like a tortoise's;
15 He took an unlit pipe out of his mouth
Politely ere I wished him 'A Happy New Year',
And with his head cast upward sideways muttered –
So far as I could hear through the trees' roar –
'Happy New Year, and may it come fastish, too',
20 While I strode by and he turned to raking leaves.

17] The Source

All day the air triumphs with its two voices
Of wind and rain:
As loud as if in anger it rejoices,
Drowning the sound of earth
5 That gulps and gulps in choked endeavour vain
To swallow the rain.

Half the night, too, only the wild air speaks
With wind and rain,
Till forth the dumb source of the river breaks
10 And drowns the rain and wind,
Bellows like a giant bathing in mighty mirth
The triumph of earth.

18] The Penny Whistle

The new moon hangs like an ivory bugle
In the naked frosty blue;
And the ghylls of the forest, already blackened
By Winter, are blackened anew.

5 The brooks that cut up and increase the forest,
As if they had never known
The sun, are roaring with black hollow voices
Betwixt rage and a moan.

But still the caravan-hut by the hollies
10 Like a kingfisher gleams between:
Round the mossed old hearths of the charcoal-burners
First primroses ask to be seen.

The charcoal-burners are black, but their linen
Blows white on the line;
15 And white the letter the girl is reading
Under that crescent fine;

And her brother who hides apart in a thicket,
Slowly and surely playing
On a whistle an olden nursery melody,
20 Says far more than I am saying.

19] A Private

This ploughman dead in battle slept out of doors
Many a frosty night, and merrily
Answered staid drinkers, good bedmen, and all bores:
'At Mrs Greenland's Hawthorn Bush,' said he,
'I slept.' None knew which bush. Above the town,
Beyond 'The Drover', a hundred spot the down
In Wiltshire. And where now at last he sleeps
More sound in France – that, too, he secret keeps.

20] Snow

In the gloom of whiteness,
In the great silence of snow,
A child was sighing
And bitterly saying: 'Oh,
They have killed a white bird up there on her nest,
The down is fluttering from her breast.'
And still it fell through that dusky brightness
On the child crying for the bird of the snow.

21] Adlestrop

Yes, I remember Adlestrop –
The name, because one afternoon
Of heat the express-train drew up there
Unwontedly. It was late June.

The steam hissed. Someone cleared his throat.
No one left and no one came

On the bare platform. What I saw
Was Adlestrop – only the name

And willows, willow-herb, and grass,
10   And meadowsweet, and haycocks dry,
No whit less still and lonely fair
Than the high cloudlets in the sky.

And for that minute a blackbird sang
Close by, and round him, mistier,
15   Farther and farther, all the birds
Of Oxfordshire and Gloucestershire.

22] Tears

It seems I have no tears left. They should have fallen –
Their ghosts, if tears have ghosts, did fall – that day
When twenty hounds streamed by me, not yet combed out
But still all equals in their rage of gladness
5   Upon the scent, made one, like a great dragon
In Blooming Meadow that bends towards the sun
And once bore hops: and on that other day
When I stepped out from the double-shadowed Tower
Into an April morning, stirring and sweet
10   And warm. Strange solitude was there and silence.
A mightier charm than any in the Tower
Possessed the courtyard. They were changing guard,
Soldiers in line, young English countrymen,
Fair-haired and ruddy, in white tunics. Drums
15   And fifes were playing 'The British Grenadiers'.
The men, the music piercing that solitude
And silence, told me truths I had not dreamed,
And have forgotten since their beauty passed.

23] Over the Hills

Often and often it came back again
To mind, the day I passed the horizon ridge
To a new country, the path I had to find
By half-gaps that were stiles once in the hedge,
5 The pack of scarlet clouds running across
The harvest evening that seemed endless then
And after, and the inn where all were kind,
All were strangers. I did not know my loss
Till one day twelve months later suddenly
10 I leaned upon my spade and saw it all,
Though far beyond the sky-line. It became
Almost a habit through the year for me
To lean and see it and think to do the same
Again for two days and a night. Recall
15 Was vain: no more could the restless brook
Ever turn back and climb the waterfall
To the lake that rests and stirs not in its nook,
As in the hollow of the collar-bone
Under the mountain's head of rush and stone.

24] The Lofty Sky

Today I want the sky,
The tops of the high hills,
Above the last man's house,
His hedges, and his cows,
5 Where, if I will, I look
Down even on sheep and rook,
And of all things that move

See buzzards only above: –
Past all trees, past furze
10   And thorn, where naught deters
The desire of the eye
For sky, nothing but sky.
I sicken of the woods
And all the multitudes
15   Of hedge-trees. They are no more
Than weeds upon this floor
Of the river of air
Leagues deep, leagues wide, where
I am like a fish that lives
20   In weeds and mud and gives
What's above him no thought.
I might be a tench for aught
That I can do today
Down on the wealden clay.
25   Even the tench has days
When he floats up and plays
Among the lily leaves
And sees the sky, or grieves
Not if he nothing sees:
30   While I, I know that trees
Under that lofty sky
Are weeds, fields mud, and I
Would arise and go far
To where the lilies are.

25] The Cuckoo

That's the cuckoo, you say. I cannot hear it.
When last I heard it I cannot recall; but I know

Too well the year when first I failed to hear it –
It was drowned by my man groaning out to his sheep
   'Ho! Ho!'

5 Ten times with an angry voice he shouted
'Ho! Ho!' but not in anger, for that was his way.
He died that Summer, and that is how I remember
The cuckoo calling, the children listening, and me saying,
   'Nay.'

And now, as you said, 'There it is' I was hearing
10 Not the cuckoo at all, but my man's 'Ho! Ho!' instead.
And I think that even if I could lose my deafness
The cuckoo's note would be drowned by the voice of my
   dead.

26] Swedes

They have taken the gable from the roof of clay
On the long swede pile. They have let in the sun
To the white and gold and purple of curled fronds
Unsunned. It is a sight more tender-gorgeous
5 At the wood-corner where Winter moans and drips
Than when, in the Valley of the Tombs of Kings,
A boy crawls down into a Pharaoh's tomb
And, first of Christian men, beholds the mummy,
God and monkey, chariot and throne and vase,
10 Blue pottery, alabaster, and gold.

But dreamless long-dead Amen-hotep lies.
This is a dream of Winter, sweet as Spring.

27] The Unknown Bird

Three lovely notes he whistled, too soft to be heard
If others sang; but others never sang
In the great beech-wood all that May and June.
No one saw him: I alone could hear him
5   Though many listened. Was it but four years
Ago? or five? He never came again.
Oftenest when I heard him I was alone,
Nor could I ever make another hear.
La-la-la! he called, seeming far-off –
10   As if a cock crowed past the edge of the world,
As if the bird or I were in a dream.
Yet that he travelled through the trees and sometimes
Neared me, was plain, though somehow distant still
He sounded. All the proof is – I told men
What I had heard.

15   I never knew a voice,
Man, beast, or bird, better than this. I told
The naturalists; but neither had they heard
Anything like the notes that did so haunt me
I had them clear by heart and have them still.
20   Four years, or five, have made no difference. Then
As now that La-la-la! was bodiless sweet:
Sad more than joyful it was, if I must say
That it was one or other, but if sad
'Twas sad only with joy too, too far off
25   For me to taste it. But I cannot tell
If truly never anything but fair
The days were when he sang, as now they seem.
This surely I know, that I who listened then,

Happy sometimes, sometimes suffering
30   A heavy body and a heavy heart,
Now straightway, if I think of it, become
Light as that bird wandering beyond my shore.

28] The Mill-Pond

The sun blazed while the thunder yet
Added a boom:
A wagtail flickered bright over
The mill-pond's gloom:

5   Less than the cooing in the alder
Isles of the pool
Sounded the thunder through that plunge
Of waters cool.

Scared starlings on the aspen tip
10   Past the black mill
Outchattered the stream and the next roar
Far on the hill.

As my feet dangling teased the foam
That slid below
15   A girl came out. 'Take care!' she said –
Ages ago.

She startled me, standing quite close
Dressed all in white:
Ages ago I was angry till
20   She passed from sight.

Then the storm burst, and as I crouched
To shelter, how

Beautiful and kind, too, she seemed,
As she does now!

29]

' 'Twill take some getting.' 'Sir, I think 'twill so.'
The old man stared up at the mistletoe
That hung too high in the poplar's crest for plunder
Of any climber, though not for kissing under:
5 Then he went on against the north-east wind –
Straight but lame, leaning on a staff new-skinned,
Carrying a brolly, flag-basket, and old coat, –
Towards Alton, ten miles off. And he had not
Done less from Chilgrove where he pulled up docks.
10 'Twere best, if he had had 'a money-box',
To have waited there till the sheep cleared a field
For what a half-week's flint-picking would yield.
His mind was running on the work he had done
Since he left Christchurch in the New Forest, one
15 Spring in the 'seventies, – navvying on dock and line
From Southampton to Newcastle-on-Tyne, –
In 'seventy-four a year of soldiering
With the Berkshires, – hoeing and harvesting
In half the shires where corn and couch will grow.
20 His sons, three sons, were fighting, but the hoe
And reap-hook he liked, or anything to do with trees.
He fell once from a poplar tall as these:
The Flying Man they called him in hospital.
'If I flew now, to another world I'd fall.'
25 He laughed and whistled to the small brown bitch
With spots of blue that hunted in the ditch.
Her foxy Welsh grandfather must have paired

Beneath him. He kept sheep in Wales and scared
Strangers, I will warrant, with his pearl eye
30   And trick of shrinking off as he were shy,
Then following close in silence for – for what?
'No rabbit, never fear, she ever got,
Yet always hunts. Today she nearly had one:
She would and she wouldn't. 'Twas like that. The bad one!
35   She's not much use, but still she's company,
Though I'm not. She goes everywhere with me.
So Alton I must reach tonight somehow:
I'll get no shakedown with that bedfellow
From farmers. Many a man sleeps worse tonight
40   Than I shall.' 'In the trenches.' 'Yes, that's right.
But they'll be out of that – I hope they be –
This weather, marching after the enemy.'
'And so I hope. Good luck.' And there I nodded
'Good-night. You keep straight on.' Stiffly he plodded;
45   And at his heels the crisp leaves scurried fast,
And the leaf-coloured robin watched. They passed,
The robin till next day, the man for good,
Together in the twilight of the wood.

30] Beauty

What does it mean? Tired, angry, and ill at ease,
No man, woman, or child, alive could please
Me now. And yet I almost dare to laugh
Because I sit and frame an epitaph –
5   'Here lies all that no one loved of him
And that loved no one.' Then in a trice that whim
Has wearied. But, though I am like a river
At fall of evening while it seems that never

Has the sun lighted it or warmed it, while
10 Cross breezes cut the surface to a file,
This heart, some fraction of me, happily
Floats through the window even now to a tree
Down in the misting, dim-lit, quiet vale,
Not like a pewit that returns to wail
15 For something it has lost, but like a dove
That slants unswerving to its home and love.
There I find my rest, as through the dusk air
Flies what yet lives in me: Beauty is there.

31]

A fortnight before Christmas Gypsies were everywhere:
Vans were drawn up on wastes, women trailed to the fair.
'My gentleman,' said one, 'You've got a lucky face.'
'And you've a luckier,' I thought, 'if such a grace
5 And impudence in rags are lucky.' 'Give a penny
For the poor baby's sake.' 'Indeed I have not any
Unless you can give change for a sovereign, my dear.'
'Then just half a pipeful of tobacco can you spare?'
I gave it. With that much victory she laughed content.
10 I should have given more, but off and away she went
With her baby and her pink sham flowers to rejoin
The rest before I could translate to its proper coin
Gratitude for her grace. And I paid nothing then,
As I pay nothing now with the dipping of my pen
15 For her brother's music when he drummed the tambourine
And stamped his feet, which made the workmen passing
    grin,
While his mouth-organ changed to a rascally Bacchanal
    dance

'Over the hills and far away'. This and his glance
Outlasted all the fair, farmer and auctioneer,
20   Cheap-jack, balloon-man, drover with crooked stick, and
        steer,
Pig, turkey, goose, and duck, Christmas Corpses to be.
Not even the kneeling ox had eyes like the Romany.
That night he peopled for me the hollow wooded land,
More dark and wild than stormiest heavens, that I searched
        and scanned
25   Like a ghost new-arrived. The gradations of the dark
Were like an underworld of death, but for the spark
In the Gypsy boy's black eyes as he played and stamped his
        tune,
'Over the hills and far away', and a crescent moon.

32] Ambition

Unless it was that day I never knew
Ambition. After a night of frost, before
The March sun brightened and the South-west blew,
Jackdaws began to shout and float and soar
5   Already, and one was racing straight and high
Alone, shouting like a black warrior
Challenges and menaces to the wide sky.
With loud long laughter then a woodpecker
Ridiculed the sadness of the owl's last cry.
10   And through the valley where all the folk astir
Made only plumes of pearly smoke to tower
Over dark trees and white meadows happier
Than was Elysium in that happy hour,
A train that roared along raised after it
15   And carried with it a motionless white bower

Of purest cloud, from end to end close-knit,
So fair it touched the roar with silence. Time
Was powerless while that lasted. I could sit
And think I had made the loveliness of prime,
20 Breathed its life into it and were its lord,
And no mind lived save this 'twixt clouds and rime.
Omnipotent I was, nor even deplored
That I did nothing. But the end fell like a bell:
The bower was scattered; far off the train roared.
25 But if this was ambition I cannot tell:
What 'twas ambition for I know not well.

33] House and Man

One hour: as dim he and his house now look
As a reflection in a rippling brook,
While I remember him; but first, his house.
Empty it sounded. 'Twas dark with forest boughs
5 That brushed the walls and made the mossy tiles
Part of the squirrels' track. In all those miles
Of forest silence and forest murmur, only
One house – 'Lonely,' he said, 'I wish it were lonely' –
Which the trees looked upon from every side,
And that was his.

10   He waved good-bye to hide
A sigh that he converted to a laugh.
He seemed to hang rather than stand there, half
Ghost-like, half a beggar's rag, clean wrung
And useless on the briar where it has hung
15 Long years a-washing by sun and wind and rain.
But why I call back man and house again

Is that now on a beech-tree's tip I see
As then I saw – I at the gate, and he
In the house darkness, – a magpie veering about,
20   A magpie like a weathercock in doubt.

34] Parting

The Past is a strange land, most strange.
Wind blows not there, nor does rain fall:
If they do, they cannot hurt at all.
Men of all kinds as equals range

5   The soundless fields and streets of it.
Pleasure and pain there have no sting,
The perished self not suffering
That lacks all blood and nerve and wit,

And is in shadow-land a shade.
10   Remembered joy and misery
Bring joy to the joyous equally;
Both sadden the sad. So memory made

Parting today a double pain:
First because it was parting; next
15   Because the ill it ended vexed
And mocked me from the Past again,

Not as what had been remedied
Had I gone on, – not that, oh no!
But as itself no longer woe;
20   Sighs, angry word and look and deed

Being faded: rather a kind of bliss,
For there spiritualized it lay

In the perpetual yesterday
That naught can stir or stain, like this.

35] First known when lost

I never had noticed it until
'Twas gone, – the narrow copse
Where now the woodman lops
The last of the willows with his bill.

5 It was not more than a hedge o'ergrown.
One meadow's breadth away
I passed it day by day.
Now the soil is bare as a bone,

And black betwixt two meadows green,
10 Though fresh-cut faggot ends
Of hazel make some amends
With a gleam as if flowers they had been.

Strange it could have hidden so near!
And now I see as I look
15 That the small winding brook,
A tributary's tributary rises there.

36] May 23

There never was a finer day,
And never will be while May is May, –
The third, and not the last of its kind;
But though fair and clear the two behind
5 Seemed pursued by tempests overpast;

And the morrow with fear that it could not last
Was spoiled. Today ere the stones were warm
Five minutes of thunderstorm
Dashed it with rain, as if to secure,
10 By one tear, its beauty the luck to endure.

At midday then along the lane
Old Jack Noman appeared again,
Jaunty and old, crooked and tall,
And stopped and grinned at me over the wall,
15 With a cowslip bunch in his button-hole
And one in his cap. Who could say if his roll
Came from flints in the road, the weather, or ale?
He was welcome as the nightingale.
Not an hour of the sun had been wasted on Jack.
20 'I've got my Indian complexion back'
Said he. He was tanned like a harvester,
Like his short clay pipe, like the leaf and bur
That clung to his coat from last night's bed,
Like the ploughland crumbling red.
25 Fairer flowers were none on the earth
Than his cowslips wet with the dew of their birth,
Or fresher leaves than the cress in his basket.
'Where did they come from, Jack?' 'Don't ask it,
And you'll be told no lies.' 'Very well:
30 Then I can't buy.' 'I don't want to sell.
Take them and these flowers, too, free.
Perhaps you have something to give me?
Wait till next time. The better the day . . .
The Lord couldn't make a better, I say;
35 If he could, he never has done.'
So off went Jack with his roll-walk-run,
Leaving his cresses from Oakshott rill
And his cowslips from Wheatham hill.

'T was the first day that the midges bit;
40 But though they bit me, I was glad of it:
Of the dust in my face, too, I was glad.
Spring could do nothing to make me sad.
Bluebells hid all the ruts in the copse.
The elm seeds lay in the road like hops,
45 That fine day, May the twenty-third,
The day Jack Noman disappeared.

37] The Barn

They should never have built a barn there, at all –
Drip, drip, drip! – under that elm tree,
Though then it was young. Now it is old
But good, not like the barn and me.

5 Tomorrow they cut it down. They will leave
The barn, as I shall be left, maybe.
What holds it up? 'Twould not pay to pull down.
Well, this place has no other antiquity.

No abbey or castle looks so old
10 As this that Job Knight built in '54,
Built to keep corn for rats and men.
Now there's fowls in the roof, pigs on the floor.

What thatch survives is dung for the grass,
The best grass on the farm. A pity the roof
15 Will not bear a mower to mow it. But
Only fowls have foothold enough.

Starlings used to sit there with bubbling throats
Making a spiky beard as they chattered
And whistled and kissed, with heads in air,
20 Till they thought of something else that mattered.

But now they cannot find a place,
Among all those holes, for a nest any more.
It's the turn of lesser things, I suppose.
Once I fancied 'twas starlings they built it for.

38] Home [1]

Not the end: but there's nothing more.
Sweet Summer and Winter rude
I have loved, and friendship and love,
The crowd and solitude:

5 But I know them: I weary not;
But all that they mean I know.
I would go back again home
Now. Yet how should I go?

This is my grief. That land,
10 My home, I have never seen;
No traveller tells of it,
However far he has been.

And could I discover it,
I fear my happiness there,
15 Or my pain, might be dreams of return
Here, to these things that were.

Remembering ills, though slight
Yet irremediable,
Brings a worse, an impurer pang
20 Than remembering what was well.

No: I cannot go back,
And would not if I could.

Until blindness come, I must wait
And blink at what is not good.

39] The Owl

Downhill I came, hungry, and yet not starved;
Cold, yet had heat within me that was proof
Against the North wind; tired, yet so that rest
Had seemed the sweetest thing under a roof.

5   Then at the inn I had food, fire, and rest,
Knowing how hungry, cold, and tired was I.
All of the night was quite barred out except
An owl's cry, a most melancholy cry

Shaken out long and clear upon the hill,
10 No merry note, nor cause of merriment,
But one telling me plain what I escaped
And others could not, that night, as in I went.

And salted was my food, and my repose,
Salted and sobered, too, by the bird's voice
15 Speaking for all who lay under the stars,
Soldiers and poor, unable to rejoice.

40] The Child on the Cliff

Mother, the root of this little yellow flower
Among the stones has the taste of quinine.
Things are strange today on the cliff. The sun shines so
    bright,
And the grasshopper works at his sewing-machine

5 So hard. Here's one on my hand, mother, look;
I lie so still. There's one on your book.

But I have something to tell more strange. So leave
Your book to the grasshopper, mother dear, –
Like a green knight in a dazzling market-place, –
10 And listen now. Can you hear what I hear
Far out? Now and then the foam there curls
And stretches a white arm out like a girl's.

Fishes and gulls ring no bells. There cannot be
A chapel or church between here and Devon,
15 With fishes or gulls ringing its bell, – hark. –
Somewhere under the sea or up in heaven.
'It's the bell, my son, out in the bay
On the buoy. It does sound sweet today.'

Sweeter I never heard, mother, no, not in all Wales.
20 I should like to be lying under that foam,
Dead, but able to hear the sound of the bell,
And certain that you would often come
And rest, listening happily.
I should be happy if that could be.

41] The Bridge

I have come a long way today:
On a strange bridge alone,
Remembering friends, old friends,
I rest, without smile or moan,
5 As they remember me without smile or moan.

All are behind, the kind
And the unkind too, no more

Tonight than a dream. The stream
Runs softly yet drowns the Past,
10 The dark-lit stream has drowned the Future and the Past.

No traveller has rest more blest
Than this moment brief between
Two lives, when the Night's first lights
And shades hide what has never been,
15 Things goodlier, lovelier, dearer, than will be or have been.

42] Good-night

The skylarks are far behind that sang over the down;
I can hear no more those suburb nightingales;
Thrushes and blackbirds sing in the gardens of the town
In vain: the noise of man, beast, and machine prevails.

5 But the call of children in the unfamiliar streets
That echo with a familiar twilight echoing,
Sweet as the voice of nightingale or lark, completes
A magic of strange welcome, so that I seem a king

Among man, beast, machine, bird, child, and the ghost
10 That in the echo lives and with the echo dies.
The friendless town is friendly; homeless, I am not lost;
Though I know none of these doors, and meet but strangers'
  eyes.

Never again, perhaps, after tomorrow, shall
I see these homely streets, these church windows alight,
15 Not a man or woman or child among them all:
But it is All Friends' Night, a traveller's good night.

43] But these things also

But these things also are Spring's –
On banks by the roadside the grass
Long-dead that is greyer now
Than all the Winter it was;

5 The shell of a little snail bleached
In the grass: chip of flint, and mite
Of chalk; and the small birds' dung
In splashes of purest white:

All the white things a man mistakes
10 For earliest violets
Who seeks through Winter's ruins
Something to pay Winter's debts,

While the North blows, and starling flocks
By chattering on and on
15 Keep their spirits up in the mist,
And Spring's here, Winter's not gone.

44] The New House

Now first, as I shut the door,
I was alone
In the new house; and the wind
Began to moan.

5 Old at once was the house,
And I was old;
My ears were teased with the dread
Of what was foretold,

Nights of storm, days of mist, without end;
10   Sad days when the sun
Shone in vain: old griefs, and griefs
Not yet begun.

All was foretold me; naught
Could I foresee;
15   But I learnt how the wind would sound
After these things should be.

45] The Barn and the Down

It stood in the sunset sky
Like the straight-backed down,
Many a time – the barn
At the edge of the town,

5   So huge and dark that it seemed
It was the hill
Till the gable's precipice proved
It impossible.

Then the great down in the west
10   Grew into sight,
A barn stored full to the ridge
With black of night;

And the barn fell to a barn
Or even less
15   Before critical eyes and its own
Late mightiness.

But far down and near barn and I
Since then have smiled,

Having seen my new cautiousness
20 By itself beguiled

To disdain what seemed the barn
Till a few steps changed
It past all doubt to the down;
So the barn was avenged.

46] Sowing

It was a perfect day
For sowing; just
As sweet and dry was the ground
As tobacco-dust.

5   I tasted deep the hour
Between the far
Owl's chuckling first soft cry
And the first star.

A long stretched hour it was;
10 Nothing undone
Remained; the early seeds
All safely sown.

And now, hark at the rain,
Windless and light,
15 Half a kiss, half a tear,
Saying good-night.

47] March the 3rd

Here again (she said) is March the third
And twelve hours singing for the bird

'Twixt dawn and dusk, from half past six
To half past six, never unheard.

5   'Tis Sunday, and the church-bells end
With the birds' songs. I think they blend
Better than in the same fair days
That shall pronounce the Winter's end.

Do men mark, and none dares say,
10 How it may shift and long delay,
Somewhere before the first of Spring,
But never fails, this singing day?

When it falls on Sunday, bells
Are a wild natural voice that dwells
15 On hillsides; but the birds' songs have
The holiness gone from the bells.

This day unpromised is more dear
Than all the named days of the year
When seasonable sweets come in,
20 Since now we know how lucky we are.

48] Two Pewits

Under the after-sunset sky
Two pewits sport and cry,
More white than is the moon on high
Riding the dark surge silently;
5 More black than earth. Their cry
Is the one sound under the sky.
They alone move, now low, now high,
And merrily they cry
To the mischievous Spring sky,

10   Plunging earthward, tossing high,
     Over the ghost who wonders why
     So merrily they cry and fly,
     Nor choose 'twixt earth and sky,
     While the moon's quarter silently
15   Rides, and earth rests as silently.

     49] Will you come?

     Will you come?
     Will you come?
     Will you ride
     So late
5   At my side?
     O, will you come?

     Will you come?
     Will you come
     If the night
10   Has a moon,
     Full and bright?
     O, will you come?

     Would you come?
     Would you come
15   If the noon
     Gave light,
     Not the moon?
     Beautiful, would you come?

     Would you have come?
20   Would you have come
     Without scorning,

Had it been
Still morning?
Beloved, would you have come?

25   If you come
Haste and come.
Owls have cried;
It grows dark
To ride.
30   Beloved, beautiful, come.

50] The Path

Running along a bank, a parapet
That saves from the precipitous wood below
The level road, there is a path. It serves
Children for looking down the long smooth steep,
5   Between the legs of beech and yew, to where
A fallen tree checks the sight: while men and women
Content themselves with the road and what they see
Over the bank, and what the children tell.
The path, winding like silver, trickles on,
10   Bordered and even invaded by thinnest moss
That tries to cover roots and crumbling chalk
With gold, olive, and emerald, but in vain.
The children wear it. They have flattened the bank
On top, and silvered it between the moss
15   With the current of their feet, year after year.
But the road is houseless, and leads not to school.
To see a child is rare there, and the eye
Has but the road, the wood that overhangs
And underyawns it, and the path that looks

20 As if it led on to some legendary
    Or fancied place where men have wished to go
    And stay; till, sudden, it ends where the wood ends.

    51]

    This moonlight makes
    The lovely lovelier
    Than ever before lakes
    And meadows were.

5   And yet they are not,
    Though this their hour is, more
    Lovely than things that were not
    Lovely before.

    Nothing on earth,
10 And in the heavens no star,
    For pure brightness is worth
    More than that jar,

    For wasps meant, now
    A star – long may it swing
15 From the dead apple-bough,
    So glistening.

    52]   A Tale [cancelled version]

    There once the walls
    Of the ruined cottage stood.
    The periwinkle crawls
    With flowers in its hair into the wood.

5   In flowerless hours
    Never will the bank fail,
    With everlasting flowers
    On fragments of blue plates, to tell the tale.

53] [A Tale] [revised version]

Here once flint walls,
Pump, orchard and wood pile stood.
Blue periwinkle crawls
From the lost garden down into the wood.

5   The flowerless hours
    Of Winter cannot prevail
    To blight these other flowers,
    Blue china fragments scattered, that tell the tale.

54] Wind and Mist

They met inside the gateway that gives the view,
A hollow land as vast as heaven. 'It is
A pleasant day, sir.' 'A very pleasant day.'
'And what a view here. If you like angled fields
5   Of grass and grain bounded by oak and thorn,
Here is a league. Had we with Germany
To play upon this board it could not be
More dear than April has made it with a smile.
The fields beyond that league close in together
10 And merge, even as our days into the past,
Into one wood that has a shining pane
Of water. Then the hills of the horizon –

That is how I should make hills had I to show
One who would never see them what hills were like.'
15 'Yes. Sixty miles of South Downs at one glance.
Sometimes a man feels proud at them, as if
He had just created them with one mighty thought.'
'That house, though modern, could not be better planned
For its position. I never liked a new
20 House better. Could you tell me who lives in it?'
'No one.' 'Ah – and I was peopling all
Those windows on the south with happy eyes,
The terrace under them with happy feet;
Girls –' 'Sir, I know. I know. I have seen that house
25 Through mist look lovely as a castle in Spain,
And airier. I have thought: " 'Twere happy there
To live." And I have laughed at that
Because I lived there then.' 'Extraordinary.'
'Yes, with my furniture and family
30 Still in it, I knowing every nook of it
And loving none, and in fact hating it.'
'Dear me! How could that be? But pardon me.'
'No offence. Doubtless the house was not to blame,
But the eye watching from those windows saw,
35 Many a day, day after day, mist – mist
Like chaos surging back – and felt itself
Alone in all the world, marooned alone.
We lived in clouds, on a cliff's edge almost
(You see), and if clouds went, the visible earth
40 Lay too far off beneath and like a cloud.
I did not know it was the earth I loved
Until I tried to live there in the clouds
And the earth turned to cloud.'
                                        'You had a garden
Of flint and clay, too.' 'True; that was real enough.

45 The flint was the one crop that never failed.
   The clay first broke my heart, and then my back;
   And the back heals not. There were other things
   Real, too. In that room at the gable a child
   Was born while the wind chilled a summer dawn:
50 Never looked grey mind on a greyer one
   Than when the child's cry broke above the groans.'
   'I hope they were both spared.' 'They were. Oh yes.
   But flint and clay and childbirth were too real
   For this cloud castle. I had forgot the wind.
55 Pray do not let me get on to the wind.
   You would not understand about the wind.
   It is my subject, and compared with me
   Those who have always lived on the firm ground
   Are quite unreal in this matter of the wind.
60 There were whole days and nights when the wind and I
   Between us shared the world, and the wind ruled
   And I obeyed it and forgot the mist.
   My past and the past of the world were in the wind.
   Now you will say that though you understand
65 And feel for me, and so on, you yourself
   Would find it different. You are all like that
   If once you stand here free from wind and mist:
   I might as well be talking to wind and mist.
   You would believe the house-agent's young man
70 Who gives no heed to anything I say.
   Good morning. But one word. I want to admit
   That I would try the house once more, if I could;
   As I should like to try being young again.'

55] A Gentleman

'He has robbed two clubs. The judge at Salisbury
Can't give him more than he undoubtedly
Deserves. The scoundrel! Look at his photograph!
A lady-killer! Hanging's too good by half
5   For such as he.' So said the stranger, one
With crimes yet undiscovered or undone.
But at the inn the Gypsy dame began:
'Now he was what I call a gentleman.
He went along with Carrie, and when she
10   Had a baby he paid up so readily
His half a crown. Just like him. A crown'd have been
More like him. For I never knew him mean.
Oh! but he was such a nice gentleman. Oh!
Last time we met he said if me and Joe
15   Was anywhere near we must be sure and call.
He put his arms around our Amos all
As if he were his own son. I pray God
Save him from justice! Nicer man never trod.'

56] Lob

At hawthorn-time in Wiltshire travelling
In search of something chance would never bring,
An old man's face, by life and weather cut
And coloured, – rough, brown, sweet as any nut, –
5   A land face, sea-blue-eyed, – hung in my mind
When I had left him many a mile behind.
All he said was: 'Nobody can't stop 'ee. It's
A footpath, right enough. You see those bits

Of mounds – that's where they opened up the barrows
10 Sixty years since, while I was scaring sparrows.
They thought as there was something to find there,
But couldn't find it, by digging, anywhere.'

To turn back then and seek him, where was the use?
There were three Manningfords, – Abbots, Bohun, and
       Bruce:
15 And whether Alton, not Manningford, it was
My memory could not decide, because
There was both Alton Barnes and Alton Priors.
All had their churches, graveyards, farms, and byres,
Lurking to one side up the paths and lanes,
20 Seldom well seen except by aeroplanes;
And when bells rang, or pigs squealed, or cocks crowed,
Then only heard. Ages ago the road
Approached. The people stood and looked and turned,
Nor asked it to come nearer, nor yet learned
25 To move out there and dwell in all men's dust.
And yet withal they shot the weathercock, just
Because 'twas he crowed out of tune, they said:
So now the copper weathercock is dead.
If they had reaped their dandelions and sold
30 Them fairly, they could have afforded gold.

Many years passed, and I went back again
Among those villages, and I looked for men
Who might have known my ancient. He himself
Had long been dead or laid upon the shelf,
35 I thought. One man I asked about him roared
At my description: ' 'Tis old Bottlesford
He means, Bill.' But another said: 'Of course,
It was Jack Button up at the White Horse.
He's dead, sir, these three years.' This lasted till

40 A girl proposed Walker of Walker's Hill,
     'Old Adam Walker. Adam's Point you'll see
     Marked on the maps.'

                        'That was her roguery'
     The next man said. He was a squire's son
     Who loved wild bird and beast, and dog and gun
45 For killing them. He had loved them from his birth,
     One with another, as he loved the earth.
     'The man may be like Button, or Walker, or
     Like Bottlesford, that you want, but far more
     He sounds like one I saw when I was a child.
50 I could almost swear to him. The man was wild
     And wandered. His home was where he was free.
     Everybody has met one such man as he.
     Does he keep clear old paths that no one uses
     But once a life-time when he loves or muses?
55 He is English as this gate, these flowers, this mire.
     And when at eight years old Lob-lie-by-the-fire
     Came in my books, this was the man I saw.
     He has been in England as long as dove and daw,
     Calling the wild cherry tree the merry tree,
60 The rose campion Bridget-in-her-bravery;
     And in a tender mood he, as I guess,
     Christened one flower Live-in-idleness,
     And while he walked from Exeter to Leeds
     One April called all cuckoo-flowers Milkmaids.
65 From him old herbal Gerard learnt, as a boy,
     To name wild clematis the Traveller's-joy.
     Our blackbirds sang no English till his ear
     Told him they called his Jan Toy "Pretty dear".
     (She was Jan Toy the Lucky, who, having lost
70 A shilling, and found a penny loaf, rejoiced.)

For reasons of his own to him the wren
Is Jenny Pooter. Before all other men
'Twas he first called the Hog's Back the Hog's Back.
That Mother Dunch's Buttocks should not lack
75 Their name was his care. He too could explain
Totteridge and Totterdown and Juggler's Lane:
He knows, if anyone. Why Tumbling Bay,
Inland in Kent, is called so, he might say.

'But little he says compared with what he does.
80 If ever a sage troubles him he will buzz
Like a beehive to conclude the tedious fray:
And the sage, who knows all languages, runs away.
Yet Lob has thirteen hundred names for a fool,
And though he never could spare time for school
85 To unteach what the fox so well expressed,
On biting the cock's head off, – Quietness is best, –
He can talk quite as well as anyone
After his thinking is forgot and done.
He first of all told someone else's wife,
90 For a farthing she'd skin a flint and spoil a knife
Worth sixpence skinning it. She heard him speak:
"She had a face as long as a wet week"
Said he, telling the tale in after years.
With blue smock and with gold rings in his ears,
95 Sometimes he is a pedlar, not too poor
To keep his wit. This is tall Tom that bore
The logs in, and with Shakespeare in the hall
Once talked, when icicles hung by the wall.
As Herne the Hunter he has known hard times.
100 On sleepless nights he made up weather rhymes
Which others spoilt. And, Hob, being then his name,
He kept the hog that thought the butcher came

To bring his breakfast. "You thought wrong" said Hob.
When there were kings in Kent this very Lob,
105 Whose sheep grew fat and he himself grew merry,
Wedded the king's daughter of Canterbury;
For he alone, unlike squire, lord, and king,
Watched a night by her without slumbering;
He kept both waking. When he was but a lad
110 He won a rich man's heiress, deaf, dumb, and sad,
By rousing her to laugh at him. He carried
His donkey on his back. So they were married.
And while he was a little cobbler's boy
He tricked the giant coming to destroy
115 Shrewsbury by flood. "And how far is it yet?"
The giant asked in passing. 'I forget;
But see these shoes I've worn out on the road
And we're not there yet.' He emptied out his load
Of shoes. The giant sighed, and dropped from his spade
120 The earth for damming Severn, and thus made
The Wrekin hill; and little Ercall hill
Rose where the giant scraped his boots. While still
So young, our Jack was chief of Gotham's sages.
But long before he could have been wise, ages
125 Earlier than this, while he grew thick and strong
And ate his bacon, or, at times, sang a song
And merely smelt it, as Jack the giant-killer
He made a name. He, too, ground up the miller,
The Yorkshireman who ground men's bones for flour.

130 'Do you believe Jack dead before his hour?
Or that his name is Walker, or Bottlesford,
Or Button, a mere clown, or squire, or lord?
The man you saw, – Lob-lie-by-the-fire, Jack Cade,
Jack Smith, Jack Moon, poor Jack of every trade,

135 Young Jack, or old Jack, or Jack What-d'ye-call,
    Jack-in-the-hedge, or Robin-run-by-the-wall,
    Robin Hood, Ragged Robin, lazy Bob,
    One of the lords of No Man's Land, good Lob, –
    Although he was seen dying at Waterloo,
140 Hastings, Agincourt, and Sedgmoor, too, –
    Lives yet. He never will admit he is dead
    Till millers cease to grind men's bones for bread,
    Not till our weathercock crows once again
    And I remove my house out of the lane
145 On to the road.' With this he disappeared
    In hazel and thorn tangled with old-man's-beard.
    But one glimpse of his back, as there he stood,
    Choosing his way, proved him of old Jack's blood,
    Young Jack perhaps, and now a Wiltshireman
150 As he has oft been since his days began.

57] Digging [1]

Today I think
Only with scents, – scents dead leaves yield,
And bracken, and wild carrot's seed,
And the square mustard field;

5 Odours that rise
When the spade wounds the roots of tree,
Rose, currant, raspberry, or goutweed,
Rhubarb or celery;

The smoke's smell, too,
10 Flowing from where a bonfire burns
The dead, the waste, the dangerous,
And all to sweetness turns.

It is enough
To smell, to crumble the dark earth,
15   While the robin sings over again
Sad songs of Autumn mirth.

58] Lovers

The two men in the road were taken aback.
The lovers came out shading their eyes from the sun,
And never was white so white, or black so black,
As her cheeks and hair. 'There are more things than one
5   A man might turn into a wood for, Jack,'
Said George; Jack whispered: 'He has not got a gun.
It's a bit too much of a good thing, I say.
They are going the other road, look. And see her run.' –
She ran – 'What a thing it is, this picking may.'

59] In Memoriam [Easter 1915]

The flowers left thick at nightfall in the wood
This Eastertide call into mind the men,
Now far from home, who, with their sweethearts, should
Have gathered them and will do never again.

60] Head and Bottle

The downs will lose the sun, white alyssum
Lose the bees' hum;
But head and bottle tilted back in the cart
Will never part

5   Till I am cold as midnight and all my hours
    Are beeless flowers.
    He neither sees, nor hears, nor smells, nor thinks,
    But only drinks,
    Quiet in the yard where tree trunks do not lie
10 More quietly.

61] Home [2]

Often I had gone this way before:
But now it seemed I never could be
And never had been anywhere else;
'Twas home; one nationality
5   We had, I and the birds that sang,
One memory.

They welcomed me. I had come back
That eve somehow from somewhere far:
The April mist, the chill, the calm,
10 Meant the same thing familiar
And pleasant to us, and strange too,
Yet with no bar.

The thrush on the oak top in the lane
Sang his last song, or last but one;
15 And as he ended, on the elm
Another had but just begun
His last; they knew no more than I
The day was done.

Then past his dark white cottage front
20 A labourer went along, his tread
Slow, half with weariness half with ease;

And, through the silence, from his shed
The sound of sawing rounded all
That silence said.

62] Health

Four miles at a leap, over the dark hollow land,
To the frosted steep of the down and its junipers black,
Travels my eye with equal ease and delight:
And scarce could my body leap four yards.

5 This is the best and the worst of it –
Never to know,
Yet to imagine gloriously, pure health.

Today, had I suddenly health,
I could not satisfy the desire of my heart
10 Unless health abated it,
So beautiful is the air in its softness and clearness, while
    Spring
Promises all and fails in nothing as yet;
And what blue and what white is I never knew
Before I saw this sky blessing the land.

15 For had I health I could not ride or run or fly
So far or so rapidly over the land
As I desire: I should reach Wiltshire tired;
I should have changed my mind before I could be in Wales.
I could not love; I could not command love.
20 Beauty would still be far off
However many hills I climbed over;
Peace would be still farther.
Maybe I should not count it anything

To leap these four miles with the eye;
25 And either I should not be filled almost to bursting with
        desire,
    Or with my power desire would still keep pace.

    Yet I am not satisfied
    Even with knowing I never could be satisfied.
    With health and all the power that lies
30 In maiden beauty, poet and warrior,
    In Caesar, Shakespeare, Alcibiades,
    Mazeppa, Leonardo, Michelangelo,
    In any maiden whose smile is lovelier
    Than sunlight upon dew,
35 I could not be as the wagtail running up and down
    The warm tiles of the roof slope, twittering
    Happily and sweetly as if the sun itself
    Extracted the song
    As the hand makes sparks from the fur of a cat:

40 I could not be as the sun.
    Nor should I be content to be
    As little as the bird or as mighty as the sun.
    For the bird knows not of the sun,
    And the sun regards not the bird.
45 But I am almost proud to love both bird and sun,
    Though scarce this Spring could my body leap four yards.

63] The Huxter

    He has a hump like an ape on his back;
    He has of money a plentiful lack;
    And but for a gay coat of double his girth
    There is not a plainer thing on the earth
5   This fine May morning.

But the huxter has a bottle of beer;
He drives a cart and his wife sits near
Who does not heed his lack or his hump;
And they laugh as down the lane they bump
10   This fine May morning.

64]

She dotes on what the wild birds say
Or hint or mock at, night and day, –
Thrush, blackbird, all that sing in May,
    And songless plover,
5 Hawk, heron, owl, and woodpecker.
They never say a word to her
    About her lover.

She laughs at them for childishness,
She cries at them for carelessness
10 Who see her going loverless
    Yet sing and chatter
Just as when he was not a ghost,
Nor ever ask her what she has lost
    Or what is the matter.

15 Yet she has fancied blackbirds hide
A secret, and that thrushes chide
Because she thinks death can divide
    Her from her lover;
And she has slept, trying to translate
20 The word the cuckoo cries to his mate
    Over and over.

65] Song [1]

She is beautiful
With happiness invincible:
If cruel she be
It is the hawk's proud innocent cruelty.

5 At poet's tears,
Sweeter than any smiles but hers,
She laughs; I sigh;
And yet I could not live if she should die.

And when in June
10 Once more the cuckoo spoils his tune,
She laughs at sighs;
And yet she says she loves me till she dies.

66] A Cat

She had a name among the children;
But no one loved though someone owned
Her, locked her out of doors at bedtime
And had her kittens duly drowned.

5 In Spring, nevertheless, this cat
Ate blackbirds, thrushes, nightingales,
And birds of bright voice and plume and flight,
As well as scraps from neighbours' pails.

I loathed and hated her for this;
10 One speckle on a thrush's breast
Was worth a million such; and yet
She lived long, till God gave her rest.

67] Melancholy

The rain and wind, the rain and wind, raved endlessly.
On me the Summer storm, and fever, and melancholy
Wrought magic, so that if I feared the solitude
Far more I feared all company: too sharp, too rude,
5 Had been the wisest or the dearest human voice.
What I desired I knew not, but whate'er my choice
Vain it must be, I knew. Yet naught did my despair
But sweeten the strange sweetness, while through the
     wild air
All day long I heard a distant cuckoo calling
10 And, soft as dulcimers, sounds of near water falling,
And, softer, and remote as if in history,
Rumours of what had touched my friends, my foes, or me.

68] Tonight

Harry, you know at night
The larks in Castle Alley
Sing from the attic's height
As if the electric light
5 Were the true sun above a summer valley:
Whistle, don't knock, tonight.

I shall come early, Kate;
And we in Castle Alley
Will sit close out of sight
10 Alone, and ask no light
Of lamp or sun above a summer valley:
Tonight I can stay late.

69] April

The sweetest thing, I thought
At one time, between earth and heaven
Was the first smile
When mist has been forgiven
5 And the sun has stolen out,
Peered, and resolved to shine at seven
On dabbled lengthening grasses,
Thick primroses and early leaves uneven,
When earth's breath, warm and humid, far surpasses
10 The richest oven's, and loudly rings 'cuckoo'
And sharply the nightingale's 'tsoo, troo, tsoo, troo';
To say 'God bless it' was all that I could do.

But now I know one sweeter
By far since the day Emily
15 Turned weeping back
To me, still happy me,
To ask forgiveness, –
Yet smiled with half a certainty
To be forgiven, – for what
20 She had never done; I knew not what it might be,
Nor could she tell me, having now forgot,
By rapture carried with me past all care
As to an isle in April lovelier
Than April's self. 'God bless you' I said to her.

70] The Glory

The glory of the beauty of the morning, –
The cuckoo crying over the untouched dew;

The blackbird that has found it, and the dove
That tempts me on to something sweeter than love;
5 White clouds ranged even and fair as new-mown hay;
The heat, the stir, the sublime vacancy
Of sky and meadow and forest and my own heart: –
The glory invites me, yet it leaves me scorning
All I can ever do, all I can be,
10 Beside the lovely of motion, shape, and hue,
The happiness I fancy fit to dwell
In beauty's presence. Shall I now this day
Begin to seek as far as heaven, as hell,
Wisdom or strength to match this beauty, start
15 And tread the pale dust pitted with small dark drops,
In hope to find whatever it is I seek,
Hearkening to short-lived happy-seeming things
That we know naught of, in the hazel copse?
Or must I be content with discontent
20 As larks and swallows are perhaps with wings?
And shall I ask at the day's end once more
What beauty is, and what I can have meant
By happiness? And shall I let all go,
Glad, weary, or both? Or shall I perhaps know
25 That I was happy oft and oft before,
A while forgetting how I am fast pent,
How dreary-swift, with naught to travel to,
Is Time? I cannot bite the day to the core.

71] July

Naught moves but clouds, and in the glassy lake
Their doubles and the shadow of my boat.
The boat itself stirs only when I break

This drowse of heat and solitude afloat
5 To prove if what I see be bird or mote,
   Or learn if yet the shore woods be awake.

   Long hours since dawn grew, – spread, – and passed on high
   And deep below, – I have watched the cool reeds hung
   Over images more cool in imaged sky:
10 Nothing there was worth thinking of so long;
   All that the ring-doves say, far leaves among,
   Brims my mind with content thus still to lie.

72] The Chalk Pit

   'Is this the road that climbs above and bends
   Round what was once a chalk pit: now it is
   By accident an amphitheatre.
   Some ash trees standing ankle-deep in brier
5 And bramble act the parts, and neither speak
   Nor stir.' 'But see: they have fallen, every one,
   And brier and bramble have grown over them.'
   'That is the place. As usual no one is here.
   Hardly can I imagine the drop of the axe,
10 And the smack that is like an echo, sounding here.'
   'I do not understand.' 'Why, what I mean is
   That I have seen the place two or three times
   At most, and that its emptiness and silence
   And stillness haunt me, as if just before
15 It was not empty, silent, still, but full
   Of life of some kind, perhaps tragical.
   Has anything unusual happened here?'

   'Not that I know of. It is called the Dell.
   They have not dug chalk here for a century.

20 That was the ash trees' age. But I will ask.'
   'No. Do not. I prefer to make a tale,
   Or better leave it like the end of a play,
   Actors and audience and lights all gone;
   For so it looks now. In my memory
25 Again and again I see it, strangely dark,
   And vacant of a life but just withdrawn.
   We have not seen the woodman with the axe.
   Some ghost has left it now as we two came.'

   'And yet you doubted if this were the road?'
30 'Well, sometimes I have thought of it and failed
   To place it. No. And I am not quite sure,
   Even now, this is it. For another place,
   Real or painted, may have combined with it.
   Or I myself a long way back in time . . .'
35 'Why, as to that, I used to meet a man –
   I had forgotten, – searching for birds' nests
   Along the road and in the chalk pit too.
   The wren's hole was an eye that looked at him
   For recognition. Every nest he knew.
40 He got a stiff neck, by looking this side or that,
   Spring after spring, he told me, with his laugh, –
   A sort of laugh. He was a visitor,
   A man of forty, – smoked and strolled about.
   At orts and crosses Pleasure and Pain had played
45 On his brown features; – I think both had lost; –
   Mild and yet wild too. You may know the kind.
   And once or twice a woman shared his walks,
   A girl of twenty with a brown boy's face,
   And hair brown as a thrush or as a nut,
50 Thick eyebrows, glinting eyes –' 'You have said enough.
   A pair, – free thought, free love, – I know the breed:
   I shall not mix my fancies up with them.'

'You please yourself. I should prefer the truth
Or nothing. Here, in fact, is nothing at all
55   Except a silent place that once rang loud,
And trees and us – imperfect friends, we men
And trees since time began; and nevertheless
Between us still we breed a mystery.'

73] Fifty Faggots

There they stand, on their ends, the fifty faggots
That once were underwood of hazel and ash
In Jenny Pinks's Copse. Now, by the hedge
Close packed, they make a thicket fancy alone
5   Can creep through with the mouse and wren. Next Spring
A blackbird or a robin will nest there,
Accustomed to them, thinking they will remain
Whatever is for ever to a bird:
This Spring it is too late; the swift has come.
10   'Twas a hot day for carrying them up:
Better they will never warm me, though they must
Light several Winters' fires. Before they are done
The war will have ended, many other things
Have ended, maybe, that I can no more
15   Foresee or more control than robin and wren.

74] Sedge-Warblers [cancelled version]

This beauty made me dream there was a time
Long past and irrecoverable, a clime
Where any brook so radiant racing clear
Through buttercup and kingcup bright as brass

5   But gentle, nourishing the meadow grass
    That leans and scurries in the wind, would bear
    Another beauty, divine and feminine,
    Child to the sun, a nymph whose soul unstained
    Could love all day, and never hate or tire,
10 A lover of mortal or immortal kin.

    And yet, rid of this dream, ere I had drained
    Its poison, quieted was my desire
    So that I only looked into the water,
    Clearer than any goddess or man's daughter,
15 And hearkened while it combed the dark green hair
    And shook the millions of the blossoms white
    Of water-crowfoot, and curdled to one sheet
    The flowers fallen from the chestnuts in the park
    Far off. And sedge-warblers, clinging so light
20 To willow twigs, sang longer than the lark,
    Quick, shrill, or grating, a song to match the heat
    Of the strong sun, nor less the water's cool,
    Gushing through narrows, swirling in the pool.
    Their song that lacks all words, all melody,
25 All sweetness almost, was dearer then to me
    Than sweetest voice that sings in tune sweet words.
    This was the best of May – the small brown birds
    Wisely reiterating endlessly
    What no man learnt yet, in or out of school.

75] Sedge-Warblers [revised version]

    This beauty makes me dream there was a time
    Long past and irrecoverable, a clime
    Where river of such radiance racing clear

Through buttercup and kingcup bright as brass
5   But gentle, nourishing the meadowgrass
That leans and scurries in the wind, would bear
Another beauty, divine and feminine,
Child of the sun, whose happy soul unstained
Could love all day, and never hate or tire,
10 Lover of mortal or immortal kin.

And yet rid of this dream, ere I had drained
Its poison, quieted was my desire
So that I only looked into the water
And hearkened, while it combed the dark-green hair
15 And shook the millions of the blossoms white
Of water crowfoot, and curdled in one sheet
The flowers fallen from the chestnuts in the park
Far off. The sedgewarblers that hung so light
On willow twigs, sang longer than any lark,
20 Quick, shrill or grating, a song to match the heat
Of the strong sun, nor less the water's cool
Gushing through narrows, swirling in the pool.
Their song that lacks all words, all melody,
All sweetness almost, was dearer now to me
25 Than sweetest voice that sings in tune sweet word:
This was the best of May, the small brown birds
Wisely reiterating endlessly
What no man learnt yet, in or out of school.

76]

I built myself a house of glass:
It took me years to make it:
And I was proud. But now, alas,
Would God someone would break it.

5 But it looks too magnificent.
   No neighbour casts a stone
   From where he dwells, in tenement
   Or palace of glass, alone.

   77] Words

   Out of us all
   That make rhymes,
   Will you choose
   Sometimes –
5 As the winds use
   A crack in a wall
   Or a drain,
   Their joy or their pain
   To whistle through –
10 Choose me,
   You English words?

   I know you:
   You are light as dreams,
   Tough as oak,
15 Precious as gold,
   As poppies and corn,
   Or an old cloak:
   Sweet as our birds
   To the ear,
20 As the burnet rose
   In the heat
   Of Midsummer:
   Strange as the races
   Of dead and unborn:

25   Strange and sweet
      Equally,
      And familiar,
      To the eye,
      As the dearest faces
30   That a man knows,
      And as lost homes are:
      But though older far
      Than oldest yew, –
      As our hills are, old, –
35   Worn new
      Again and again;
      Young as our streams
      After rain:
      And as dear
40   As the earth which you prove
      That we love.

      Make me content
      With some sweetness
      From Wales
45   Whose nightingales
      Have no wings, –
      From Wiltshire and Kent
      And Herefordshire,
      And the villages there, –
50   From the names, and the things
      No less.

      Let me sometimes dance
      With you,
      Or climb
55   Or stand perchance
      In ecstasy,

Fixed and free
In a rhyme,
As poets do.

78] The Word

There are so many things I have forgot,
That once were much to me, or that were not,
All lost, as is a childless woman's child
And its child's children, in the undefiled
5   Abyss of what can never be again.
I have forgot, too, names of the mighty men
That fought and lost or won in the old wars,
Of kings and fiends and gods, and most of the stars.
Some things I have forgot that I forget.
10 But lesser things there are, remembered yet,
Than all the others. One name that I have not –
Though 'tis an empty thingless name – forgot
Never can die because Spring after Spring
Some thrushes learn to say it as they sing.
15 There is always one at midday saying it clear
And tart – the name, only the name I hear.
While perhaps I am thinking of the elder scent
That is like food, or while I am content
With the wild rose scent that is like memory,
20 This name suddenly is cried out to me
From somewhere in the bushes by a bird
Over and over again, a pure thrush word.

79] Under the Wood

When these old woods were young
The thrushes' ancestors
As sweetly sung
In the old years.

5 There was no garden here,
Apples nor mistletoe;
No children dear
Ran to and fro.

New then was this thatched cot,
10 But the keeper was old,
And he had not
Much lead or gold.

Most silent beech and yew:
As he went round about
15 The woods to view
Seldom he shot.

But now that he is gone
Out of most memories,
Still lingers on
20 A stoat of his,

But one, shrivelled and green,
And with no scent at all,
And barely seen
On this shed wall.

80] Haymaking

After night's thunder far away had rolled
The fiery day had a kernel sweet of cold,
And in the perfect blue the clouds uncurled,
Like the first gods before they made the world
5 And misery, swimming the stormless sea
In beauty and in divine gaiety.
The smooth white empty road was lightly strewn
With leaves – the holly's Autumn falls in June –
And fir cones standing stiff up in the heat.
10 The mill-foot water tumbled white and lit
With tossing crystals, happier than any crowd
Of children pouring out of school aloud.
And in the little thickets where a sleeper
For ever might lie lost, the nettle-creeper
15 And garden warbler sang unceasingly;
While over them shrill shrieked in his fierce glee
The swift with wings and tail as sharp and narrow
As if the bow had flown off with the arrow.
Only the scent of woodbine and hay new-mown
20 Travelled the road. In the field sloping down,
Park-like, to where its willows showed the brook,
Haymakers rested. The tosser lay forsook
Out in the sun; and the long waggon stood
Without its team; it seemed it never would
25 Move from the shadow of that single yew.
The team, as still, until their task was due,
Beside the labourers enjoyed the shade
That three squat oaks mid-field together made
Upon a circle of grass and weed uncut,
30 And on the hollow, once a chalk-pit, but

Now brimmed with nut and elder-flower so clean.
The men leaned on their rakes, about to begin,
But still. And all were silent. All was old,
This morning time, with a great age untold,
35   Older than Clare and Cowper, Morland and Crome,
Than, at the field's far edge, the farmer's home,
A white house crouched at the foot of a great tree.
Under the heavens that know not what years be
The men, the beasts, the trees, the implements
40   Uttered even what they will in times far hence –
All of us gone out of the reach of change –
Immortal in a picture of an old grange.

81] A Dream

Over known fields with an old friend in dream
I walked, but came sudden to a strange stream.
Its dark waters were bursting out most bright
From a great mountain's heart into the light.
5   They ran a short course under the sun, then back
Into a pit they plunged, once more as black
As at their birth: and I stood thinking there
How white, had the day shone on them, they were,
Heaving and coiling. So by the roar and hiss
10   And by the mighty motion of the abyss
I was bemused, that I forgot my friend
And neither saw nor sought him till the end,
When I awoke from waters unto men
Saying: 'I shall be here some day again.'

82] The Brook

Seated once by a brook, watching a child
Chiefly that paddled, I was thus beguiled.
Mellow the blackbird sang and sharp the thrush
Not far off in the oak and hazel brush,
5   Unseen. There was a scent like honeycomb
From mugwort dull. And down upon the dome
Of the stone the cart-horse kicks against so oft
A butterfly alighted. From aloft
He took the heat of the sun, and from below.
10 On the hot stone he perched contented so,
As if never a cart would pass again
That way; as if I were the last of men
And he the first of insects to have earth
And sun together and to know their worth.
15 I was divided between him and the gleam,
The motion, and the voices, of the stream,
The waters running frizzled over gravel,
That never vanish and for ever travel.
A grey flycatcher silent on a fence
20 And I sat as if we had been there since
The horseman and the horse lying beneath
The fir-tree-covered barrow on the heath,
The horseman and the horse with silver shoes,
Galloped the downs last. All that I could lose
25 I lost. And then the child's voice raised the dead.
'No one's been here before' was what she said
And what I felt, yet never should have found
A word for, while I gathered sight and sound.

83] Aspens

All day and night, save winter, every weather,
Above the inn, the smithy, and the shop,
The aspens at the cross-roads talk together
Of rain, until their last leaves fall from the top.

5   Out of the blacksmith's cavern comes the ringing
Of hammer, shoe, and anvil; out of the inn
The clink, the hum, the roar, the random singing –
The sounds that for these fifty years have been.

The whisper of the aspens is not drowned,
10 And over lightless pane and footless road,
Empty as sky, with every other sound
Not ceasing, calls their ghosts from their abode,

A silent smithy, a silent inn, nor fails
In the bare moonlight or the thick-furred gloom,
15 In tempest or the night of nightingales,
To turn the cross-roads to a ghostly room.

And it would be the same were no house near.
Over all sorts of weather, men, and times,
Aspens must shake their leaves and men may hear
20 But need not listen, more than to my rhymes.

Whatever wind blows, while they and I have leaves
We cannot other than an aspen be
That ceaselessly, unreasonably grieves,
Or so men think who like a different tree.

84] The Mill-Water

Only the sound remains
Of the old mill;
Gone is the wheel;
On the prone roof and walls the nettle reigns.

5   Water that toils no more
Dangles white locks
And, falling, mocks
The music of the mill-wheel's busy roar.

Pretty to see, by day
10 Its sound is naught
Compared with thought
And talk and noise of labour and of play.

Night makes the difference.
In calm moonlight,
15 Gloom infinite,
The sound comes surging in upon the sense:

Solitude, company, –
When it is night, –
Grief or delight
20 By it must haunted or concluded be.

Often the silentness
Has but this one
Companion;
Wherever one creeps in the other is:

25 Sometimes a thought is drowned
By it, sometimes
Out of it climbs;
All thoughts begin or end upon this sound,

Only the idle foam
30   Of water falling
Changelessly calling,
Where once men had a work-place and a home.

85] For These [Prayer]

An acre of land between the shore and the hills,
Upon a ledge that shows my kingdoms three,
The lovely visible earth and sky and sea,
Where what the curlew needs not, the farmer tills:

5   A house that shall love me as I love it,
Well-hedged, and honoured by a few ash-trees
That linnets, greenfinches, and goldfinches
Shall often visit and make love in and flit:

A garden I need never go beyond,
10   Broken but neat, whose sunflowers every one
Are fit to be the sign of the Rising Sun:
A spring, a brook's bend, or at least a pond:

For these I ask not, but, neither too late
Nor yet too early, for what men call content,
15   And also that something may be sent
To be contented with, I ask of fate.

86] Digging [2]

What matter makes my spade for tears or mirth,
Letting down two clay pipes into the earth?
The one I smoked, the other a soldier

Of Blenheim, Ramillies, and Malplaquet
5   Perhaps. The dead man's immortality
Lies represented lightly with my own,
A yard or two nearer the living air
Than bones of ancients who, amazed to see
Almighty God erect the mastodon,
10   Once laughed, or wept, in this same light of day.

87] Two Houses

Between a sunny bank and the sun
The farmhouse smiles
On the riverside plat:
No other one
5   So pleasant to look at
And remember, for many miles,
So velvet-hushed and cool under warm tiles.

Nor far from the road it lies, yet caught
Far out of reach
10   Of the road's dust
And the dusty thought
Of passers-by, though each
Stops, and turns, and must
Look down at it like a wasp at a muslined peach.

15   But another house stood there long before:
And as if above graves
Still the turf heaves
Above its stones:
Dark hangs the sycamore,
20   Shadowing kennel and bones
And the black dog that shakes his chain and moans.

And when he barks, over the river
Flashing fast,
Dark echoes reply,
25   And the hollow past
Half yields the dead that never
More than half hidden lie:
And out they creep and back again for ever.

88] Cock-Crow

Out of the wood of thoughts that grows by night
To be cut down by the sharp axe of light, –
Out of the night, two cocks together crow,
Cleaving the darkness with a silver blow:
5   And bright before my eyes twin trumpeters stand,
Heralds of splendour, one at either hand,
Each facing each as in a coat of arms:
The milkers lace their boots up at the farms.

89] October

The green elm with the one great bough of gold
Lets leaves into the grass slip, one by one. –
The short hill grass, the mushrooms small milk-white,
Harebell and scabious and tormentil,
5   That blackberry and gorse, in dew and sun,
Bow down to; and the wind travels too light
To shake the fallen birch leaves from the fern;
The gossamers wander at their own will.
At heavier steps than birds' the squirrels scold.

10   The late year has grown fresh again and new
     As Spring, and to the touch is not more cool
     Than it is warm to the gaze; and now I might
     As happy be as earth is beautiful,
     Were I some other or with earth could turn
15   In alternation of violet and rose,
     Harebell and snowdrop, at their season due,
     And gorse that has no time not to be gay.
     But if this be not happiness, who knows?
     Some day I shall think this a happy day,
20   And this mood by the name of melancholy
     Shall no more blackened and obscured be.

90] There's Nothing Like the Sun

     There's nothing like the sun as the year dies,
     Kind as it can be, this world being made so,
     To stones and men and beasts and birds and flies,
     To all things that it touches except snow,
5   Whether on mountain side or street of town.
     The south wall warms me: November has begun,
     Yet never shone the sun as fair as now
     While the sweet last-left damsons from the bough
     With spangles of the morning's storm drop down
10   Because the starling shakes it, whistling what
     Once swallows sang. But I have not forgot
     That there is nothing, too, like March's sun,
     Like April's, or July's, or June's, or May's,
     Or January's, or February's, great days:
15   And August, September, October, and December
     Have equal days, all different from November.
     No day of any month but I have said –

Or, if I could live long enough, should say –
'There's nothing like the sun that shines today.'
20   There's nothing like the sun till we are dead.

91] The Thrush

When Winter's ahead,
What can you read in November
That you read in April
When Winter's dead?

5   I hear the thrush, and I see
Him alone at the end of the lane
Near the bare poplar's tip,
Singing continuously.

Is it more that you know
10   Than that, even as in April,
So in November,
Winter is gone that must go?

Or is all your lore
Not to call November November,
15   And April April,
And Winter Winter – no more?

But I know the months all,
And their sweet names, April,
May and June and October,
20   As you call and call

I must remember
What died into April
And consider what will be born
Of a fair November;

25 And April I love for what
It was born of, and November
For what it will die in,
What they are and what they are not,

While you love what is kind,
30 What you can sing in
And love and forget in
All that's ahead and behind.

92] Liberty

The last light has gone out of the world, except
This moonlight lying on the grass like frost
Beyond the brink of the tall elm's shadow.
It is as if everything else had slept
5 Many an age, unforgotten and lost
The men that were, the things done, long ago,
All I have thought; and but the moon and I
Live yet and here stand idle over the grave
Where all is buried. Both have liberty
10 To dream what we could do if we were free
To do some thing we had desired long,
The moon and I. There's none less free than who
Does nothing and has nothing else to do,
Being free only for what is not to his mind,
15 And nothing is to his mind. If every hour
Like this one passing that I have spent among
The wiser others when I have forgot
To wonder whether I was free or not,
Were piled before me, and not lost behind,
20 And I could take and carry them away

I should be rich; or if I had the power
To wipe out every one and not again
Regret, I should be rich to be so poor.
And yet I still am half in love with pain,
25   With what is imperfect, with both tears and mirth,
With things that have an end, with life and earth,
And this moon that leaves me dark within the door.

93]

This is no case of petty right or wrong
That politicians or philosophers
Can judge. I hate not Germans, nor grow hot
With love of Englishmen, to please newspapers.
5   Beside my hate for one fat patriot
My hatred of the Kaiser is love true: –
A kind of god he is, banging a gong.
But I have not to choose between the two,
Or between justice and injustice. Dinned
10   With war and argument I read no more
Than in the storm smoking along the wind
Athwart the wood. Two witches' cauldrons roar.
From one the weather shall rise clear and gay;
Out of the other an England beautiful
15   And like her mother that died yesterday.
Little I know or care if, being dull,
I shall miss something that historians
Can rake out of the ashes when perchance
The phoenix broods serene above their ken.
20   But with the best and meanest Englishmen
I am one in crying, God save England, lest
We lose what never slaves and cattle blessed.

The ages made her that made us from the dust:
She is all we know and live by, and we trust
25 She is good and must endure, loving her so:
And as we love ourselves we hate her foe.

94] Rain

Rain, midnight rain, nothing but the wild rain
On this bleak hut, and solitude, and me
Remembering again that I shall die
And neither hear the rain nor give it thanks
5   For washing me cleaner than I have been
Since I was born into this solitude.
Blessed are the dead that the rain rains upon:
But here I pray that none whom once I loved
Is dying tonight or lying still awake
10 Solitary, listening to the rain,
Either in pain or thus in sympathy
Helpless among the living and the dead,
Like a cold water among broken reeds,
Myriads of broken reeds all still and stiff,
15 Like me who have no love which this wild rain
Has not dissolved except the love of death,
If love it be towards what is perfect and
Cannot, the tempest tells me, disappoint.

95] Song [2]

The clouds that are so light,
Beautiful, swift and bright,
Cast shadows on field and park
Of the earth that is so dark,

5   And even so now, light one!
Beautiful, swift and bright one!
You let fall on a heart that was dark,
Unillumined, a deeper mark.

But clouds would have, without earth
10 To shadow, far less worth:
Away from your shadow on me
Your beauty less would be,

And if it still be treasured
An age hence, it shall be measured
15 By this small dark spot
Without which it were not.

96] Roads

I love roads:
The goddesses that dwell
Far along invisible
Are my favourite gods.

5 Roads go on
While we forget, and are
Forgotten like a star
That shoots and is gone.

On this earth 'tis sure
10 We men have not made
Anything that doth fade
So soon, so long endure:

The hill road wet with rain
In the sun would not gleam
15 Like a winding stream
If we trod it not again.

They are lonely
While we sleep, lonelier

For lack of the traveller
20 Who is now a dream only.

From dawn's twilight
And all the clouds like sheep
On the mountains of sleep
They wind into the night.

25 The next turn may reveal
Heaven: upon the crest
The close pine clump, at rest
And black, may Hell conceal.

Often footsore, never
30 Yet of the road I weary,
Though long and steep and dreary
As it winds on for ever.

Helen of the roads,
The mountain ways of Wales
35 And the Mabinogion tales,
Is one of the true gods,

Abiding in the trees,
The threes and fours so wise,
The larger companies,
40 That by the roadside be,

And beneath the rafter
Else uninhabited
Excepting by the dead;
And it is her laughter

45 At morn and night I hear
When the thrush cock sings
Bright irrelevant things,
And when the chanticleer

Calls back to their own night
50 Troops that make loneliness
With their light footsteps' press,
As Helen's own are light.

Now all roads lead to France
And heavy is the tread
55 Of the living; but the dead
Returning lightly dance:

Whatever the road bring
To me or take from me,
They keep me company
60 With their pattering,

Crowding the solitude
Of the loops over the downs,
Hushing the roar of towns
And their brief multitude.

97] The Ash Grove

Half of the grove stood dead, and those that yet lived made
Little more than the dead ones made of shade.
If they led to a house, long before they had seen its fall:
But they welcomed me; I was glad without cause and
    delayed.

5 Scarce a hundred paces under the trees was the interval –
Paces each sweeter than sweetest miles – but nothing at all,
Not even the spirits of memory and fear with restless wing,
Could climb down in to molest me over the wall

That I passed through at either end without noticing.
10   And now an ash grove far from those hills can bring
The same tranquillity in which I wander a ghost
With a ghostly gladness, as if I heard a girl sing

The song of the Ash Grove soft as love uncrossed,
And then in a crowd or in distance it were lost,
15   But the moment unveiled something unwilling to die
And I had what most I desired, without search or desert
       or cost.

98] February Afternoon

Men heard this roar of parleying starlings, saw,
A thousand years ago even as now,
Black rooks with white gulls following the plough
So that the first are last until a caw
Commands that last are first again, – a law
Which was of old when one, like me, dreamed how
A thousand years might dust lie on his brow
Yet thus would birds do between hedge and shaw.

Time swims before me, making as a day
10   A thousand years, while the broad ploughland oak
Roars mill-like and men strike and bear the stroke
Of war as ever, audacious or resigned,
And God still sits aloft in the array
That we have wrought him, stone-deaf and stone-blind.

99]

I may come near loving you
When you are dead

And there is nothing to do
And much to be said.

5   To repent that day will be
Impossible
For you, and vain for me
The truth to tell.

I shall be sorry for
10 Your impotence:
You can do and undo no more
When you go hence,

Cannot even forgive
The funeral.
15 But not so long as you live
Can I love you at all.

100]

These things that poets said
Of love seemed true to me
When I loved and I fed
On love and poetry equally.

5   But now I wish I knew
If theirs were love indeed,
Or if mine were the true
And theirs some other lovely weed:

For certainly not thus,
10 Then or thereafter, I
Loved ever. Between us
Decide, good Love, before I die.

Only, that once I loved
By this one argument
15 Is very plainly proved:
I, loving not, am different.

101]

No one so much as you
Loves this my clay,
Or would lament as you
Its dying day.

5 You know me through and through
Though I have not told,
And though with what you know
You are not bold.

None ever was so fair
10 As I thought you:
Not a word can I bear
Spoken against you.

All that I ever did
For you seemed coarse
15 Compared with what I hid
Nor put in force.

Scarce my eyes dare meet you
Lest they should prove
I but respond to you
20 And do not love.

We look and understand,
We cannot speak

Except in trifles and
Words the most weak.

25   I at the most accept
Your love, regretting
That is all: I have kept
A helpless fretting

That I could not return
30   All that you gave
And could not ever burn
With the love you have,

Till sometimes it did seem
Better it were
35   Never to see you more
Than linger here

With only gratitude
Instead of love –
A pine in solitude
40   Cradling a dove.

102] The Unknown

She is most fair,
And when they see her pass
The poets' ladies
Look no more in the glass
5   But after her.

On a bleak moor
Running under the moon
She lures a poet,

Once proud or happy, soon
10 Far from his door.

Beside a train,
Because they saw her go,
Or failed to see her,
Travellers and watchers know
15 Another pain.

The simple lack
Of her is more to me
Than others' presence,
Whether life splendid be
20 Or utter black.

I have not seen,
I have no news of her;
I can tell only
She is not here, but there
25 She might have been.

She is to be kissed
Only perhaps by me;
She may be seeking
Me and no other: she
30 May not exist.

103] Celandine

Thinking of her had saddened me at first,
Until I saw the sun on the celandines lie
Redoubled, and she stood up like a flame,
A living thing, not what before I nursed,
5 The shadow I was growing to love almost,

The phantom, not the creature with bright eye
That I had thought never to see, once lost.

She found the celandines of February
Always before us all. Her nature and name
10 Were like those flowers, and now immediately
For a short swift eternity back she came,
Beautiful, happy, simply as when she wore
Her brightest bloom among the winter hues
Of all the world; and I was happy too,
15 Seeing the blossoms and the maiden who
Had seen them with me Februarys before,
Bending to them as in and out she trod
And laughed, with locks sweeping the mossy sod.

But this was a dream: the flowers were not true,
20 Until I stooped to pluck from the grass there
One of five petals and I smelt the juice
Which made me sigh, remembering she was no more,
Gone like a never perfectly recalled air.

104] 'Home' [3]

Fair was the morning, fair our tempers, and
We had seen nothing fairer than that land,
Though strange, and the untrodden snow that made
Wild of the tame, casting out all that was
5 Not wild and rustic and old; and we were glad.

Fair too was afternoon, and first to pass
Were we that league of snow, next the north wind.

There was nothing to return for except need.
And yet we sang nor ever stopped for speed,

10 As we did often with the start behind.
   Faster still strode we when we came in sight
   Of the cold roofs where we must spend the night.

   Happy we had not been there, nor could be,
   Though we had tasted sleep and food and fellowship
   Together long.
15   'How quick' to someone's lip
   The word came, 'will the beaten horse run home.'

   The word 'home' raised a smile in us all three,
   And one repeated it, smiling just so
   That all knew what he meant and none would say.
20 Between three countries far apart that lay
   We were divided and looked strangely each
   At the other, and we knew we were not friends
   But fellows in a union that ends
   With the necessity for it, as it ought.

25 Never a word was spoken, not a thought
   Was thought, of what the look meant with the word
   'Home' as we walked and watched the sunset blurred.
   And then to me the word, only the word,
   'Homesick', as it were playfully occurred:
30 No more. If I should ever more admit
   Than the mere word I could not endure it
   For a day longer: this captivity
   Must somehow come to an end, else I should be
   Another man, as often now I seem,
35 Or this life be only an evil dream.

105] Thaw

Over the land freckled with snow half-thawed
The speculating rooks at their nests cawed
And saw from elm-tops, delicate as flower of grass,
What we below could not see, Winter pass.

Household Poems

106] [1 Bronwen]

If I should ever by chance grow rich
I'll buy Codham, Cockridden, and Childerditch,
Roses, Pyrgo, and Lapwater,
And let them all to my elder daughter.
5   The rent I shall ask of her will be only
Each year's first violets, white and lonely,
The first primroses and orchises –
She must find them before I do, that is.
But if she finds a blossom on furze
10   Without rent they shall all for ever be hers,
Codham, Cockridden, and Childerditch,
Roses, Pyrgo and Lapwater, –
I shall give them all to my elder daughter.

107] [2 Merfyn]

If I were to own this countryside
As far as a man in a day could ride,

And the Tyes were mine for giving or letting, –
Wingle Tye and Margaretting
5 Tye, – and Skreens, Gooshays, and Cockerells,
Shellow, Rochetts, Bandish, and Pickerells,
Martins, Lambkins, and Lillyputs,
Their copses, ponds, roads, and ruts,
Fields where plough-horses steam and plovers
10 Fling and whimper, hedges that lovers
Love, and orchards, shrubberies, walls
Where the sun untroubled by north wind falls,
And single trees where the thrush sings well
His proverbs untranslatable,
15 I would give them all to my son
If he would let me any one
For a song, a blackbird's song, at dawn.
He should have no more, till on my lawn
Never a one was left, because I
20 Had shot them to put them into a pie, –
His Essex blackbirds, every one,
And I was left old and alone.

Then unless I could pay, for rent, a song
As sweet as a blackbird's, and as long –
25 No more – he should have the house, not I:
Margaretting or Wingle Tye,
Or it might be Skreens, Gooshays, or Cockerells,
Shellow, Rochetts, Bandish, or Pickerells,
Martins, Lambkins, or Lillyputs,
30 Should be his till the cart tracks had no ruts.

108] [3 Myfanwy]

What shall I give my daughter the younger
More than will keep her from cold and hunger?
I shall not give her anything.
If she shared South Weald and Havering,
5   Their acres, the two brooks running between,
Paine's Brook and Weald Brook,
With pewit, woodpecker, swan, and rook,
She would be no richer than the queen
Who once on a time sat in Havering Bower
10   Alone, with the shadows, pleasure and power.
She could do no more with Samarcand,
Or the mountains of a mountain land
And its far white house above cottages
Like Venus above the Pleiades.
15   Her small hands I would not cumber
With so many acres and their lumber,
But leave her Steep and her own world
And her spectacled self with hair uncurled,
Wanting a thousand little things
20   That time without contentment brings.

109] [4 Helen]

And you, Helen, what should I give you?
So many things I would give you
Had I an infinite great store
Offered me and I stood before
5   To choose. I would give you youth,
All kinds of loveliness and truth,

A clear eye as good as mine,
Lands, waters, flowers, wine,
As many children as your heart
10 Might wish for, a far better art
Than mine can be, all you have lost
Upon the travelling waters tossed,
Or given to me. If I could choose
Freely in that great treasure-house
15 Anything from any shelf,
I would give you back yourself,
And power to discriminate
What you want and want it not too late,
Many fair days free from care
20 And heart to enjoy both foul and fair,
And myself, too, if I could find
Where it lay hidden and it proved kind.

110]

Dull-thoughted, walking among the nunneries
Of many a myriad anemones
In the close copses, I grew weary of Spring
Till I emerged and in my wandering
5 I climbed the down up to a lone pine clump
Of six, the tallest dead, one a mere stump.
On one long stem, branchless and flayed and prone
I sat in the sun listening to the wind alone,
Thinking there could be no old song so sad
10 As the wind's song; but later none so glad
Could I remember as that same wind's song
All the time blowing the pine boughs among.
My heart that had been still as the dead tree
Awakened by the West wind was made free.

111] 'Go now'

Like the touch of rain she was
On a man's flesh and hair and eyes
When the joy of walking thus
Has taken him by surprise:

5   With the love of the storm he burns,
He sings, he laughs, well I know how,
But forgets when he returns
As I shall not forget her 'Go now'.

Those two words shut a door
10   Between me and the blessed rain
That was never shut before
And will not open again.

112] When we two walked

When we two walked in Lent
We imagined that happiness
Was something different
And this was something less.

5   But happy were we to hide
Our happiness, not as they were
Who acted in their pride
Juno and Jupiter:

For the gods in their jealousy
10   Murdered that wife and man,
And we that were wise live free
To recall our happiness then.

113] Tall Nettles

Tall nettles cover up, as they have done
These many springs, the rusty harrow, the plough
Long worn out, and the roller made of stone:
Only the elm butt tops the nettles now.

5   This corner of the farmyard I like most:
As well as any bloom upon a flower
I like the dust on the nettles, never lost
Except to prove the sweetness of a shower.

114]

By the ford at the town's edge
Horse and carter rest:
The carter smokes on the bridge
Watching the water press in swathes about his horse's chest.

5   From the inn one watches, too,
In the room for visitors
That has no fire, but a view
And many cases of stuffed fish, vermin, and kingfishers.

115]

I never saw that land before,
And now can never see it again;
Yet, as if by acquaintance hoar
Endeared, by gladness and by pain,
5   Great was the affection that I bore

To the valley and the river small,
The cattle, the grass, the bare ash trees,
The chickens from the farmsteads, all
Elm-hidden, and the tributaries
10 Descending at equal interval;

The blackthorns down along the brook
With wounds yellow as crocuses
Where yesterday the labourer's hook
Had sliced them cleanly; and the breeze
15 That hinted all and nothing spoke.

I neither expected anything
Nor yet remembered: but some goal
I touched then; and if I could sing
What would not even whisper my soul
20 As I went on my journeying,

I should use, as the trees and birds did,
A language not to be betrayed;
And what was hid should still be hid
Excepting from those like me made
25 Who answer when such whispers bid.

116] The Cherry Trees

The cherry trees bend over and are shedding
On the old road where all that passed are dead,
Their petals, strewing the grass as for a wedding
This early May morn when there is none to wed.

117] It Rains

It rains, and nothing stirs within the fence
Anywhere through the orchard's untrodden, dense
Forest of parsley. The great diamonds
Of rain on the grassblades there is none to break,
5   Or the fallen petals further down to shake.

And I am nearly as happy as possible
To search the wilderness in vain though well,
To think of two walking, kissing there,
Drenched, yet forgetting the kisses of the rain:
10 Sad, too, to think that never, never again,

Unless alone, so happy shall I walk
In the rain. When I turn away, on its fine stalk
Twilight has fined to naught, the parsley flower
Figures, suspended still and ghostly white,
15 The past hovering as it revisits the light.

118] Some eyes condemn

Some eyes condemn the earth they gaze upon:
Some wait patiently till they know far more
Than earth can tell them: some laugh at the whole
As folly of another's making: one
5 I knew that laughed because he saw, from core
To rind, not one thing worth the laugh his soul
Had ready at waking: some eyes have begun
With laughing; some stand startled at the door.

Others, too, I have seen rest, question, roll,
10 Dance, shoot. And many I have loved watching. Some
   I could not take my eyes from till they turned
   And loving died. I had not found my goal.
   But thinking of your eyes, dear, I become
   Dumb: for they flamed, and it was me they burned.

119] The sun used to shine

The sun used to shine while we two walked
Slowly together, paused and started
Again, and sometimes mused, sometimes talked
As either pleased, and cheerfully parted

5 Each night. We never disagreed
  Which gate to rest on. The to be
  And the late past we gave small heed.
  We turned from men or poetry

To rumours of the war remote
10 Only till both stood disinclined
   For aught but the yellow flavorous coat
   Of an apple wasps had undermined;

Or a sentry of dark betonies,
The stateliest of small flowers on earth,
15 At the forest verge; or crocuses
   Pale purple as if they had their birth

In sunless Hades fields. The war
Came back to mind with the moonrise
Which soldiers in the east afar
20 Beheld then. Nevertheless, our eyes

Could as well imagine the Crusades
Or Caesar's battles. Everything
To faintness like those rumours fades –
Like the brook's water glittering

25 Under the moonlight – like those walks
Now – like us two that took them, and
The fallen apples, all the talks
And silences – like memory's sand

When the tide covers it late or soon,
30 And other men through other flowers
In those fields under the same moon
Go talking and have easy hours.

120]

'No one cares less than I,
Nobody knows but God
Whether I am destined to lie
Under a foreign clod'
5 Were the words I made to the bugle call in the morning.

But laughing, storming, scorning,
Only the bugles know
What the bugles say in the morning,
And they do not care, when they blow
10 The call that I heard and made words to early this morning.

121] As the team's head brass

As the team's head brass flashed out on the turn
The lovers disappeared into the wood.

I sat among the boughs of the fallen elm
That strewed an angle of the fallow, and
5 Watched the plough narrowing a yellow square
Of charlock. Every time the horses turned
Instead of treading me down, the ploughman leaned
Upon the handles to say or ask a word,
About the weather, next about the war.
10 Scraping the share he faced towards the wood,
And screwed along the furrow till the brass flashed
Once more.

        The blizzard felled the elm whose crest
I sat in, by a woodpecker's round hole,
The ploughman said. 'When will they take it away?'
15 'When the war's over.' So the talk began –
One minute and an interval of ten,
A minute more and the same interval.
'Have you been out?' 'No.' 'And don't want to, perhaps?'
'If I could only come back again, I should.
20 I could spare an arm. I shouldn't want to lose
A leg. If I should lose my head, why, so,
I should want nothing more . . . Have many gone
From here?' 'Yes.' 'Many lost?' 'Yes, a good few.
Only two teams work on the farm this year.
25 One of my mates is dead. The second day
In France they killed him. It was back in March,
The very night of the blizzard, too. Now if
He had stayed here we should have moved the tree.'
'And I should not have sat here. Everything
30 Would have been different. For it would have been
Another world.' 'Ay, and a better, though
If we could see all all might seem good.' Then
The lovers came out of the wood again:
The horses started and for the last time

35 I watched the clods crumble and topple over
    After the ploughshare and the stumbling team.

122] After you speak

    After you speak
    And what you meant
    Is plain,
    My eyes
5   Meet yours that mean –
    With your cheeks and hair –
    Something more wise,
    More dark,
    And far different.
10 Even so the lark
    Loves dust
    And nestles in it
    The minute
    Before he must
15 Soar in lone flight
    So far,
    Like a black star
    He seems –
    A mote
20 Of singing dust
    Afloat
    Above,
    That dreams
    And sheds no light.
25 I know your lust
    Is love.

123] The Pond

Bright clouds of may
Shade half the pond.
Beyond,
All but one bay
5   Of emerald
Tall reeds
Like criss-cross bayonets
Where a bird once called,
Lies bright as the sun.
10   No one heeds.
The light wind frets
And drifts the scum
Of may-blossom.
Till the moorhen calls
15   Again
Naught's to be done
By birds or men.
Still the may falls.

124]

Early one morning in May I set out,
And nobody I knew was about.
        I'm bound away for ever,
        Away somewhere, away for ever.

5   There was no wind to trouble the weathercocks.
I had burnt my letters and darned my socks.

No one knew I was going away,
I thought myself I should come back some day.

I heard the brook through the town gardens run.
10 O sweet was the mud turned to dust by the sun.

A gate banged in a fence and banged in my head.
'A fine morning, sir,' a shepherd said.

I could not return from my liberty,
To my youth and my love and my misery.

15 The past is the only dead thing that smells sweet,
The only sweet thing that is not also fleet.
        I'm bound away for ever,
        Away somewhere, away for ever.

125] It was upon

It was upon a July evening.
At a stile I stood, looking along a path
Over the country by a second Spring
Drenched perfect green again. 'The lattermath
5 Will be a fine one.' So the stranger said,
A wandering man. Albeit I stood at rest
Flushed with desire I was. The earth outspread,
Like meadows of the future, I possessed.

And as an unaccomplished prophecy
10 The stranger's words, after the interval
Of a score years, when those fields are by me
Never to be recrossed, now I recall,
This July eve, and question, wondering,
What of the lattermath to this hoar Spring?

126] Bob's Lane

Women he liked, did shovel-bearded Bob,
Old Farmer Hayward of the Heath, but he
Loved horses. He himself was like a cob,
And leather-coloured. Also he loved a tree.

5   For the life in them he loved most living things,
But a tree chiefly. All along the lane
He planted elms where now the stormcock sings
That travellers hear from the slow-climbing train.

Till then the track had never had a name
10 For all its thicket and the nightingales
That should have earned it. No one was to blame.
To name a thing beloved man sometimes fails.

Many years since, Bob Hayward died, and now
None passes there because the mist and the rain
15 Out of the elms have turned the lane to slough
And gloom, the name alone survives, Bob's Lane.

127]

There was a time when this poor frame was whole
And I had youth and never another care,
Or none that should have troubled a strong soul.
Yet, except sometimes in a frosty air
5   When my heels hammered out a melody
From pavements of a city left behind,
I never would acknowledge my own glee
Because it was less mighty than my mind

Had dreamed of. Since I could not boast of strength
10   Great as I wished, weakness was all my boast.
I sought yet hated pity till at length
I earned it. Oh, too heavy was the cost.
But now that there is something I could use
My youth and strength for, I deny the age,
15   The care and weakness that I know – refuse
To admit I am unworthy of the wage
Paid to a man who gives up eyes and breath
For what can neither ask nor heed his death.

128] The Green Roads

The green roads that end in the forest
Are strewn with white goose feathers this June,

Like marks left behind by some one gone to the forest
To show his track. But he has never come back.

5   Down each green road a cottage looks at the forest.
Round one the nettle towers; two are bathed in flowers.

An old man along the green road to the forest
Strays from one, from another a child alone.

In the thicket bordering the forest,
10   All day long a thrush twiddles his song.

It is old, but the trees are young in the forest,
All but one like a castle keep, in the middle deep.

That oak saw the ages pass in the forest:
They were a host, but their memories are lost,

15   For the tree is dead: all things forget the forest
Excepting perhaps me, when now I see

The old man, the child, the goose feathers at the edge of the
   forest,
And hear all day long the thrush repeat his song.

129] When first

When first I came here I had hope,
Hope for I knew not what. Fast beat
My heart at sight of the tall slope
Of grass and yews, as if my feet

5 Only by scaling its steps of chalk
Would see something no other hill
Ever disclosed. And now I walk
Down it the last time. Never will

My heart beat so again at sight
10 Of any hill although as fair
And loftier. For infinite
The change, late unperceived, this year,

The twelfth, suddenly, shows me plain.
Hope now, – not health, nor cheerfulness,
15 Since they can come and go again,
As often one brief hour witnesses, –

Just hope has gone for ever. Perhaps
I may love other hills yet more
Than this: the future and the maps
20 Hide something I was waiting for.

One thing I know, that love with chance
And use and time and necessity
Will grow, and louder the heart's dance
At parting than at meeting be.

130] The Gallows

There was a weasel lived in the sun
With all his family,
Till a keeper shot him with his gun
And hung him up on a tree,
5 Where he swings in the wind and rain,
In the sun and in the snow,
Without pleasure, without pain,
On the dead oak tree bough.

There was a crow who was no sleeper,
10 But a thief and a murderer
Till a very late hour; and this keeper
Made him one of the things that were,
To hang and flap in rain and wind,
In the sun and in the snow.
15 There are no more sins to be sinned
On the dead oak tree bough.

There was a magpie, too,
Had a long tongue and a long tail;
He could both talk and do –
20 But what did that avail?
He, too, flaps in the wind and rain
Alongside weasel and crow,
Without pleasure, without pain,
On the dead oak tree bough.

25 And many other beasts
And birds, skin, bone and feather,
Have been taken from their feasts
And hung up there together,

To swing and have endless leisure
30 In the sun and in the snow,
Without pain, without pleasure,
On the dead oak tree bough.

131]

Dark is the forest and deep, and overhead
Hang stars like seeds of light
In vain, though not since they were sown was bred
Anything more bright.

5 And evermore mighty multitudes ride
About, nor enter in;
Of the other multitudes that dwell inside
Never yet was one seen.

The forest foxglove is purple, the marguerite
10 Outside is gold and white,
Nor can those that pluck either blossom greet
The others, day or night.

132] When he should laugh

When he should laugh the wise man knows full well:
For he knows what is truly laughable.
But wiser is the man who laughs also,
Or holds his laughter, when the foolish do.

133] The Swifts

How at once should I know,
When stretched in the harvest blue
I saw the swift's black bow,
That I would not have that view
5 Another day
Until next May
Again it is due?

The same year after year –
But with the swift alone.
10 With other things I but fear
That they will be over and done
Suddenly
And I only see
Them to know them gone.

134] Blenheim Oranges

Gone, gone again,
May, June, July,
And August gone,
Again gone by,

5 Not memorable
Save that I saw them go,
As past the empty quays
The rivers flow.

And now again,
10 In the harvest rain,

The Blenheim oranges
Fall grubby from the trees,

As when I was young –
And when the lost one was here –
15 And when the war began
To turn young men to dung.

Look at the old house,
Outmoded, dignified,
Dark and untenanted,
20 With grass growing instead

Of the footsteps of life,
The friendliness, the strife;
In its beds have lain
Youth, love, age and pain:

25 I am something like that;
Only I am not dead,
Still breathing and interested
In the house that is not dark: –

I am something like that:
30 Not one pane to reflect the sun,
For the schoolboys to throw at –
They have broken every one.

135]

That girl's clear eyes utterly concealed all
Except that there was something to reveal.
And what did mine say in the interval?
No more: no less. They are but as a seal

5   Not to be broken till after I am dead;
And then vainly. Every one of us
This morning at our tasks left nothing said,
In spite of many words. We were sealed thus,
Like tombs. Nor until now could I admit
10 That all I cared for was the pleasure and pain
I tasted in the stony square sunlit,
Or the dark cloisters, or shade of airy plane,
While music blazed and children, line after line,
Marched past, hiding the 'Seventeen Thirty-Nine'.

136]

What will they do when I am gone? It is plain
That they will do without me as the rain
Can do without the flowers and the grass
That profit by it and must perish without.
5 I have but seen them in the loud street pass;
And I was naught to them. I turned about
To see them disappearing carelessly.
But what if I in them as they in me
Nourished what has great value and no price?
10 Almost I thought that rain thirsts for a draught
Which only in the blossom's chalice lies,
Until that one turned back and lightly laughed.

137] The Trumpet

Rise up, rise up,
And, as the trumpet blowing
Chases the dreams of men,

As the dawn glowing
5   The stars that left unlit
The land and water,
Rise up and scatter
The dew that covers
The print of last night's lovers –
10 Scatter it, scatter it!

While you are listening
To the clear horn,
Forget, men, everything
On this earth newborn,
15 Except that it is lovelier
Than any mysteries.
Open your eyes to the air
That has washed the eyes of the stars
Through all the dewy night:
20 Up with the light,
To the old wars;
Arise, arise!

138]

'He rolls in the orchard: he is stained with moss
And with earth, the solitary old white horse.
Where is his father and where is his mother
Among all the brown horses? Has he a brother?
5   I know the swallow, the hawk, and the hern;
But there are two million things for me to learn.

'Who was the lady that rode the white horse
With rings and bells to Banbury Cross?
Was there no other lady in England beside

10   That a nursery rhyme could take for a ride?
The swift, the swallow, the hawk, and the hern.
There are two million things for me to learn.

'Was there a man once who straddled across
The back of the Westbury White Horse
15   Over there on Salisbury Plain's green wall?
Was he bound for Westbury, or had he a fall?
The swift, the swallow, the hawk, and the hern.
There are two million things for me to learn.

'Out of all the white horses I know three,
20   At the age of six; and it seems to me
There is so much to learn, for men,
That I dare not go to bed again.
The swift, the swallow, the hawk, and the hern.
There are millions of things for me to learn.'

139] Lights Out

I have come to the borders of sleep,
The unfathomable deep
Forest, where all must lose
Their way, however straight
5   Or winding, soon or late;
They can not choose.

Many a road and track
That since the dawn's first crack
Up to the forest brink
10   Deceived the travellers,
Suddenly now blurs,
And in they sink.

Here love ends –
Despair, ambition ends;
15 All pleasure and all trouble,
Although most sweet or bitter,
Here ends, in sleep that is sweeter
Than tasks most noble.

There is not any book
20 Or face of dearest look
That I would not turn from now
To go into the unknown
I must enter, and leave, alone,
I know not how.

25 The tall forest towers:
Its cloudy foliage lowers
Ahead, shelf above shelf:
Its silence I hear and obey
That I may lose my way
30 And myself.

140] The long small room

The long small room that showed willows in the west
Narrowed up to the end the fireplace filled,
Although not wide. I liked it. No one guessed
What need or accident made them so build.

5 Only the moon, the mouse and the sparrow peeped
In from the ivy round the casement thick.
Of all they saw and heard there they shall keep
The tale for the old ivy and older brick.

When I look back I am like moon, sparrow and mouse
10   That witnessed what they could never understand
Or alter or prevent in the dark house.
One thing remains the same – this my right hand

Crawling crab-like over the clean white page,
Resting awhile each morning on the pillow,
15   Then once more starting to crawl on towards age.
The hundred last leaves stream upon the willow.

141] The Sheiling

It stands alone
Up in a land of stone
All worn like ancient stairs,
A land of rocks and trees
5   Nourished on wind and stone.

And all within
Long delicate has been;
By arts and kindliness
Coloured, sweetened, and warmed
10   For many years has been.

Safe resting there
Men hear in the travelling air
But music, pictures see
In the same daily land
15   Painted by the wild air.

One maker's mind
Made both, and the house is kind
To the land that gave it peace,
And the stone has taken the house
20   To its cold heart and is kind.

142]

Some day, I think, there will be people enough
In Froxfield to pick all the blackberries
Out of the hedges of Green Lane, the straight
Broad lane where now September hides herself
5   In bracken and blackberry, harebell and dwarf gorse.
Today, where yesterday a hundred sheep
Were nibbling, halcyon bells shake to the sway
Of waters that no vessel ever sailed . . .
It is a kind of spring: the chaffinch tries
10 His song. For heat it is like summer too.
This might be winter's quiet. While the glint
Of hollies dark in the swollen hedges lasts –
One mile – and those bells ring, little I know
Or heed if time be still the same, until
15 The lane ends and once more all is the same.

143]

Out in the dark over the snow
The fallow fawns invisible go
With the fallow doe;
And the winds blow
5   Fast as the stars are slow.

Stealthily the dark haunts round
And, when a lamp goes, without sound
At a swifter bound
Than the swiftest hound,
10 Arrives, and all else is drowned;

And I and star and wind and deer
Are in the dark together, – near,
Yet far, – and fear
Drums on my ear
15   In that sage company drear.

How weak and little is the light,
All the universe of sight,
Love and delight,
Before the might,
20   If you love it not, of night.

144]

The sorrow of true love is a great sorrow
And true love parting blackens a bright morrow:
Yet almost they equal joys, since their despair
Is but hope blinded by its tears, and clear
5 Above the storm the heavens wait to be seen.
But greater sorrow from less love has been
That can mistake lack of despair for hope
And knows not tempest and the perfect scope
Of summer, but a frozen drizzle perpetual
10 Of drops that from remorse and pity fall
And cannot ever shine in the sun or thaw,
Removed eternally from the sun's law.

                                        13.1.17

The private diary kept by Edward Thomas during his last three months as a soldier is here printed for the third time. It is written in a small (3 in. × 5¾ in.) Walker's Back-Loop pocket-book, bound in pigskin and priced at two shillings; the cover and pages are curiously creased, which suggests that he was carrying the diary either on 8 April, when he was knocked over by the blast from a 5.9 shell, or on the morning of 9 April, when he was killed at an Observation Post while directing the fire of 244 Battery during the opening barrage of the Battle of Arras. The diary was given to his son, Merfyn, who died in 1965, and it was re-discovered in 1970 by *his* son, Edward, among various documents and papers that had been deposited for safety while the poet's grandson was abroad. The diary is here printed with the kind permission of the poet's daughter, Myfanwy, and of his grandson, Edward, who owns it. I do not think that the previous biographers of Edward Thomas have seen this diary, although many of the facts and laconic observations of the notebook are sometimes expanded and differently angled in the poet's letters to his family and friends, especially in letters to his wife Helen, to his brother Julian, and to such close friends as Robert Frost, Gordon Bottomley, and Eleanor Farjeon.

The diary is written in cramped handwriting with numerous abbreviations.[1] It is not easy to read with the naked eye and in places the heavy creasing and thin ink make it almost indecipherable. In the present version – which is based on a careful transcription made first by the poet's grandson, then checked by his two daughters, and finally prepared by me from a magnified copy of the original – all abbreviations have been silently expanded. I have also retained the diary's spelling of French names and the poet's spelling of 'Bosh'.

1 Four pages of the diary are reproduced in *The Anglo-Welsh Review*, Autumn 1971, pp. 9–11. The diary is carefully phrased and Thomas corrects words and phrases as in all his working drafts. The twenty cancelled readings in the diary are not shown in the present text.

Perhaps the most interesting single item in the notebook is the poem written on the last page and dated '13.1.17'; undoubtedly this is the last poem that Edward Thomas wrote. A fair copy of ll. 1–5 was made by Helen Thomas; the poem was not published until 1971. As far as one can tell from the poet's correspondence, this is only a draft version. In the various notebooks that contain his poems – both those in private hands and those available in various public libraries in England and America – there is sufficient evidence to state that it is very rare to find that a first draft of any of his poems remained unaltered in the final version. The poem shows the strong influence of Shakespeare's sonnets, for, as the diary and the letters show, he read Shakespeare regularly each night during these last months of his life.

To my mind, the diary itself offers a more compelling interest than the new poem: like his own anthology, *This England*, it is as full of his character 'as an egg is of meat' and seems to contain the germs of ideas, books, and poems that were never to be written but that were surely present in his mind. Even more clearly it reveals the consistency of the poet's entire writing life, grounded as that was upon his powerful sensuous response to the world of living and natural things. At the same time we are made aware of the self-contained, efficient officer who astonished his literary friends, who mostly seem to recall in their memoirs the self-doubting and despondent literary 'failure' that they had assumed Edward Thomas to be during the two years before the war. Apart from the various tributes sent to Helen in letters from his fellow soldiers, the best portrait of 2/Lt. P. E. Thomas was given in 1930 by his commanding Officer (Major Franklin Lushington) in Chapter Five of *The Gambardier* by 'Mark Severn':

'Among the subalterns T. Tyler [i.e. Thomas] alone was reliable and helpful. He was old enough to be Shadbolt's [i.e. Lushington's] father and before the war had achieved a name for himself as a writer ... He carried on quietly and patiently until he was killed about two months later. His serene and kindly presence and quiet dry humour did much to alleviate the squalid miseries of life for his companions.'

True to lifelong habit, Edward Thomas kept his own moments of self-doubt and distrust to himself. The inner mood of his life in the front line is conveyed more unequivocally in his letters to Robert Frost, to whom, at this time, he seemed ever ready to open some of the otherwise unspoken thoughts of head and heart. Here are three significant extracts from his unpublished letters:

(1) 6 March 1917. 'I have time to spare but I can't talk. You don't answer, and I am inhibiting introspection except when I wake up and hear the shelling and wonder whether I ought to move my bed away from the window to the inner side where there is more masonry – more to resist and more to fall on me. But it is no use thinking like this . . . So far it excites but doesn't disturb, or at any rate doesn't upset or unfit.

'I hear my book is coming out soon. Did the duplicate verses[2] ever reach you? You never said so. But don't think I mind. I should like to be a poet, just as I should like to live, but I know as much about my chances in either case, and I don't really trouble about either. Only I want to come back more or less complete.'

(2) 8 March 1917. 'Yesterday was cold and raw and I had to be indoors except for one hour and I became very depressed and solitary by the evening. Very soon, I expect to have no time or room left for depression.'

'I know some things about houses now that you don't know. The houses I observe from, for example, are still modern small houses, the last left standing before you come to the first line trenches. . . . No Man's Land is 150 yards wide. These modern houses have all been hit and downstairs is a mixture of bricks, mortar, bedsteads and filth. Upstairs you spy out through tiles at the enemy, who knows perfectly well you are there in one of the houses and some day will batter them all

2 A duplicate set of the typescripts of *Poems by Edward Eastaway*, Thomas's first volume of poetry, published by Selwyn & Blount. Frost never received this set: at least I have been unable to trace them among his papers, and I assume they were lost at sea.

down. . . . You can't paint death living in them. – As I went to the village house today I heard a very young child talking in another equally exposed house in the same street. Someone too poor or too helpless or what to leave even these places. But I positively am not going to describe any more except for a living.'

(3) 2 April 1917. 'Otherwise I have done all the things so far asked of me without making any mess and I have mingled satisfaction with dissatisfaction in about the usual proportion, comfort and discomfort . . . I think I get surer of some primitive things that one has to get sure of, about myself and other people, and I think this is not due simply to being older. In short, I am glad I came out and I think less about return than I thought I should – partly no doubt I inhibit the idea of return. I only think by flashes of the things at home that I used to enjoy and should again. I enjoy many of them out here when the sun shines and at early morning and late afternoon. I doubt if anybody here thinks less of home than I do and yet I doubt if anybody loves it more.'

These letters to Frost provide a significant counterbass to the rather jerky melody of the diary. Taken together they confirm the opinion of his fellows about his steadying influence on this raw battery of young men under fire for the first time. Surprisingly, too, for one who began his career with so much shyness even at giving map-reading instruction, Thomas emerges from the diary as a good soldier with a sharp eye and quiet courage to meet the essentials of military duty. Again, the diary and the letters underline the poet's capacity for silent enjoyment of – is 'communion with' too strong a phrase? – the seen world of nature. The numerous jottings about the weather, the record of birds and plants, the direct response to the ruin of human dwellings – all these are not the random notes of an escapist. He was undoubtedly making a raw record on which to base his letters home, but, in another sense, he was writing for dear life. Had he survived, the diary would have provided the material for another imaginative work, unlike anything he had written before and certainly not a book that 'merely described for a living'. For this last diary continues his lifelong habit of observing accurately and recording his response to the natural world. His first book, *Woodland Life*, contained such a record of the natural world from 1 April 1895 to 30 March 1896, and many of his travelling records – often written in pencil in notebooks exactly like this diary – have survived from the twenty years of his writing life. His various topographical works were based on such records and his poetry, too, returns frequently to moods, incidents, scenes, and memories that date back almost twenty years before the first nature poem was composed in November 1914.

Elsewhere[3] I have argued that to understand the intense significance of these timeless, but accurately recalled, moments of communion with the natural world is necessary before one can understand the peculiar quality of 'sincerity' that is the hallmark of Thomas's poetry. This diary, I hope, helps to confirm this view and substantiates the remark to Frost that 'I think I get surer of some primitive things that one has got to get sure of, about myself and other people'. I find the diary most moving because of its subdued tone. Through his gifted eye and sure pen one can catch a glimpse both of the fearful tragedy of the 'Great War' and the low-keyed heroic strength of one poet's inner certitude.

JANUARY

1. Shooting with 15 pounders and then 6″ howitzers. All week at Lydd, I being f/c [fire control officer] or observer daily, with map work for next day at night. Thorburn away. Beautiful clear bright weather always, but sometimes cold.

5. Left Lydd on mobilisation leave. Night at Rusham Road with Father and Mother.

---

3 *Edward Thomas* (*Writers of Wales*), ch. III, pp. 36–66.

6. Julian to breakfast. With Mother to stores. Lunch with Eleanor and tea with Joan and Bertie [Farjeon]. Home with Bronwen (returning from Chiswick). All well.

7. Walks with Helen and children. Fine day.

8. Eleanor came and stayed night. Wrote cheques for next 6 months.

9. Eleanor left. Helen and I walked in forest.

10. Dentist's. Lunch with Jones and Harry [Hooton]. Tea with Ivy Ransome and then Ingpen and Davies. Saw V. H. Collins. Home.

11. Said goodbye to Helen, Mervyn and Baba. Bronwen to Rusham Road. Lunched with Mrs. Freeman: afterwards saw [E. S. P.] Haynes and McCabe. Tea with Jesse [Berridge] and T. Clayton and met Lipchitz. Supper at Rusham Road with all my brothers.

12. A letter from Helen. Goodbye to Bronwen, Mother and Father. Lunch with Mary [Valon, Helen's sister] and Margaret [Mary Valon's daughter]. Saw Irene [MacArthur]. To Lydd and found only Horton[4] and Grier; Thorburn gone on to Codford. Letters from Helen and [G. R.] Blanco White; to Helen, Mother, Mrs. de la Mare, Frost, [Vivian Locke] Ellis, [C.] Hodson, Eleanor, and John Freeman.

13. Nothing to do but test compass which never gives same results. Walk and tea with Flawn. Cold drizzle. Horton and the battery left early for Codford. Even wrote verses.[5] Early to bed.

---

4 A fellow officer. Others mentioned in the Diary are Berrington, Cassells, Fenner, Flawn, Lushington, Rubin, Smith, Thorburn, and Witchall.
5 See Poem 144.

14. A Sunday and no letters as I am supposed to be at Codford. Letters to Helen and Blanco White. A bright cold day. Walked with Flawn through Old Romney and Ivychurch. Flawn to tea with me. Packing.

15. Up 6. Packing. Left Lydd at 9 with Q.M.S. [Quartermaster Sergeant] and Grier and 3 men. Light snow and red sun. 4 hours to spare in London but could only see T. Clayton and D. [A. Duncan] Williams: could not find J. Freeman. Then to Codford in the dark, writing to Helen and beginning 'A Sentimental Journey'. Arrived too late for dinner.

16. Letters from Helen, Eleanor, Mervyn, [Edward] Garnett, [John W.] Haines, Mrs. Ellis. Took route march to Wigtye, Stockton, Sherrington, and had great luck in short cuts and byeroads over river. A frosty clear day: men singing 'Dixie', 'There's a long long trail of winding [*sic*] to the land of my dreams', and 'We're here because we're here' to the tune of Auld Lang Syne. Only Smith and I and Capt. Fenner left of the 6 officers. Afternoon walked with Smith to Chitterne and had tea there. Evening dined together and talked about practical education – pronunciation of 'girl', 'soot' and 'historian' – and about rhymes to eye.

17. Light snow in night; hard frost. Men on fatigues or drawing overseas clothes etc. Office full of boots, blankets, pails, axes, shovels, dixies, stretchers etc. Route march to Tytherington, Heytesbury and Knook. Afternoon walked over Downs by Stockton Wood to Chilmark with Smith: tea at the inn and Smith played ragtime etc. A cloudy clear frosty day. Back over the downs on a dark night, but only went astray 200 yards. Letter from Helen, Mother and John Freeman. Letters to Helen, Mother, Haines, Eleanor.

18. Letters from Helen, Hodson, Mrs. de la Mare, Father. Letters to Helen, Irene, Father. To Warminster to the bank.

Still frosty. Afternoon lectured on map-reading. Orderly officer for camp from 6 p.m. Indoors all evening, talking to Smith about marching songs etc.

19. Letters from Mother, Helen, Miss Coltman, [W. H.] Hudson. Letters to Mother, Helen, M. Freeman, Lady Newbolt, Oscar [Thomas, Edward's fourth brother]. Morning orderly officer – latrines etc. – lectured on maps – paid Battery. Afternoon learnt to ride motor cycle. Mild and drizzly. Guns are due to arrive. A cake from Mother. Shakespeare's Sonnets from Helen. Capt. Fenner talks of having to take sick leave.

20. Letter from J. Freeman. Letters to Garnett, [James] Guthrie, Harry, Coltman. Mild snowy. Arranging stores. Guns arriving. Smith to Bath. So I had to see to unloading and parking the guns till dark. No use walking after dark. The roads are pitch dark and crowded with men going to cinemas, darkness worse from blaze of motor lamps and electric light in camps nearby. Long queues waiting outside cinema at 5.30. Tested battery compass. Talk with Fenner about martens in Ireland, badgers, plovers, barrows etc.

21. No church parade for me. 9.30–1.30 walked over Stockton Down, the Bake, and under Grovely Wood to Barford St. Martin, Burcombe, and to lunch at Netherhampton House with Newbolts. Freezing drizzle – freezes on ground, white grass and icy roads. 2 families of vagrants in green road roasting a corpse of something by slow wood fire. Beautiful Downs, with one or two isolated thatched barns, ivied ash trees, and derelict threshing machine. Old milestones lichened as with battered gold and silver nails. Back by train at 5. Tea alone. Guns in line out on parade square. Smith back. Letter from Helen, Ingpen, Eleanor, Hudson. Letter to Helen,

Ingpen. Talk with Fenner after dinner about fishing – river and sea.

22. Set the men branding and sorting stores. Left at 10.30 for Gloster to see Haines. Still frosty and dull. Gloster at 2.50. Sat till 12.15 gossiping about Frost, de la Mare, and the army, marching songs etc. Haines gave me Frost's 'Mountain Interval'.

23. With Mrs. Haines and Robin most of morning. 3.30 left Gloster via Mangotsfield and Bath for Codford. Read 'Mountain Interval'. Horton, Rubin and Thorburn back. Fenner merry; he is probably to go on sick leave. He and Rubin returned late and had a noisy parting from 2 others. Thorburn had a screaming nightmare.

24. All men on fatigues. A short walk with Thorburn to test compasses. Letters from Helen, Father, Mother, Harry. Letters to Helen, Father, Mother, M. Freeman. Parcel of medicines etc. from Helen, cigars from Harry. Walked in afternoon with Thorburn to Chilmark for tea, and back over frosty Downs with new moon and all stars. But my ankles chafed by new boots lame me.

25. Resting my sore ankles. Dial sights tested and stores arranged for packing tomorrow. Guns leave on 27th and Battery on 29th. Fenner is to go to hospital and Horton to take charge. Very cold with East wind. Letters from Oscar, letters to Oscar, Helen, Mother, Mrs. de la Mare, Frost, John Freeman, Mrs. M. Freeman, Harry, Eleanor. Capt. Lushington is to be our new o/c [Officer Commanding 244 Battery (Acting Major Lushington)] and to take us out.

26. Letters from Helen, Eleanor, letters to Helen, Mervyn. Loading lorries and attaching guns to 4-wheel drives – standing out in dusty icy East wind doing nothing but getting

cold and dirty. I sleep badly too. Also I have taken charge of mess and mess accounts. Thorburn is on my nerves – he had a nightmare lately – asking 'Can you tell me how much 55 lbs. is?' – the weight of officers' luggage. I feel useless. Am still in slacks and shoes on account of bad ankles. Thorburn and I dining alone, the others with Capt. Lushington in the village – our mess kit being packed. Can't even walk far enough to get warm. Thorburn goes tomorrow with guns. Dined with him and then talked about philosophy and poetry, and Yes and Perhaps, and the lyric and the Bible. I have a cold. The frost is worse tonight.

27. A clear windy frosty dawn, the sun like a bright coin between the knuckles of opposite hills seen from sidelong. A fox. A little office work. Telegram to say Baba was at Ransome's, so I walked over Downs by Chicklade Bottom and the Fonthills to Hatch, and blistered both feet badly. House full of ice and big fires. Sat up with Ivy till 12 and slept till 8. Another fine bright frosty day on the

28th. Wrote to Bronwen, Helen, Ivy, Eleanor. Letters from Bronwen, Helen, Mother, Eleanor. Slept late. Rested my feet, talking to the children or Ivy cooking with Kitty Gurd. Hired a bicycle to save walking. Such a beautiful ride after joining the Mere and Amesbury Road at Fonthill Bishop – hedgeless roads over long sloping downs with woods and sprinkled thorns, carved with old tracks which junipers line – an owl and many rabbits – a clear pale sky and but a faint sunset – a long twilight lasting till 6. We are to move at 6.30 a.m. tomorrow. Horton and Smith and I dined together laughing at imbecile jests and at Smith's own laughing. Had to change in order to send home my soiled things. Letters. Mess accounts and cheques to tradesmen.

29. Up at 5. Very cold. Off at 6.30, men marching in frosty dark to station singing 'Pack up your troubles in your old kit-bag'. The rotten song in the still dark brought one tear. No food or tea – Freezing carriage. Southampton at 9.30 and there had to wait till dusk, walking up and down, watching ice-scattered water, gulls and dark wood beyond, or London Scottish playing improvised Rugger, or men dancing to con-certina, in a great shed between railway and water. Smith and I got off for lunch after Horton and Capt. Lushington returned from theirs. Letter to Helen from 'South Western Hotel', where sea-captains were talking of the 'Black Adder' and of 'The Black Ball Line' that used to go to Australia. Hung about till dark – the seagulls as light failed nearly all floated instead of flying – then sailed at 7. Thorburn turned up. Now I'm in 2nd officer's cabin with Capt. and Horton, the men outside laughing and joking and saying fucking. Q.W.R.'s [Queen's Westmorland (?) Rifles] and Scottish and a Field Battery and 236 S.B. [Siege Battery], also on 'The Mona Queen'. Remember the entirely serious and decorous writing in urinal whitewash – name, address, unit, and date of sailing. A tumbling crossing, but rested.

30. Arrived Havre 4 a.m. Light of stars and windows of tall pale houses and electric arcs on quay. March through bales of cotton in sun to camp. The snow first emptying its castor of finest white. Tents. Mess full of subalterns censoring letters. Breakfast at 9.45 a.m. on arrival. Afternoon in Havre, which Thorburn likes because it is French. Mess unendurably hot and stuffy, tent unendurably cold till I got into my blankets. Slept well in fug. Snow at night.

31. Had to shift our lines in snow. 12 to a tent with 2 blankets each. Ankles bad. Nearly all water frozen in taps and basins. Mess crowded – some standing. Censoring letters about the

crossing and the children and ailments etc. at home. Had to make a speech explaining that men need not be shy about writing familiar letters home. At 'Nouvel Hotel', Havre, while we had tea, waitress kissing a Capt. and arranging for another visit. 4f. for 2 teas. Battery had to be specially warned against venereal in Havre. Read Sonnets in evening: to bed at 9 to escape hot stuff room. Officers coming and going. Some faces you just see, drinking once and never again. More fine snow like sago.

FEBRUARY

1. Freezing and overcast. Hospital train goes through camp (wounded men say we have advanced at N. Chapelle). Battery on route march. I arrange to eat midday ration in tent to save lunch in Mess (2f.50). Guns and stores not here yet. Other officers mostly in Havre but my ankle prevents me. Down in lorry to Ordnance Store for field boots. Snow. Route march, but not for me. I write and censor letters. No fire in the mess till 3 p.m. Guns are coming today. Detachments reorganised. – Mess fills up. – Cockney rankers with two stars come in and drink standing and talk of Singapore and Pekin and duration officers look up. Some rapacious and sneering, some gentle. Read Sonnets.

2. A still colder night and my new boots hurt my ankles like the old. Tried to get shoes from Ordnance in vain – rode past quays and stores of hay, grain, cotton etc. – cattle – German prisoners – French sentries hooded with long loose cloaks and long rifles and curved bayonets. Afternoon into Havre to look for low shoes – but all too tight: bought low soft boots. Tea in teashop with Thorburn. In a hole over value of English

shillings. Bought a good root stick with leather sling for 2f.50. Hard clear night again. All other officers out. Argument with Thorburn about morals, shame, whether poets must go through not only 'sin' but 'repentance' – Dante, Shakespeare. Cold supper in our cold tent – iron ration and cheese and marmalade.

3. Not quite so cold. Overhauling guns and rearranging stores on roadside by camp. A pleasant change, but not very much for me to do. Shall the guns be George, Andrew, Patrick, David? Again on the guns in afternoon. 236 Battery leave tonight: most of the officers are in Havre ignorant. All 244 except Smith dined and wined at the Normandie for 10fr. The view is that it could possibly be better placed. Back to Rest Camp 9.30 – great stark ships black with level flecked snow below and big engines and troops arriving.

4. Cold and bright again. Took the section sliding, then work on guns. At 11 came warning to move at 5.30. Packing, Censoring. New servant – Taylor. Asked if he had done anything of the kind before, said 'I've a wife and family and I know what comforts are.' Started at 4.45 for station with guns – held up 1½ hours by train across road – 2 hours at station doing nothing, 1½ hours entraining guns – platform all cotton bales and men singing 'The nightingales are singing in the pale moonlight'. ('There's a long long trail awinding'). Sgt. Major did practically all the work. – The long waiting before train starts – men quite silent after first comic cries of 'All tickets' and imitating cattle (35 men in each cattle truck: we have a compartment to 2 officers). As we start at 11 suddenly the silent men all yell 'Hurray' but are silent before we are clear of long desolate platform of cotton and trampled snow and electric light.

5. At 7 a.m. after many stops and starts we were close under partly wooded chalk hills, among railway trucks, and near a village with here and there an upper storey quite open like a loft. Snow. Gradually flatter and poplars regular as telegraph poles, orchards, level crossings, children. Buchy at 10 a.m. – Y.M.C.A. – Leave train. Nearly lost train. Fine snowfall. Furzy cuttings. Mistletoe in field, poplars by Alaincourt. Amiens at 2 and train left a score of men behind for a time. Pale sky and crimson sun at sunset. Doullens at 8. Guns all the time. Night with Thorburn at Resthouse. Thorburn had been very worried on journey – by things like tunnels while shaving etc. – then by dirty stories after tea. A restless night.

6. Still very cold. Men had only just drawn rations at 10 when parade was. Much ice on road and pavement. Hanging about in cafés or cold Resthouse. Fine dusty cold day. 2.50 fr. break-fast; 6 fr. lunch. Horton's amusing jaunty talk full of old army proverbs and metaphors and 'I mean to say.' Letter to Helen. No letters received since Codford. Suddenly at 7.30 we have to shift to Mondicourt without guns – I go on in lorry and choose billets – all in half-ruined barns – barns and farms here are a quad, entered through high arch and self-complete. We got an elephant sergeants mess to sleep in. Bitter cold, this being highest in Northern France. Roads ice and frozen snow. Farmyards all frozen. Kaffirs digging.

7. Bright cold. Horton's way of suddenly saying 'I will arise and go to my Father and say "Form Fours".' Indoors mostly, talking silly, arranging mess funds etc. – I being secretary – cooking our dinner. Battery on short route march. We are to move up very soon. A very merry evening.

8. Weather as before. Physical drill, a hasty Welsh Rabbit with honey, and then off in lorries through Alaincourt, Barly,

Fosseux, to Berneville – men billet in huge barn of a big uneven farmyard surrounded by spread arched stone barns and buildings with old pump at one side, kitchen at upper end. We forage. Enemy plane like pale moth beautiful among shrapnel bursts. A fine ride over high open snowy country with some woods. Rigging up table in mess and borrowing crockery. The battery is to split for the present: Rubin has taken guns to Saulty. We are for Dainville. A scramble dinner of half cold stuff, mostly standing. Taylor makes a table and says 'Very good, Sir' and 'It's the same for all. You gentlemen have to put up with same as us'. Bed early. Rubin returns late. Heavy firing at night. Restless.

9. Bright bitter cold. Rubin and Smith move off to join 146. Heavy firing near. Afternoon marched through Warlus to Dainville, billets on Arras road, with shell holes behind. Bitter cold. Tea with 146. Beds in the mess for night. (Remember Berneville courtyard, with ruined pigeon house by well and church behind and what was manor house). Graveyard for 3 'Mort pour la patrie' below our billet. A wonderful night of all the stars and low full moon. Officers of trench mortar battery detained here dine with us on bully, cheese and white wine.

10. Slept warm. Making latrines. With Debenham of 146 to see O.P.s [Observation Posts] and what was visible from them – through Achicourt and over railway towards Beaurains. One dead man under railway bridge. Maison brulé[e] dangerous. Map, field glass and compass over snowy broken land with posts and wires and dead trees. No infantry visible in our lines or Germans, except those we passed in trenches – Somersets and Cornwalls. Cloudy night and light wind but no thaw yet.

11. Milder and misty first – sun warm at noon. Maps in morning. Afternoon with digging party at our position by

Faubourg d'Amiens at southern edge of Arras in an orchard.
After tea paid the battery for first time in France. Tested com-
pass bearings by map. Cold. Rubin influenza. Thorburn to
Arras. No letters yet. Censoring as usual. Gramophone play-
ing 'Wait till I am as old as father' and 'Where does daddy go
when he goes out?' 9 p.m. Great cannonade thudding and
flashing quite continuously away South in Ancre.

12. Disappointed in not going again on trench Reconnaissance.
Maps in morning. Working party at gun position in afternoons.
Got a chill and was very weary. Thorburn and Rubin have colds.
Evening as usual censoring men's letters. Halfbattery moves to
Faubourg d'Amiens – Thorburn there too, thank God. Smith
back from Saulty – no news of our letters or lorries. Not much
firing near us today, but 146 lost a man killed and one wounded.
Gramophone plays the rotten things and then Gounod's 'Ave
Maria' and 'Dormezvous' which makes us rather silent after
smut.

13. Awoke tired and cold though it is thawing and cloudy
with a breeze. No work this morning, but I pore over map and
think how I may enjoy doing it when this is all over, which is
not a good feeling, I suspect. Taylor says (as he makes my bed
and as usual asks if he does it right): 'I am not proud, but I
likes to be comfortable. I have been domesticated since I
joined the Army.' Nothing to do all morning, afternoon at our
position – hare, partridges and wild duck in field S.E. of guns.
I feel the cold – the morning sun turns to a damp thaw wind.
Letters home to Father, Mother and Eleanor. Some grass
showing green through melting snow. Thorburn worries
because he can't laugh at silly low talk. Evening censoring let-
ters and reading Sonnets; others writing – when I began to
talk to Rubin, the Captain said 'You get on with your Sonnets'
and then all was silent. Awful fug.

14. A bad night but feeling better. All day with Horton, and then Horton and Smith, examining O.P.s above Agny and Wailly, and then between Achicourt and Beaurains. Fine sunny day – snow melting. Black-headed buntings talk, rooks caw, lovely white puffs of shrapnel round planes high up. Right Section does aeroplane shoot in afternoon. Dead campion umbels, and grass rustling on my helmet through trenches. Pretty little copse in deep hollow high up between Ficheux and Dainville, where guns look over to Berneville and Warlus.

15. With Captain observing for a BT. [Battery Training] shoot on Ficheux Mill and edge of Blairville Wood. Fine sun but cold in trench. With working party in afternoon. Letters arrived at 6. We sorted them and then spent an hour silently reading. 750 letters for men; 17 for me – from Helen, the children, Father, Mother, Eleanor, Freeman, Mrs. Freeman, Guthrie, Vernon and Haines. Evening, reading and writing letters. A quiet evening indoors and out. Taylor says as he mends the fire, 'Well, we have to put up with many discomforts. We are all alike, Sir, all human.' A still starry night with only machine guns and rifles. Slept badly again, and then suddenly with no notice got up from breakfast on the

16th to do fire control on aeroplane shoot (only 10 rounds, observation being bad). Dull day. Left Thorburn on guns at 11.30. Bad temper. Afternoon up to O.P., but too hazy to observe. A mad Captain with several men driving partridges over the open and whistling and crying 'Mark over'. Kestrels in pairs. Four or five planes hovering and wheeling as kestrels used to over Mutton and Ludcombe. Women hanging clothes to dry on barbed entanglement across the road. Rain at last at 4.15. This morning the old Frenchman living in this ruin burst into our room while we were dressing to complain of our dirt

and depredation, and when Rubin was rude in English said he
was a Frenchman and had been an officer. Nobody felt the
slightest sympathy with his ravings, more than with the old
white horse who works a mill walking up and up treadmill.

17. A dull muddy day. No observation, no shooting. On guns
all day and in dug-out, writing up our fighting book. Another
letter from home. Could only just see A.P. [(First) Aid Post].
Kit arrived late last night. I slept badly, coughing. Very mild
and the roads chalk and water, Grandes Graves 2.50 a bottle.
Thorburn asks where he shall put the letters he has censored
– decides on the crowded table – then I have to tell him the
mantelpiece is the obvious place.

18. Another dull day down in 146 Dug-out. Afternoon to
Arras – Town Hall like Carreg Cennin. Beautiful small white
square empty. Top storey of high house ruined cloth armchair
and a garment across it left as fly shell arrived. Car to
Mendicourt and back by light of star shells. Shopping at
Bellevue B.E.F. canteen. Returned to find I am to go as Orderly
Officer to Group 35 H.A. [Heavy Artillery] in Arras tomorrow.

19. To Arras and began showing sectors and arcs on 1/10000
maps. Field Cashier's, waiting in long queue of officers to cash
cheques etc. Learning office work. Place Victor Hugo white
houses and shutters and sharpened fuller and dome in mid-
dle. Beautiful. In class it was like Bath – retired people,
schools, priests. Gardens, courtyards, open spaces with trees.
I still funk the telephone and did not use it once today.
Sentries challenge in street and answer 'Sussex' etc.

20. Rain. To Fosseux in the car for cash and gas helmets. Rain
and mud and troops and Hun prisoners and turbaned
Indians at a barn door holding a sheep by a rope round its
neck, all still and silent. Afternoon through Fosseux again

with Col. Witchall to Mondicourt in rain and mud and back
in darkness along main Arras Road – could usually only see 2
or 3 of the roadside trees except when we ran into the blaze of
18-pounder battery by roadside. Blast of 18-pounders near the
billet blows mortar from ruins against our window linen.
Called at 244 for letters – none. C/O [Commanding Officer
(Colonel Witchall)] and Berrington and Cassels as before sat
up till 12.30 and I could not get my bed before

21. Clearer and no rain. Checking inventory of new billet in
fine modern house at corner of Rue de l'Abbé Hallain and
Boulevard Vauban. Big vacant house, red brick and shutters,
oak floors, panelling and pictured ceilings and mirrors – a few
beds, chairs and tables left. A small backyard with a few trees
and grass. We supplant Cameronians. One ruined house has
still an engraved 1850 portrait hanging on wall high up, with-
out glass broken. Rubin brought in letters from Helen and
Eleanor. Hung on at old billet till telephone connection was
made at new. It being very cold, we got to bed at 11.30.

22. Cold and wet. Fuel damp. Office work and maps. Court
on Inquiry on gassing of 4 men. Am I to stay on here and do
nothing but have cold feet and ask Cassels What is to be done?
No thrushes yet, but a chaffinch says 'Chink' in the chestnut
in our garden. Pipits sing up at Daneville, where I have come
to see 244, but they are all out – they came in, all but O/C, and
we had tea, and Rubin drove me back. Letter from Father.
Evening in Mess with Wallace as guest. Cold and still: no
artillery all day. At night I quite thought someone was knock-
ing excitedly at one of the doors, when it was really machine
guns. Troops going out to trenches singing and whistling 'It's
nice to get up in the morning' or a thing with part of 'The
Minstrel Boy' tune in it.

23. Chaffinch sang once. Another dull cold day. Inspected stables, checked inventory of new billet for men in Rue Jeanne d'Arc, went with Colonel round 244, 141 and 234 positions and O.P. in Achicourt. Afternoon maps. Partridges twanging in fields. Flooded fields by stream between the 2 sides of Achicourt. Ruined churches, churchyard and railway. Sordid ruin of Estaminet with carpenter's shop over it in Rue Jeanne d'Arc – wet, mortar, litter, almanacs, bottles, broken glass, damp beds, dirty paper, knife, crucifix, statuette, old chairs. Our cat moves with the Group wherever it goes, but inspects new house inside and out, windows, fireplace etc. Paid the Pool gunners (scrapings from several batteries doing odd jobs here). 2 owls in garden at 6. The shelling must have slaughtered many jackdaws but has made home for many more. Finished Frost's 'Mountain Interval'. Wrote to Frost. A quiet still evening. Rubin brought over letters from Helen and Oscar.

24. Why do Huns not retaliate on Arras guns? Some day this will be one of the hottest places this side of Hell, if it is this side. Nothing to do here today. Clearer, but still dull and cold with more breeze. Gas Alert off. Wrote to Father. Lushington calls and goes out with Colonel W—. Dined with 244 and Major Berrington and Capt. Angus – a dull long meal with maraschino chocolates at end. Benedictine, whisky and coffee, after soup, hors d'oeuvres, tinned turkey, roast mutton, Christmas pudding, apricots and cream. Gramophone but no fun. Walked back to Arras in dark with Thorburn, challenged by *only 2 sentries* who were content with 'Friend' though they could not see a yard among the ruins. Owls on Daneville Road. Machine guns and hanging lights above No Man's Land. Cassells and Colonel alone up when I returned at 11. New moon – *last* as I walked from Hatch to Codford.

25. A dull morning turns sunny and warm. Chaffinches and partridges, moles working on surface. Beautiful 18th century citadel with church ruined in middle of great barrack square. Huge bastions with sycamores in moat and tangled grass. Walked over citadel to new position with Colonel. Talked to Horton in our orchard. Wrote to Oscar. Artillery lively in the clear sunny noon. I got hot and spring-languid walking up at 4.30 to 244. Gramophone here played 'Anitra's Dance', 'Death of Troll' etc. and 'Allanwater'. Does a mole ever get hit by a shell?

26. A clear morning. 8.15–9.30 a.m. incessant field-gun firing – raid – German prisoners back at 10.15. Sunshine in white ruins and white squares with Scots standing about. A few shells arrive in Arras, but nobody looked as if anything were happening. While our guns were firing we could not hear one another speak. Afternoon to Achicourt to see if a gun position was visible to Huns. Shells and machine gun bullets came over. An 18-pounder on a fire point fired when I was 3 yards off (in front). Fitting aeroplane photos together. Paid out. A sunny day but cold in this house. Wrote to G. Bottomley. Gramophone. Talk with Berrington and Colonel.

27. Fine but chilly. 2 English planes fell, one on fire, as I walked up to 244 in afternoon: machine gun bullets cut telephone wire close by. Letters from Helen and Irene. Nothing to do but go and see about a billet of 244's collared by another Battery. Tea at 244 after seeing 2 of our planes down, one on fire with both burnt to death after alighting. Letters from Helen, Irene and Eleanor.

28. 244 to go into position. Out identifying gun positions. Up to 244 to pack for a change of billet. Tea with Rubin, Thorburn, Lushington and Horton. Letter from Helen, parcel

from Mother. Shelling town at night. Walk out to Daneville by citadel and marsh – moorhens in clear chalk stream by incinerator; blackbirds too, but no song except hedge-sparrow. Evening, ruin with Colonel and Cassells.

MARCH

1. Sunny and breezy. Wrote to Helen, Mother, Eleanor and Ellis. Indoors all morning doing nothing. Mostly a quiet morning. Out with Berrington round the marsh towards 244 who were doing their 1st shoot. Enemy planes over. 2 rounds across 244 position on to Doullens Road. Great deal of anti-aircraft shells singing by. Sat down on hill above 244 and watched German lines and Beaurains ghastly trees and ruins above Achicourt church tower. A bullet passes. Quite warm to sit down for quarter hour. Evening in mess. Colonel talks of the General (Poole) who was all for 'Fire, fire, fire! Loose her off! Deliver the goods! Annoy the Hun.' with artillery. Shelling heavy from about 5 a.m. I only dressed because I thought it would be better to have my clothes on. In any case I had to be up at 6 to go to Achicourt. A very misty still morning: could see nothing from bedroom except the trees and the stone dog – our artillery really made most of the noise, and I being just wakened and also inexperienced mistook it.

2. Up at 5.30 and went out to Achicourt Chateau to see 141's gun into its forward position. A misty frosty morning luckily and no plane could observe. Afternoon to Faubourg Ronville, its whistling deserted ruined streets. deserted roadway, pavement with single files of men. Cellars as dugouts, trenches behind and across road. Dead dry calf in stable. Rubble, rubbish, filth and old plush chair. Perfect view of No Man's Land

winding level at foot of Hun slope, and Beaurains above to one side and woods just behind crest on other side (M.B. 110) [a map reference (?Bench Mark)]. With Horton and Lushington to see 3 O.P.s there: – Letters from Helen, Mother, Eleanor and J. Freeman.

3.[6] No post. Morning dull spent in office. But afternoon with Colonel to Achicourt to see O.P.s and then to new battery positions. A chilly day not good for observing. Court of Inquiry on a man burnt with petrol – Lushington presiding and afterwards I went back with him to 244's new billet and saw my new quarters to be. Wrote to Mother and Helen.

4. Cold but bright clear and breezy. Nothing to do all morning but trace a map and its contours. Colonel and I went down to 244 before lunch to see the shell holes of last night and this morning. Hun planes over. More shells came in the afternoon. The fire is warm but the room cold. Tea with Lushington and Thorburn. Shelling at 5.30 – I don't like it. I wonder where I shall be hit as in bed I wonder if it is better to be on the window or outer side of room or on the chimney on inner side, whether better to be upstairs where you may fall or on the ground floor where you may be worse crushed. Birthday parcels from home.

5. Out early to see a raid by VI Corps [the main Army Command Group in this area], but snow hid most but singing of Field shells and snuffling of 6''. – Ronville's desolate streets. To 244's orchard which has had numerous 4.2 shells over, meant for the road. Wrote to Helen, Mervyn and Bronwen. Afternoon indoors paying etc. After tea to 244 to dine, not very happy with Lushington, Horton and Smith.

6 Thomas's thirty-ninth birthday.

They have the wind up because of the shells (which may have been meant for the road behind). Letters from de la Mare, Helen, Bronwen and de la Mare. A beautiful clear moonlit night after a beautiful high blue day with combed white clouds.

6. Bright and clear early and all day and warm at 1. Walked over to 244's position with Colonel and then up to 234 beyond Daneville station, and listened to larks and watched aeroplane fights. 2 planes down, one in flames, a Hun. Sometimes 10 of our planes together very high. Shells into Arras in afternoon.

7. A cold raw dull day with nothing to do except walk round to 244 to get a pair of socks. The wind made a noise in the house and trees and a dozen black crumpled sycamore leaves dance round and round on terrace. Wrote to Pearce and Irene. Rather a cold and depressed, solitary.

8. Snow blizzard – fine snow and fierce wind – to Achicourt O.P. but suddenly a blue sky and soft white cloud through the last of the snow – with Colonel and Berrington. Returned to hear that the Group has to leave this billet. I liked the walk. Indoors afternoon fitting together aeroplane trench photographs. Letters from Helen, Eleanor, Oscar and Frost (saying he had got an American publisher for my verses). A still quiet night up to 11 with just one round fired to show we have not left Arras. Up till 1 for a despatch from Corps. Colonel snotted interpreter.

9. Snow and very cold indoors doing nothing but look at a sandbag O.P. My last day at the Group. Weir of 2/1 Lowland takes my place. I return to 244 – Lushington, Horton and Rubin. I am fed up with sitting on my arse doing nothing that anybody couldn't do better. Wrote to de la Mare, Frost and Eleanor.

10. Up at 5.45 for a raid, but nothing doing. A misty mild morning clearing slightly to a white sky. 10 rounds gunfire C-B [?Command Battery]. Snowdrops at foot of peartrees by Decanville Railway. R.F.C. [Royal (?) Flying Corps] wireless man reading 'Hiawatha'. 3 shoots of 10 rounds gunfire suddenly at N.F. targets [no fixed targets] unobserved. Men mending a caved-in dugout in the dark. Parcel from Janet Hooton.

11. Out at 8.30 to Ronville O.P. and studied the ground from Beaurains N. Larks singing over No Man's Land – trench mortars. We were bombarding their front line: they were shooting at Arras. R.F.A. [Royal Field Artillery] officer with me who was quite concerned till he spotted a certain familiar Hun sentry in front line. A clear, cloudy day, mild and breezy. 8th shell carrying into Arras. Later Ronville heavily shelled and we retired to dugout. At 6.15 all quiet and heard blackbirds chinking. Scene peaceful, desolate like Dunwich moors except sprinkling of white chalk on the rough brown ground. Lines broken and linesmen out from 2.30 to 7 p.m. A little raid in the night . . .,

12. . . . then a beautiful moist clear limpid early morning till the Raid at 7 and the retaliation on Ronville at 7.30–8.45 with 77 cm. 25 to the minute. Then back through 6 ins. of chalk mud in trenches along battered Ronville Street. Rooks in tall trees on N. side of Arras – they and their nests and the trees black against the soft clouded sky. W. wind and mild but no rain yet (11 a.m.). Letters, mess accounts, maps. Afternoon at maps and with Horton at battery. Evening of partridges calling and pipsqueaks coming over behind.

13. Blackbird trying to sing early in dull marsh. A dull cold day. One N.F. shoot at nightfall. I was in position all day.

Letters from Eleanor, Mother and Ellis: wrote to Bronwen, Mother and Eleanor.

14. Ronville O.P. Looking out towards No Man's Land what I thought first was a piece of burnt paper or something turned out to be a bat shaken at last by shells from one of the last sheds in Ronville. A dull cold morning, with some shelling of Arras and St. Sauveur and just 3 for us. Talking to Birt and Randall about Glostershire and Wiltshire, particularly Painswick and Marlborough. A still evening – blackbirds singing far off – a spatter of our machine guns – the spit of one enemy bullet – a little rain – no wind – only far-off artillery.

15. Huns strafe I sector at 5.30. We reply and they retaliate on Arras and Ronville. Only tired 77s reach OP. A sunny breezy morning. Tried to climb Arras chimney to observe, but funked. 4 shells nearly got me while I was going and coming. A rotten day. No letters for 5 days.

16. Larks and great tits. Ploughing field next to orchard in mist – horses and man go right up to crest in view of Hun at Beaurains. Cold and dull. Letters to Helen and Janet. In the battery for the day. Fired 100 rounds from 12–1.30. Sun shining but misty still. Letter from Bronwen. The first thrush I have heard in France sang as I returned to Mess at 6 p.m. Parcel from Mother – my old Artist boots. Wrote to Hodson. A horrible night of bombardment, and the only time I slept I dreamt I was at home and couldn't stay to tea . . .

17. . . . Then a most glorious bright high clear morning. But even Horton, disturbed by 60-pounders behind his dugout, came in to breakfast saying: 'I am not going to stay in this — army; on the day peace is declared I am out of it like a — rabbit'. A beautiful day, sunny with pale cloudless sky and W. wind, but cold in O.P. Clear nightfall with curled,

cinereous cloud and then a cloudless night with pale stains in sky over where Bosh is burning a village or something. Quiet till 3: then a Hun raid and our artillery over us to meet it: their shells into St. Sauveur, Ronville and Arras. Sound of fan in underground cave.

18. Beautiful clear cloudless morning and no firing between daybreak and 8. Drew another panorama at 7. Linnets and chaffinches sing in waste trenched ground with trees and water tanks between us and Arras. Magpies over No Man's Land in pairs. The old green (grey) track crossing No Man's Land – once a country way to Arras. The water green and clear (like Silent Pool) of the Moat of the Citadel with skeletons of whole trees lying there. Afternoon washing and reading letters from Helen and Eleanor. I did 2 shoots. News came that we are in Beaurains and near Mercatel. Letters to Helen and Eleanor. The pigeons are about in the streets of this Faubourg more than ever and I could hear a lark till the Archies drowned it. Fired 600 rounds and got tired eyes and ears. Then early to bed and up at 4 to go to O.P. on

19. Nothing to do all day at Ronville but look at quiet No Man's Land and trenches with engineers beginning to straighten road up. Back to sleep at billet, but preferred to return to O.P. as I've to go to the front trench O.P. at 4 on the

20th. Stiff deep mud all the way up and shelled as we started. Telegraph Hill as quiet as if only rabbits lived there. I took revolver and left this diary behind in case. For it is very exposed and only a few Cornwalls and MGC [Machine Gun Corps] about. But Hun shelled chiefly over our heads into Beaurains all night – like starlings returning 20 or 30 a minute. Horrible flap of 5.9 a little along the trench. Rain and mud and I've to stay till I am relieved tomorrow. Had not brought warm clothes or enough food and had no shelter, nor had telephonists. Shelled all night. But the M.G.C. boy gave me tea. I've no bed. I leant against wall of trench. I got up and looked over. I stamped up and down. I tried to see patrol out. Very light – the only sign of Hun on Telegraph Hill, though 2 appeared and were sniped at. A terribly long night and cold. Not relieved till 8. Telephonists out repairing line since 4 on the morning of the

21st. At last 260 relieved us. Great pleasure to be going back to sleep and rest. No Man's Land like Goodwood Racecourse with engineers swarming over it and making a road between shell holes full of blood-stained water and beer bottles among barbed wire. Larks singing as they did when we went up in dark and were shelled. Now I hardly felt as if a shell could hurt, though several were thrown about near working parties. Found letters from Helen, Eleanor and Julian. Had lunch, went to bed at 2 intending to get up to tea, but slept till 6.30 on the . . .

22nd. (Beautiful was Arras yesterday coming down from Beaurains and seeing Town Hall ruin white in sun like a thick smoke beginning to curl. Sprinkle of snow today in sun.) A cold bright day with snow early. We fired twice. I on duty at Battery. Letters to Helen and home and Gordon and Deacon. Partridges twanging in open fields. Not much shooting to do. Several windy snow showers half-hail and then sun. Talk with Thorburn about his fate if he loses his commission. Gramophone plays Ambrose Thomas's 'Mignon' gavotte (by Raymond Jeremy's Philharmonic Quartette), 'D'ye ken John Peel', Chopin's 'Berceuse', Tchaikovsky's 'Fantasia Italiana'.

23. Frosty clear. Ploughs going up over crest towards Beaurains. Rubin back from F.O.P. [Forward Observation

Post (in No Man's Land)] believes in God and tackles me about atheism – thinks marvellous escapes are ordained. But I say so are the marvellous escapes of certain telegraph posts, houses, etc. Sunny and cold – motored to Avesnes and Fosseux to buy luxuries and get letters. Crowded bad roads through beautiful hedgeless rolling chalk country with rows of trees, some along roads following curving ridges – villages on crests with church spires and trees. Troops, children holding hands, and darkskinned women, mud walled ruined barns. Parcels from Mother and Helen, letters from Mother and J. Freeman.

24. Out early to Beaurains. The chill clear air pains my skin while it delights my mind – both walking and in car. Only tombstones recognisable in Beaurains and that little conical summer house among trees. Sat all day in copse in old chalk pit between Agny and Achicourt which is perhaps to be our new position. Warm in the sun, but no thrushes in all those ash, hazel and dogwood. Parcels from Mrs. Freeman and Eleanor. Letters to Helen, Mrs. Freeman and Mother.

25. Up at 5 and to O.P. beyond Beaurains with Thorburn and stood all day in trench behind hedge till head ached with staring at Wancourt and Neuville Vitasse and the ground between and beyond. A cold but sunny day. Many R.F.A. and infantry used the O.P. We were discovered and the O.P. 20 yards away had a shell on to it, and we had several over our shoulders. Larks singing. Drawing panoramas. Left Thorburn there at 6 p.m. tired enough. Letters from Bronwen, [R. C.] Trevelyan and Guthrie.

26. Preparing reports and panoramas for 35 H.A.G. [Heavy Artillery Group]. Rainy and dull. Letter to Bronwen. Packing up for move to the chalk pit. Up late in emptied billet waiting

for ASC [Army Service Corps] lorries to come up. Off at last
on foot to the Achicourt billet at 1, in white cordite flashes in
dark roads.

27. Rain and sleet and sun, getting guns camouflaged, steal-
ing a Decanville truck, laying out nightlines. Letters from
Hodson, Eleanor and Sgt. Pellissier. Still that aching below the
nape of my neck since my last O.P. day. Sat till 11 writing let-
ters. As I was falling asleep great blasts shook the house and
windows, whether from our own firing or enemy bursts near,
I could not tell in my drowse, but I did not doubt my heart
thumped so that if they had come closer together it might
have stopped. Rubin and Smith dead tired after being up all
the night before. Letters to Helen and Eleanor.

28. Frosty and clear and some blackbirds singing at Agny
Chateau in the quiet of exhausted battery, everyone just
having breakfast at 9.30: all very still and clear: but these
mornings always very misleading and disappearing so that
one might almost think afterwards they were illusive. Planes
humming. In high white cloud aeroplanes leave tracks curv-
ing like rough wheel tracks in snow – I had a dream this
morning that I have forgot but Mother was in distress. All
day loading shells from old position – sat doing nothing
till I got damned philosophical and sad. Thorburn dreamt
2 nights ago that a maid was counting forks and spoons and
he asked her 'Must an officer be present.' Letter to Helen.
Tired still.

29. Wet again. Getting refuge trenches dug for detachments.
Marking crests on map. How beautiful, like a great crystal
sparkling and spangling, the light reflected from some glass
which is visible at certain places and times through a hole in
cathedral wall, ruined cathedral.

30. Bright early, then rain. New zero line, planting pickets. Arranging for material for new O.P. dugout – old one fell in yesterday. Clear and bright and still from 6 p.m. on. Air full of planes and sound of whistles against Hun planes. Blackbirds singing and then chuckling as they go to roost. Two shells falling near Agny Chateau scatter them. Letters from Helen and Mother and parcels from Mother and Eleanor. Too late to bed and had no sleep at all, for the firing, chiefly 60-pounders of our own. Shakespeare's plays for 10 minutes before sleep.

31. Up at 5 worn out and wretched. 5.9s flopping on Achicourt while I dressed. Up to Beaurains. There is a chalk-stone cellar with a dripping Bosh dug-out far under and by the last layer of stones is the lilac bush, rather short. Nearby a graveyard for the 'tapferer franzos soldat' with crosses and Hun names. Blackbirds in the clear cold bright morning early in black Beaurains. Sparrows in the elder of the hedge I observe through – a cherry tree just this side of hedge makes projection in trench with its roots. Beautiful clear evening everything dark and soft round Neuville Vitasse, after the rainbow there and the last shower. Night in lilac-bush cellar of stone like Berryfield. Letter to Helen. Machine gun bullets snaking along – hissing like little wormy serpents.

APRIL

1. among the ragged and craggy gables of Beaurains – a beautiful serene clear morning with larks at 5.15 and blackbirds at 6 till it snowed or rained at 8. All day sat writing letters to Helen, Father and Mother by the fire and censoring men's letters etc., an idle day – I could not sleep till I went to bed at 10. Letters from Helen, Baba and Deacon. A fine bright day with showers.

2. Letter to H. K. Vernon. Another frosty clear windy morning. Some sun and I enjoyed filling sandbags for dug out we are to have in battery for the battle. But snow later after we had fired 100 rounds blind. Snow half melting as it falls makes fearful slush. I up at battery alone till 9.30 p.m. Writing to Helen and Frost. Rubin and Smith sang duets from 'Bing Boys' till 11.

3. Snow just frozen – strong S.E. wind. Feet wet by 8.15 a.m. Letters from Gordon and Freeman. The eve. Letters to Gordon, Freeman, Helen. A fine day later, filling sandbags. MACBETH.

4. Up at 4.30. Blackbirds sing at battery at 5.45 – shooting at 6.30. A cloudy fresh morning. But showery cold muddy and slippery later. 600 rounds. Nothing in return yet. Tired by 9.15 p.m. Moved to dug-out in position. Letter from Helen. Artillery makes air flap all night long.

5. A dull morning turns misty with rain. Some 4.2s coming over at 10. Air flapping all night as with great sails in strong gusty wind (with artillery) – thick misty windless air. Sods on f/c's dugout begin to be fledged with fine green feathers of yarrow – yarrow. Sun and wind drying the mud. Firing all day, practising barrage etc. Beautiful pale hazy moonlight and the sag and flap of air. Letters to Mother and Helen. HAMLET.

6. A lazy morning, being a half day: warm and breezy, with sun and cloud but turned wet. Billets shelled by 4.2: 60-pounders hit. In car with Horton to Fosseux and Avesnes and met infantry with yellow patches behind marching soaked up to line – band and pipes at Wanquetin to greet them, playing 'They wind up the Watch on the Rhine' (as Horton calls it). After the shelling Horton remarks: 'The Bosh

is a damned good man, isn't he, a damned smart man, you must admit'. Roads worse than ever – no crust left on side roads. Letters from Helen, Mervyn, Mother, Eleanor.

7. Up at 6 to O.P. A cold bright day of continuous shelling N. Vitasse and Telegraph Hill. Infantry all over the place in open preparing Prussian Way with boards for wounded. Hardly any shells into Beaurains. Larks, partridges, hedge-sparrows, magpies by O.P. A great burst in red brick building in N. Vitasse stood up like a birch tree or a fountain. Back at 7.30 in peace. Then at 8.30 a continuous roar of artillery.

8. A bright warm Easter day but Achicourt shelled at 12.39 and then at 2.15 so that we all retired to cellar. I had to go over to battery at 3 for a practice barrage, skirting the danger zone, but we were twice interrupted. A 5.9 fell 2 yards from me as I stood by the f/c post. One burst down the back of the office and a piece of dust scratched my neck. No firing from 2–4. Rubin left for a course.

On the last pages of diary are these notes:

> The light of the new moon and every star
>
> And no more singing for the bird . . .
>
> I never understood quite what was meant by God
>
> The morning chill and clear hurts my skin while it delights my mind.
>
> Neuville in early morning with its flat straight crest with trees and houses [see Diary, April 1] – the beauty of this silent empty scene of no inhabitants and hid troops, but don't know why I could have cried and didn't.

Loose inside the diary, strangely creased by shell-blast like the diary, is a photograph of Helen and an army pass to Loughton/Lydd dated

3.12.16. Also a slip of paper with addresses of S. N. Jones of Newport, H. K. Vernon of Oxford, J. N. Benson of Upper Tooting, Lewis John of Upminster, his brother Julian Thomas in Tooting. On the reverse of this in pencil is written

Where any turn may lead to Heaven

Or any corner may hide Hell

Roads shining like river up hill after rain.[7]

7 Cf. Poem 96, fourth and seventh stanzas.

NOTES, APPENDICES AND INDEX

Notes

By quotations from his numerous letters, these notes are intended to provide information about Thomas's life and thinking while he was writing the poems. For many poems he seemed to draw on memories of incidents and moods that are recorded in his published prose or in his unpublished notebooks. Whenever such links can be directly established, they are included in the notes.

Abbreviations used in the notes

AANP	*An Annual of New Poetry*, Constable, 1917.
Berg	Manuscript poems in the Berg Collection of the New York Public Library.
Berg FNB	Manuscript Field Note Books in the Berg Collection.
BM	Manuscript poems in the British Museum (now British Library) Add. MS. 44990.
Bod	Manuscript poems in Bodley MS. Don. d. 28.
Cooke	William Cooke, *Edward Thomas, A Critical Biography*, Faber & Faber, 1970.
CP$_1$	Edward Thomas, *Collected Poems*, Selwyn & Blount, 1920.
CP$_2$	Edward Thomas, *Collected Poems* (New Edition), Ingpen & Grant, 1928.
CP$_3$	Edward Thomas, *Collected Poems* (New Edition), Faber & Faber, 1944.
CP$_4$	Edward Thomas, *Collected Poems* (Fifth Impression), Faber & Faber, 1949.
Eckert	Robert P. Eckert, *Edward Thomas: A Biography and a Bibliography*, Dent, 1937.
Eckert Coll.	Eckert Collection: a collection of papers of Judge R. P. Eckert, now in the Bodleian Library (Eng. lett., c. 281, d. 281).
EE	'Edward Eastaway' [Edward Thomas], *Poems*, Selwyn & Blount, 1917.
EF$_1$	Manuscript poems once owned by Eleanor Farjeon.
EF$_2$	Typescript poems once owned by Eleanor Farjeon.
Form	*Form, A Quarterly of the Arts*, vol. i, No. 1 (April 1916), ed. Austin O. Spare and Francis Marsden.

GB   *Letters from Edward Thomas to Gordon Bottomley*, ed. R. George
       Thomas, Oxford University Press, 1968.

Helen Manuscript and typescript poems among Helen Thomas's papers.

IM   *In Memoriam: Edward Thomas, Being Number Two of the Pasture
       Series*, The Morland Press, July 1919.

IPS   Edward Thomas, *In Pursuit of Spring*, Thomas Nelson & Sons, 1914.

JT   Typescript poems once owned by the poet's brother, Julian
       Thomas.

KS   *Known Signatures: New Poems*, ed. John Gawsworth, Rich &
       Cowan, 1932 (includes *Two Poems*).

LML   Edward Thomas manuscripts in the Lockwood Memorial Library,
       Buffalo, New York.

LP   Edward Thomas, *Last Poems*, Selwyn & Blount, 1918.

M_1 Manuscript poems in a green notebook once owned by the poet's
       son, Merfyn.

M_2 Manuscript poems in a blue notebook once owned by the poet's
       son, Merfyn.

MET   Typescript poems once owned by the poet's mother, Mary
       Elizabeth Thomas.

Moore John Moore, *The Life and Letters of Edward Thomas*, Heinemann,
       1939.

NS   'Edward Eastaway' [Edward Thomas], *Four Poems*, in *New
       Statesman*, 28 April 1917, p. 87.

Poetry *Poetry: A Magazine of Verse*, ed. Harriet Monroe, vol. ix, No. V,
       February 1917, pp. 247–50 [Poems by Edward Eastaway],
       Chicago.

RB   *Root and Branch, A Seasonal of the Arts*, ed. James Guthrie 1913–18
       (vol. i: 1913–15; vol. ii: 1916–18).

RF_1 Poems included in letters from Thomas to Robert Frost, in
       Dartmouth College Library, Hanover, New Hampshire, U.S.A.

RF_2 Typescript poems among the Robert Frost papers in Dartmouth
       College Library.

RGT_1 Manuscript poem given to the editor by Helen Thomas.

RGT_2 Typescript poems given to the editor by Helen Thomas.

RLW   Manuscript poems given by Eleanor Farjeon to the late
       Rowland L. Watson (Secretary to the Edward Thomas
       Memorial Fund).

SP   'Edward Eastaway' [Edward Thomas], *Six Poems*, The Pear Tree Press, Flansham, Sussex, 1916.

TE   *This England, An Anthology from her Writers*, compiled by Edward Thomas, Oxford University Press, 1915.

TLFY   Eleanor Farjeon, *Edward Thomas: The Last Four Years*, Oxford University Press, 1958.

TP   *Twelve Poets, A Miscellany of New Verse*, Selwyn & Blount, 1918.

Two Poems   Edward Thomas, *Two Poems*, Ingpen & Grant, 1927.

1 Up in the Wind

35 The White Horse is an inn at Froxfield, near Steep.

The following jottings are in *Berg FNB 79*:

> 27 November 1914. *Ryton*: Clothes on the line violently blowing in wind and crackle like a rising woodfire. [Cf. 11. 95–6.]

On the left-hand side, facing an entry dated 2 Nov. 1914:

> I could wring the old girl's neck
> That put it here
> A public house! (Charcoal burner)
> by bringing up and quite outdoing
> The idea of London
> Two woods around and never a road in sight
> Trees roaring like a train without an end
> But she's dead long ago
> Only a motorist from far away
> Or marketers in carts once a fortnight
> Or a few fresh tramps ignorant
> of the house turning.

The next page (undated) is headed:

Subjects

> (1) The White Horse
> (2) Old Man (see this notebook for Nov. 11)
> (1) dirty earth and clean bright sky.
>   see 1 December back. [i.e. back of the notebook]

2 November Sky

See the following jottings from *Berg FNB 79*:

> 1 December 1914. The roads all muddy with mashed leaves, twigs, sparse hedges, and sodden fields–

> Beautiful hobnail pattern in path over reddish light ploughland

Undated, but transferred to 1 Dec. 1914:

A fine liquid morning then sunny drops slanting a *few* in a
sprinkle then heavy rain and a blue and black sky where wind
comes from. Then at 12–3 bright sun, clear sweet cold sky with a
few white clouds line – the sky so bright and clear and cleaner.
The roads all muddy with mashed leaves and twigs, and bare
hedges and sodden fields. Clear till moon rise (big full white
moon towards East and sun going crimson cloudless in West –
When Jupiter was visible at 4.45 there was some wet
sandcoloured cloud in West – a big rag of it. – Beautiful hobnail
pattern on path near reddish bright ploughland. An evening of
alternate blazing moon and wind and of lashing rain. Each long
stick in faggots has been dipped in moonlight once: also water
spouts. gutters.

3 March

In this poem Thomas takes seriously Frost's advice that he should
write verse based on his prose book *In Pursuit of Spring* (1914). The
first three lines reflect the structure of that travel book which is
hung around the thin thread of a search for the true spring after
so many false starts. See *IPS*, pp. 24–5 ('In search of Spring') and
pp. 290–301 ('The Grave of Winter'). This poem is dated in *LML*
with a heavy relief pen which is used for all the final corrections
made to 'Up in the Wind' and 'November Sky' and which suggests
that by 5 Dec. 1914 Thomas had decided to commit himself firmly
both to writing verse and to following Frost's advice.

4 Old Man

The poem owes a great deal to Thomas's spate of autobiographical
writing in the autumn and winter of 1912 (see *GB*, Letter 126), of
which *The Childhood of Edward Thomas* (published in 1937 but
probably written 1912–13) is a part. Its opening paragraphs are
relevant to 'Old Man':

When I penetrate backward into my childhood I come perhaps
sooner than many people to impassable night. A sweet darkness
enfolds with a faint blessing my life up to the age of about four

... But out of doors, somewhere at the verge of the dark years, I can recall more simply and completely than any spent indoors at that time one day above others. I lay in the tall grass and buttercups of a narrow field at the edge of London and saw the sky and nothing but the sky. There was some one near, probably a servant, necessary but utterly insignificant. I was alone and happy to be so, just as indoors I was happy among people and shadows between walls. Was it one day or many? I know of no beginning or end to it; but an end I suppose it had an age past. [pp. 13–14]

See, (1) in *Berg holograph notebook* No. 3, dated on the flyleaf by Thomas, 10 Aug. 1909, the following extract from an unpublished story called *The Old House*:

Mrs Rose [a housekeeper] was stirring in the garden. She appeared among the trees. 'Do you know what this is, Sir?' she asked as he [Mr. Banks, the owner of the house] got up. It was a feathery sprig of grey green. Without thinking he crushed it gently between his fingers and held it to his nose. 'Ah! – Beautiful.' [Beginning of an insertion from the left-hand side.] He sniffed a long and solemn exploring sniff, to the heart of the scent, and then again; and then he meditated with the sprig at his nose but no longer smelling it; and then he tried to think and smell at the same time, closing his eyes, as if he were diving through some new medium into a strange land, – but in vain.' [End of insertion.] 'No, what is it?' 'Lad's love, sir. Crush it and it is sweeter.'

Again 'Blenheim 1705' [a date of a lintel of the Old House] ran in his brain he knew not why. The scent was like memory.

(2) *Berg FNB* 79, entry dated 11 Nov. 1914:

'*Old Man* scent, I smell again and again not really liking it but venerating it because it holds the secret of something of very long ago which I feel it may someday recall, but I have got no idea what.'

5 The Signpost

A rough outline of this poem is in *Berg FNB* 79, not later than
December 1914. The right-hand side of page 5 from the end of the
notebook has the single line

> A   to
> The mouthful of earth that remedies all.

The left-hand side reads:

> When the grass is heard first
> And the crimson haunts the boughs
> With smoke of traveller's joy
> Today I wished I was (fifty) 20
>
> When I ---
>   -------
> Then I wished I had not been born
>   _____
>
> When –
> And I ~~am~~ 50, what shall I wish
>   _____
>
> When –
> Will there come a day
> When I could wish to be alive
> Somehow 20 or 40 or not

6 The Other

This poem had a special interest for Frost, who had directed
Thomas's attention specifically to *IPS* as evidence of Thomas's
poetic ability. 'The Other' is closely based on 'The Other Man' in
IPS, and both poets shared an interest in the hallucinatory
recurrence it describes.

Passages on the following pages in *IPS* demonstrate the prose
genesis of the poem: pp. 43–4, 47–9, 51–2, 60, 119–27, 140, 201–15,
218–32, and 282.

53–4   Cf. the conversations between Thomas and the 'other man' in *IPS*
       (pp. 119–27), especially his 'confession' about his fondness for clay
       pipes; see also pp. 219–20, where the 'other man' speaks of the poet
       and his life-long habit of using field notebooks:

> He rambled on and on about himself, his past, his writing, his
> digestion; his main point being that he did not like writing. He
> had been attempting the impossible task of reducing undigested
> notes about all sorts of details to a grammatical, continuous
> narrative. He abused notebooks violently. He said that they
> blinded him to nearly everything that would not go into the
> form of notes; or, at any rate, he could never afterwards
> reproduce the great effects of Nature and fill in the interstices
> merely – which was all they were good for – from the notes. The
> notes – often of things which he would otherwise have forgotten
> – had to fill the whole canvas. Whereas, if he had taken none,
> then only the important, what he truly cared for, would have
> survived in his memory, arranged not perhaps as they were in
> Nature, but at least according to the tendencies of his own spirit.
> 'Good God!' said he. But luckily we were by this time on the
> level. I mounted. He followed.

61–70 Cf. Thomas's 'pleasure of my disembodied spirit (so to call it)' on
       the cycle ride from Semington and Melksham to Staverton (*IPS*,
       pp. 201–15). The passage concludes:

> The inn door, which was now open, was as the entrance to a
> bright cave in the middle of the darkness: the illumination had a
> kind of blessedness such as it might have had to a cow, not
> without foreignness; and a half-seen man within it belonged to a
> world, blessed indeed, but far different from this one of mine,
> dark, soft, and tranquil. I felt that I could walk on thus, sipping
> the evening silence and solitude, endlessly. But at the house
> where I was staying I stopped as usual. I entered, blinked at the
> light, and by laughing at something, said with the intention of
> being laughed at, I swiftly again naturalized myself.

80   Cf. *IPS*, p. 60, where Thomas writes of George Meredith: 'From
       first to last he wrote as an inhabitant of this earth, where, as

Wordsworth says, "we have our happiness or not at all," just or unjust.'

Two entries in the *Berg FNB* bear on this poem. (1) *Berg FNB* 62, June 1913, reads: '*Other Man* – wraith – when seen at Salterley I was not sure he had existed before – he avoids a difficulty in telling truth.' (2) *Berg FNB* 67, 18 Dec. 1913, reads:

> *East Grinstead*. 4.30. One of those eternal evenings – the wind gone, no one upon the road. I grasp the stately tall holly or look over the ploughland to the near ridge, the crocketed spruces, the dark house mass, and behind them a soft dulling flame-coloured sky where large shapeless soft dull dark clouds in roughly horizontal lines are massing with one bright star in an interstice – and far behind me an owl calls again and again and somewhere far to one side in a hid hollow a dog barks and nearer, one or two blackbirds climb as they fly along hedges. What does it mean? I feel an old inhabitant of earth at such times. How many hundred times have I seen the same since I was fifteen.

10 The Mountain Chapel

The poem appears to be based on memories of early visits to Wales. Cf. Thomas's *Beautiful Wales* (1905), p. 26 and pp. 148–9:

> But Siloh stands firm, and ventures once a week to send up a thin music that avails nothing against the wind; although close to it, threatening it, laughing at it, able to overwhelm it, should the laugh become cruel, is a company of elder trees, which, seen at twilight, are sentinels, embossed upon the sky – sentinels of the invisible, patient, unconquerable powers: or (if one is lighter-hearted) they seem the empty homes of what the mines and the chapels think they have routed . . .

> But by this mountain you cannot be really at ease until in some way you have travelled through all history. For it has not been as nothing to it that Persia, Carthage, Greece and Rome, and Spain have been great and are not. It has been worn by the foot-prints

of time which have elsewhere made the grass a little deeper or renewed the woods. It has sat motionless, looking on the world; it has grown wrinkled; it is all memory. Were it and its fellows to depart, we should not know how old we were; for we should have only books. Therefore I love it. It offers no illusions. Its roads are winding and rough. The grass is thin; the shelter scarce, the valley crops moderate; the cheese and mutton good; the water pure; the people strong, kind, intelligent, and without newspapers; the fires warm and bright and large, and throwing light and shadow upon pewter and brass and oak and books. It offers no illusions; for it is clear, as it is not in a city or in an exuberant English county, that the world is old and troubled, and that light and warmth and fellowship are good. Sometimes comes a thought that it is a huge gravestone, so it is worn, so obscure and brief its legend. It belongs to the past, to the dead; and the dead, as they are more numerous, so here they are greater than we, and we only great because we shall one day be of their number. You cannot look at it without thinking that the time will come when it may be, and we are not, nor the races of men—

sed haec prius fuere: nunc recondita
senet quiete.

11 The Manor Farm

This England, An Anthology from her Writers, compiled by Thomas (1915) is described by him in a prefatory note:

This is an anthology from the work of English writers rather strictly so called. Building round a few most English poems like 'When icicles hang by the wall', – excluding professedly patriotic writing because it is generally bad and because indirect praise is sweeter and more profound, – never aiming at what a committee from Great Britain and Ireland might call complete, – I wished to make a book as full of English character and country as an egg is of meat. If I have reminded others, as I did myself continually, of some of the echoes called up by the name of England, I am satisfied.

Apart from some prose quotations from C. M. Doughty and W. H. Hudson, and a few songs from three volumes of folk-songs, the only contemporary poems in the selection are by Gordon Bottomley, Walter de la Mare, Thomas Hardy, and Edward Eastaway ('Haymaking' and 'The Manor Farm' in Section III, 'Her Sweet Three Corners', pp. 111–12).

12 An Old Song [1]

4   *BM*'s cancelled 'O' (in favour of 'But') gave the original refrain of the Lincolnshire folk-song, 'The Lincolnshire Poacher', whose words and music are included in Thomas's *The Pocket Book of Poems and Songs for the Open Air* (p. 81) which, together with his letters to Gordon Bottomley, give some indication of his informed interest in ballads and folk-music.

13   The incident with a gamekeeper occurred on a visit to Robert Frost at The Gallows, near Dymock. Apparently Frost resented the threats of Lord Beauchamp's shot-gun-carrying gamekeeper and gave him a piece of his mind. Thomas was frightened, but Frost, in a typical rage, went back and threatened to beat up the man. The police later intervened and finally Lord Beauchamp sent Frost an apology. References to this incident occur frequently in Thomas's letters to Frost. The affair and its background is described in Lawrance Thompson, *Robert Frost: The Early Years* (London, 1967), pp. 467–8.

13 An Old Song [2]

19–22   Cf. this excerpt from Thomas's letter to his brother-in-law, Hugh McArthur, from Steep, dated 26 Mar. 1912: 'We've had a very good time for us. I kept it up till 1 o'clock this morning with sea songs by a new neighbour – a man who was on the "Nimrod" with Shackleton . . .'

14 The Combe

Roman figure II is inserted before the title in *JT* and the poem is signed 'Edward Eastaway', the only known autograph of this pseudonym. Presumably the poem was among the first group of verses sent to editors (e.g. Monro and Blackwood's) and rejected in December 1914 and January 1915.

15 The Hollow Wood

'The Hollow Land' is a poem by William Morris, whose *Collected Works* Thomas had reviewed between September and December 1914. The name was also given to a copse near Gordon Bottomley's home at Carnforth.

16 The New Year

7–8 This image is taken from the prose version of 'Up in the Wind' in *LML* (see Appendix A, p. 435).

1–12 These games are described in *The Childhood of Edward Thomas*, pp. 79–80:

> The playground was asphalt; again there were no organized games, but a dozen groups playing leap frog, fly the garter, or tops, or chasing one another, or simply messing about. 'Fly the garter' – if that is its right name – was a grand game to see played by a dozen of the biggest boys. I forget how it came about, but by degrees at length there were four or five boys bent double, forming a continuous line of backs. Each grasped the one in front of him and the first of them had his head, protected by his hands, against the playground wall. From half-way across the playground a big boy ran at a gallop, his ironshod heels pounding the asphalt, towards this line of boys who could see him approaching between their legs. Reaching the line and putting his hands upon the first back to help him leap he leaped forward into the air. A brilliant leaper would use only one hand for the take off: the other gave a sonorous smack on the right place in passing. With legs outspread he flew along the line of backs, and alighted upon the fourth or fifth of them. The lighter his weight, the more fortunate was the steed thus accidentally mounted: the heavier, the greater was the chance that both together crashed to the ground. Then, I think, the leaper added

another to the line of backs and set the next leaper an impossible task.

(This game was common in the editor's own primary school in the Rhymney Valley between 1920 and 1924. It was called 'Cutter' – an anglicized form of Welsh 'cwtaf', i.e. 'the tailender'; probably a Middle Welsh borrowing from Middle English 'cut', i.e. 'a lot'.)

20 Snow

3 The child in the poem is the poet's younger daughter, Myfanwy. The best source of incidental background information to these early poems is *TLFY*, pp. 107–55. For Thomas's interest in tales written for children see especially his *Celtic Stories* (1911), *Norse Tales* (1912), and *Four-and-Twenty Blackbirds* (1915), and, variously, his numerous favourable reviews of Walter de la Mare's prose and poetry.

21 Adlestrop

Adlestrop is on the main road between Stow-on-the-Wold and Chipping Norton (about five miles from Stow-on-the-Wold). The station, now closed, was close to the River Evenlode and half a mile away from the village. It was on the main G.W.R. line from Oxford to Worcester and Wolverhampton, and in Thomas's day was part of the Central Line.

An undated entry (probably early January 1915) in *Berg FNB* 80 reads: 'Train stopping outside station at Adlestrop June 1914.' This incident is expanded in *Berg FNB* 75:

> 23 June 1914. A glorious day from 4.20 a.m. and at 10 tiers above tiers of white cloud with dirtiest grey bars above the sea of slate and dull brick by Battersea Park. Then at Oxford tiers of pure white with loose longer masses above and gaps of dark clear blue above hay-making and elms.

> Then we stopped at Adlestrop, through the willows could be heard a chain of blackbirds' songs at 12.45 and one thrush and no man seen, only a hiss of engine letting off steam.

Stopping outside Campden by banks of long grass, willowherb and meadowsweet, extraordinary silence between two periods of travel – looking out on grey dry stones between metals and the shining metals and over it all the elms willows and long grass – one man clears his throat – a greater than rustic silence. No house in view. Stop only for a minute till signal is up.

Now stop like this outside Colwall on 27th with thrush singing on hillside above road.

24–27th. At Ledington with Frost in always hot weather.

24 The Lofty Sky

This poem was written, after seven days in bed with an injured ankle, on Thomas's first day 'downstairs but worse off because I know how helpless I still am. I can only hop and am in a filthy temper.' (Letter in *TLFY*, 10 Jan. 1915.)

25 The Cuckoo

For a different memory see Thomas's essay, 'The First Cuckoo' in *The Last Sheaf* (1928), pp. 60–4.

26 Swedes

Cf. Thomas's *The Heart of England* (1906), Ch. 1, p. 19:

Or as, when a man has mined in the dead desert for many days, he suddenly enters an old tomb, and making a light, sees before him vases of alabaster, furniture adorned with gold and blue enamel and the figures of gods, a chariot of gold, and a silence perfected through many ages in the company of death and of the desire of immortality.

11 *Amen-hotep* was the name used in Thomas's day for the Egyptian ruler Armen-ophis II (1436–1413 BC). The tomb-robber in the poem may refer to an incident in the Valley of Kings' tombs in November 1901 (see J. H. Breasted, *A History of the Ancient Egyptians* (1912)).

27 The Unknown Bird

15–19   Although Thomas had edited *The Book of the Open Air* (1907) and
        written much on country topics, he did not consider himself a
        professional naturalist like his friend W. H. Hudson whose
        Adventures among Birds is praised in *IPS*, pp. 244–50: 'While his
        birds are intensely alive in many different ways, and always
        intensely birdlike, presenting a loveliness beyond that of idealized
        or supernaturalized women and children, yet at the same time their
        humanity was never before so apparent.'

   See *Berg FNB* early in January 1915 for a single line: 'The strange
   bird la! – la! – la!'

29 ' 'Twill take some getting.' 'Sir, I think 'twill so'

For Thomas's interest in the authentic life of tramps, blended with
some autobiographical overtones, see the following quotation from
'Hawthornden', *Light and Twilight* (1911), pp. 123–6:

> When he moved into the country he was prepared for
> adventures. Gypsies should be allowed to camp near his house
> and he would be familiar with them. He would invite the tramps
> into his study for a talk and a smoke. He used to sit by the
> roadside, or in the taproom of an inn, waiting for what would
> turn up. But something always stood in the way – himself. He
> grew tired of paying for a tramp's quart, and was disconcerted,
> now by too great familiarity and now by too great respect. When
> a tramp came to the back door, his maids or his wife reported it
> to him, and they sometimes had interesting fragments of a story
> to relate; for the women had human sympathies along with
> unquestioning commonplace views of social distinctions.
> Sometimes he saw the man coming or going, and formed
> romantic conjectures which made him impatient of what he
> actually heard.

See a detailed prose account of this meeting in *Berg FNB* 79,
dated 21 Nov. 1914:

> Going up Stoner in cold strong N.E. wind but a fine cloudy sky
> at 3, overtook short stiff oldish man taking short quick strides –

carrying flag basket and brolly and old coat on back and with a
green ash stick in hand. Says it's a fine day and as I passed he
decides to ask me for – I don't know. I stopped his request with
questions, found him a 6d. He had a little bitch brown with
spots of grey reminding me of a Welsh sheep-dog – not much
one, but company. He says the mother was almost pure (blue)
Welsh. Hunts in Hangers, nearly got one this morning 'he would
and he wouldn't, 'twas like that.' 'They say those Welsh bitches
will breed with a fox. He knew one the other side of Guildford
and she had her litter of seven in a rabbit-hole. He had one. It
tried to bite anything it killed so hard it was useless: red mouth
like a fox.' He had come from Childgrove where he's done two
halfdays dock-picking this week: is going to Alton and hopes for
a lift from Crowley's men to Longmoor to look for a job. But
perhaps he won't reach Alton – rheumatism in one leg – rubs oil
they sell at harness makers and 'supples' it a bit – round face
with white bristles all over and eyes with red rims. Has worked a
lot at S'hampton docks, navvying, but likes farm work best, has
promises of flint picking when the sheep are out of field, but
can't hang about – comes from Christchurch in the New Forest –
did a year's soldiering in '74 with Berkshires – has three sons at
Front, one just come from Bombay had really finished his eight
years with the colours, one son a marine. If he can't reach Alton,
will get a shakedown from a farmer.

Talked about the soldiers just coming to billet in Petersfield –
he thought two or three thousand – twenty, or so, in kilts –
might be a Border Regiment.

A rustic, burring, rather monotonous speech, head a little
hung down, but hardly a stoop as he keeps on at his stiff quick
short steps among crisp dry scurrying leaves up to Ludcombe
Corner where I turned off.

He was thinking about soldiers in France – terrible affair – in
cold weather, supposing they would be 'marching after the
enemy' and surely not lying in trenches this winter weather.

30 Beauty

See Thomas's letter to James Guthrie, dated 21 Mar. 1915 [1916?]:

> The book [*Six Poems*] arrived yesterday. . . . There are two words
> omitted that should be inserted by hand. In the last line [*sic*] of
> 'Beauty' 'my' should be inserted before 'rest' 'There I find my
> rest'. In 'Aspens' [Poem 83], last verse, the line should be 'We
> cannot other than an aspen be'. insert 'an'. That can be managed,
> can't it?

31 'A fortnight before Christmas Gypsies were everywhere'

Thomas's fascination with gipsy life can be seen in the 'Conclusion'
to his *George Borrow: The Man and His Books* (1912). See especially
pp. 319–20:

> Wistful or fancifully envious admiration for the fortunate
> simple yeomen, or careless poor men, or noble savages, or
> untradesmanlike fishermen, or unromanized *Germani*, or
> animals who do not fret about their souls, admiration for those
> in any class who are not for the fashion of these days, is a deep-
> seated and ancient sentiment, akin to the sentiment for
> childhood and the golden age. Borrow met a hundred men fit to
> awaken and satisfy this admiration in an age when thousands
> can over-eat and over-dress in comfort all the days of their life.
> Sometimes he shows that he himself admires in this way, but
> more often he mingles with them as one almost on an equality
> with them, though his melancholy or his book knowledge is at
> times something of a foil. He introduces us to fighting men,
> jockeys, thieves, and rat-catchers, without our running any risk
> of contamination. Above all, he introduces us to the Gypsies,
> people who are either young and beautiful or strong, or else
> witchlike in a fierce old age. . . .
>   Borrow's Gypsies are wild and uncoddled and without
> sordidness, and will not soon be superseded. They are painted
> with a lively if ideal colouring, and they live only in his books.
> They will not be seen again until the day of Jefferies' wild
> England, 'after London,' shall come, and tents are pitched amidst

the ruins of palaces that had displaced earlier tents. Borrow's England is the old England of Fielding, painted with more intensity because even as Borrow was travelling the change was far advanced, and when he was writing had been fulfilled. And now most people have to keep off the grass, except in remotest parts or in the neighbourhood of large towns where landowners are, to some extent, kept in their place. The rivers, the very roads, are not ours, as they were Borrow's. We go out to look for them still, and of those who adventure with caravan, tent, or knapsack, the majority must be consciously under Borrow's influence.

See *Berg FNB* 67 for the incidents behind this poem:

East Grinstead. 11th December 1913. *East Grinstead Fair*

Drawn up at fork to Turner's Hill etc. are a lot of little traps and small rough ponies. A balloon seller.

Gypsies coming in with sham flowers and 'My lucky gentleman' 'You've got a lucky face'. But she had a much luckier face in reality. Lots of caravans drawn up between Selsfield and Grinstead – begging money or half pipe of tobacco. One caravan on Selsfield Common, several down by Tickeridge, others by Hill Farm, more at fork to Saint Hill. All begging. One boy and girl I ran away from. One boy playing rapid rascally Bacchanal tune on mouth organ while he drums on a tambourine and stamps feet and workmen grin. A few carthorses at auction. Cheapjack, little blackhaired pale man of 30 who asks a rough and simple labourer if he's married and says 'You have my sympathy' and shakes hands and says 'Do you love your wife?' Lots of laughing, knives, clocks, jewellry [*sic*] etc.

17 December. Two more gypsies with that rascally Bacchic music at Selsfield House door, one has mouth organ, the other drums on tambourine, lacking cymbals – they play 'Over the hills and far away' and 'If I were Mr. Balfour'.

4.15 p.m. How different two days ago when I looked from a highish road (? or from railway near Warnham) over a houseless lowish but hollow wooded country, nothing but gradations of inhuman dark (beginning to get misty at nightfall), as of an underworld and my soul fled over it experiencing the afterdeath – friendless, vacant hopeless.

32 Ambition

18–23   The mood reflected in these lines resembles the following passage from *IPS*, pp. 210–11:

> Motion was extraordinarily easy that afternoon, and I had no doubts that I did well to bicycle instead of walking. It was as easy as riding in a cart, and more satisfying to a restless man. At the same time I was a great deal nearer to being a disembodied spirit than I can often be. I was not at all tired, so far as I knew. No people or thoughts embarrassed me. I fed through the senses directly, but very temperately, through the eyes chiefly, and was happier than is explicable or seems reasonable. This pleasure of my disembodied spirit (so to call it) was an inhuman and diffused one, such as may be attained by whatever dregs of this our life survive after death. In fact, had I to describe the adventure of this remnant of a man I should express it somewhat thus, with no need of help from Dante, Mr. A. C. Benson, or any other visitors to the afterworld. In a different mood I might have been encouraged to believe the experience a foretaste of a sort of imprisonment in the viewless winds, or of a spiritual share in the task of keeping the cloudy winds 'fresh for the opening of the morning's eye.' Supposing I were persuaded to provide this afterworld with some of the usual furniture, I could borrow several visible things from that ride through Semington, Melksham, and Staverton.

(Cf. notes to 'The Other', Poem 6.)

34 Parting

13   The poet's son, Merfyn, left Steep with his mother for Liverpool on 11 Feb. and embarked for America two days later with Robert Frost and his family. (Thomas was unable to walk because of an ankle

injury.) The poem recalls the complicated relationship between father and son which is best expressed in Thomas's letters to Bottomley (*GB*, especially Letters 146, 162, and 163).

24   'like this' refers to the poem. 'stir or stain' may refer to the actual manuscript (as well as the act of memory); the page in *BM* is blotted in a few places.

36 May 23

The day after writing this poem Thomas left Steep for the first time since an ankle injury had confined him there since early January. He spent a few days checking source material for his anthology *This England* and returned to Steep on 29 Feb. 1915.

30–5   For Jack's reluctance to sell his ware, compare the Watercress Man in *The Heart of England* (1906), Ch. I ('Leaving Town'), which suggests that Jack Noman was a composite character based on memories that began with Thomas's youthful encounter with some such wanderer when he was a boy of nine.

38 Home [1]

14, 16   The words 'there' and 'here', I suggest, refer directly to Thomas's parents' home at Balham – he had spent two days with them the previous week and discovered that his mother needed an operation for cataract – and his own home at Steep.

17–20   An oblique reference to Thomas's many disagreements with his father. (See also note on Poem 99.)

39 The Owl

See *An Introduction* by Edward Garnett to *Selected Poems* (The Gregynog Press, 1927), p. vi: 'Three months before his death, Thomas was still insistent that "Edward Eastaway's" real name should not be disclosed to editors. I took "Home" and "The Owl" (re-entitled "Those Others") to *The Nation* in January 1917.'

See *Berg FNB 77*: '*20 October 1914*. (After returning from Swansea and Ryton). Day ends silent and misty: owl hoots, blackbirds chink, a robin sings, far off train roars hollowly in the Vale [of Steep].'

40 The Child on the Cliff

The child was probably Edward's brother Julian. See letter to Eleanor Farjeon (*TLFY*, pp. 127–8), dated 25 Mar. 1915: 'I like the Child on the Cliff. It is a memory between one of my young brothers and myself which he reminded me of lately. [A note in Julian's diary on 24 Feb. stated that 'Edwy was at Balham last week'.] He was most of the child and I have been truthful. I think I can expect some allowances for the "strangeness" of the day.' The poet's childhood summer holidays were spent with relations in West Wales and I suggest that the cliffs in the poem refer either to Gower or Laugharne, both places that Thomas visited frequently throughout his life.

41 The Bridge

The reflective mood of this poem probably refers to the first letter received from Frost and Merfyn after they landed in New York. See letter to Eleanor Farjeon (*TLFY*, p. 124) dated 12 Mar. 1915: 'But I am sick of reading at the Museum and then Maeterlinck's poems. I was glad to get back here and go up to the study again and write and have fine days for sowing the garden. I am not sure that I want to leave this part after all [to join Frost in the U.S.A.], especially as it would cost so much.' The 'strange bridge' (l. 2) may well refer to his first half-unconscious decision to enlist and to exorcise the indecision that had marked his life for nearly three years.

44 The New House

This is the house at Wick Green which was built for Thomas by Geoffrey Lupton in 1909. See 'Wind and Mist' (Poem 54) and *GB* (especially Letters 104, 105, 107, 126).

45 The Barn and the Down

See *Berg FNB* 80, undated, before 25 Mar. 1915: 'At end of Charles Street is a big slate-barn. You see the length of it and its ridge is in evening like Down against sky and sometimes I mistake a Down (which is also visible from thereabouts) for the barn – sometimes barn is exalted, sometimes Down humbled.'

46 Sowing

The *BM* manuscript has a fifth stanza:

A kiss for all the seeds'
Dry multitude,
A tear at ending this
March interlude.

This final rejected stanza, with its 'calendar-verse' tone, echoes Thomas's sense of happiness before he began work on another 'filthy job – a book on the Duke of Marlborough to be done in haste'. See *TLFY*, pp. 127–8 and especially a letter to Eleanor Farjeon of 25 Mar. 1915: 'The weather has been tempting and tiring. We have done a lot of gardening, and never had the ground in better order so early.'

47 March the 3rd

3 Mar. was the poet's birthday.

48 Two Pewits

See Thomas's letter to Edward Garnett (in *Selected Poems* (The Gregynog Press, 1927), p. xi, written in March–April 1915):

But I can't tell you how pleased I am that you like the long piece [Lob] in the main and 'Pewits' too. I am going to try and be just about the lines you have marked in 'Pewits', though I am not sure whether you question the form of them or the 'divagations' of the idea, but probably the latter. If only I could hit upon some continuous form as you suggest. I doubt if it will come by direct consideration. But I think perhaps intermingled prose and verse would add a difficulty. Even as it is I fancy the better passages in my prose lose by not really being happy in their place.

(Garnett probably marked ll. 12–15.)

50 The Path

The path was probably the short cut taken by Thomas each morning as he walked from his home in Steep village to his study up on Wick Green adjacent to the new house Lupton had built for him. See his letter to Eleanor Farjeon (*TLFY*, p. 127), dated 25 Mar. 1915, about some more poems he had written: 'It has perhaps become a really bad habit as I walk up the hill and I can sometimes hardly wait to light my fire.'

51 'This moonlight makes'

See *Berg FNB* 80: '*25 March 1915*: Beautiful moonlight and in hedge glistens bottle put there long ago for wasps – old time – old crockery opposite cottages – far ponds etc.'

52 [A Tale] [cancelled version]

See *Berg FNB* 80: '*25 March 1915* [cont.]. Outside the [old] ruined cottage is periwinkle and when that is not flowering there is some blue and white peering among the leaves.'

54 Wind and Mist

1   The 'view' is the one seen across the South Downs from near the poet's study where the poem was written, close to the new house at Wick Green where he lived from 1909 to 1913. The encounter imagined in the poem would have taken place near Berryfield Cottage (where Thomas had lived before the building of this new house).

44–7   For the garden see *GB*, especially Letters 104, 107, 108; and 115 (dated 23 Feb. 1911): 'The garden improves but the clay breaks first the back and then the heart.'

46–7   See *Berg FNB* 80, undated, before 25 Mar. 1915:

> First I broke my back and then my heart
> But the back will not mend.

54   For the significance of the phrase 'cloud castle' in Thomas's earlier private symbolism see his short sketch 'Cloud Castle', written in

1912 and printed posthumously in *Cloud Castle and Other Papers* (1922).

56 Lob

Thomas's life-long interest in folk-tales, and place-names, and country lore of all kinds is copiously illustrated in his *Richard Jefferies* (1909), *Celtic Stories* (1911), *The Country* (1913), *The Icknield Way* (1913), *Four-and-Twenty Blackbirds* (1915), and *This England* (1915). His most general statement of this interest is best shown in the following quotation from his introduction to Isaac Taylor, *Words and Places* (No. 517 of *Everyman's Library*), 1911:

> Remembering the 'too ingenious antiquary' and the fearless folk etymology which created the 'liver' for Liverpool, Mr. [J. H.] Round disputes the philologist's claim to explain place names by his laws, because . . . 'they ignore the human element.' But they ignore only what is incalculable, and when they confess defeat they are bowing partly to darkest antiquity and partly to this very human element . . . I found a sturdy fellow sitting on Offa's Dyke in Monmouthshire who told me that the mound was 'Dogger's Bank.' We have need of men like that to explain 'Eggpie' Lane near the village of Sevenoaks Weald, or Tumbling Bay in a neighbouring parish far inland. . . . Science goes deep, but the pure sense goes deeper.' A useful guide to the many folk-tales in *Lob* is *English Fairy Tales*, ed. J. Jacobs (1890–94).

Lob: a name variously used for a country bumpkin, a kind of a clown, or mischievous Puck-like fairy (especially in this last in the form *Lob-lie-by-the-fire*). See, too, the poem 'Lob Lie by the Fire' in De la Mare's *A Child's Day* (1912).

26   *Weathercock*: see note to 1. 123 (*Gotham*).

65–6 *Gerard.* Thomas quotes John Gerard's *The Herball* (1597) on 'Traveller's Joy' in *TE*, p. 97.

73–4 See *Berg FNB* 80, undated, between 25 Mar. and 18 Apr. 1915:

> 'T was she first called the Hog's back the Hog's Back
> And gave the name to Mother Dunch's Buttocks.

74   *Mother Dunch's Buttocks*, according to Camden's *Brittania* a vulgar
     name for Sinodun Hill, Berkshire, gave offence to one editor to
     whom he offered 'Lob' soon after it was written.

96   *tall Tom*: see *Love's Labour's Lost*, v. ii. 909–27, quoted in *TE*,
     p. 51.

99   *Herne the Hunter*: a ghostly medieval hunter, originally a keeper in
     Windsor Forest, who is described by Mistress Page in *The Merry
     Wives of Windsor*, IV. iv. 28–40. Quoted under the title *Herne the
     Hunter* in *TE*, p. 72.

104–12, For the various tales of 'Jack', including 'The Princess of
122–9   Canterbury', see Jacobs, *English Fairy Tales*.

123 *Gotham's sages*. From medieval times, at least, the people of
     Gotham in Nottinghamshire acquired a reputation for foolish
     behaviour. Many tales, some involving weathercocks or hedging in
     a cuckoo or finding the moon in a pond, had accumulated around
     the Wise Men of Gotham. The first known collection, 'Merry Tales
     of Gotham by A.B.' is extant in a 1630 edition.

113–22 This tale, from Charlotte S. Burne, *Shropshire Folk-Lore*, is quoted
     in *TE*, pp. 68–9.

137 *Robin Hood*. Thomas quotes one of the many Robin Hood ballads
     in *TE*, pp. 22–4. Apart from the names of flowers, folk-tales of
     'Robin' can be found in Jacobs (above).

61 Home [2]

This poem seems to confirm the subtle relationship between
Thomas's sudden development as a poet and his way of life at
Steep. It was composed after his first longish working period spent
away from home since he had begun to write verse in late
November and early December 1914. (From 5 Apr. 1915 he had
spent a few days with his parents at Balham in order to work at the
British Museum on his newly commissioned life of the Duke of
Marlborough.)

See *Berg FNB* 80, 12 Apr. 1915: 'Evening of misty stillness after drizzly day – last thrushes on oaks – then man goes by a dark white cottage front to thatched wood lodge and presently began sawing and birds were all still.'

62 Health

See *Berg FNB* 80, undated, after 18 Apr. and before 23 May 1915: 'The best and worst of sickness is to think how glorious health is or might be. – glorious ambitious feeling on April 18 when Butser [Hill] was but a great jump away over hollow land early in morning and sky all blue but one white cloud.'

63 The Huxter

See *Berg FNB* 77, 24 Aug. 1914: 'Ledbury – met a huckster.' (During a holiday spent with the family of Robert Frost.)

65 Song [1]

The poet's comment on the poem in his letter to Eleanor Farjeon (28 Apr. 1915) is half-ironic: 'But I promise you I am under a thick cloud of Marlborough mostly, tho I wrote a sort of a song in it; . . . [the song follows]. Does it make you larf?'

The same day Thomas replied to the first long letter he had received from Robert Frost after his return to the U.S.A. (Frost's letter arrived in early April 1915, just before W. H. Davies spent a few days at Steep.) He wrote: 'You're a literary man like me. Do you know I go on with verses to the detriment of Marlborough: take the 2 best hours out of my morning with I am afraid rather poetical things sometimes. Did you think it might become a habit?'

67 Melancholy

2   *fever*: see letter to Eleanor Farjeon dated 28 Apr. 1915 (*TLFY*, p. 131): 'I was rather ill for 4 days with a chill or I would have written – a chill and a boil together.' Thomas spent the next four days from Monday (26 Apr.) to Thursday (29 Apr.) working at the British Museum on his *Marlborough*, and staying again with his parents at Balham.

9–10   See *Berg FNB* 80, undated but after 18 Apr. 1915:

> ~~Dripping water sweet as dulcimer~~
> In the wind
> I thought I heard the cuckoo all day long
> 40 years had crimsoned his cheeks with pain and pleasure

68 Tonight

1   There is no evidence to suggest reasons for the change of name
     from 'Margaret' (in the early manuscripts) to 'Harry'.

69 April

12   See Thomas's letter to Frost dated 3 May 1915:

> I find I can't write. Re-reading Rupert Brooke and putting a few
> things together about him [Thomas's article 'Rupert Brooke' in
> *The English Review*, 20, pp. 325–8, June 1915] have rather messed
> me up and there's Marlborough behind and Marlborough before
> . . . Are the children at school now? Or are you still 'neglecting'
> them? God bless them all. By the way, there was a beautiful
> return of sun yesterday after a misty moisty morning, and
> everything smelt wet and warm and cuckoos called and I found
> myself with nothing to say but 'God bless it'. I laughed a little as I
> came over the field, thinking about the 'it' in 'God bless it'. . . .
>
> P.S. Here is [V. Locke] Ellis very elderly and masterly about my
> verses, not ~~troubling to say~~ finding one to say he likes, but
> seeing the 'elements of poetry'. The rhythm is too rough and not
> obvious enough. He wants to talk them over. I don't. Well, I feel
> sure I'm old enough not to know better, though I don't profess
> to know how good or bad it may be.

14   *Emily*: possibly a half-memory of Emily Bottomley. See Letter 148
     to Gordon Bottomley, dated 6 May 1915: 'I have been wondering
     many times about you all, your Mother, Aunt Sarah, Mrs. Burton,
     and You and Emily with those four points to her compass. I hope
     she isn't tired out.'

69–71 April, The Glory, *and* July

See *Berg FNB* 80, undated, between 18 Apr. and 23 May 1915:

As we met – the nightingale sang
As we loved _____
As we parted _____ the same.

Coming to ask forgiveness for something I had not
    noticed
Smiling with a half-certainty to be forgiven.
'God bless it' was all I could say and laughed to find
no other words.
Now it is when Kate comes to me —
            God bless her
Nightingale's tsoo tsoo tsooed
        Turned in tears back

Dog that barked so hoarse and old by Luff's house (near old
farmyard and trees) and also by river and rother under echoing
banks
The happy seeming short lived things we do not understand
Nightingale[,] aspern joy of life and grief of dark
I exult and then I despair in beauty that bears no
correspondence in any strength or wisdom known to me
~~down in the val~~
Doves invite to something sweeter than truer
How swift time passes when nothing is

            _____

In Time _____ still hour after hour
Filled to content with what ring doves say
        ~~I thought the above worth thinking of saying~~.

72 The Chalk Pit

See *Berg FNB* 80, dated between 23 May and 2 June 1915:

A girl of 20 with a boy's brown face
Thick eyebrows glinting eyes:

> You have said enough

Oh yes.

2 June 1915

The smell like honeycomb of mugwort dull
and brown hair, brown as a thrush or as a nut
the frizzled water over sun all *stones*

The way light is there before you in a dark cupboard as soon as
you open it.

Berg FNB 80, undated, between 25 Mar. and 23 May 1915: 'Did
something once happen there at the bend of the road Round the
chalk pit old.'
    See also Thomas's essay 'Chalk Pits', printed in *The Last Sheaf*,
pp. 27–37, which contains many prose adumbrations of this poem.
(The renewal of correspondence with Frost may well have
occasioned Thomas's return to the use of older, prose material as
the basis of new verse.)

18 See *The Last Sheaf*, p. 31: 'They have names of their own; often they
    are dells, such as Stubridge Dell, or Slade Dell . . . These islands are
    attractive largely, I think, because they suggest fragments of
    primaeval forest that have been left untouched by the plough on
    account of their roughness.'

43 An echo of many wry self-portraits that are in Thomas's prose
    writings.

44 *orts*: then a colloquial form of 'noughts'.

47–52 These lines are based on memories of his open-air courtship of
    Helen Noble in and around London, Wiltshire, and Oxford.

56–8 See 'The Friend of the Blackbird' in *The Last Sheaf*, p. 211: 'He did
    not forget the trees – "those tethered dreamers, standing on one leg
    like Indian mystics". With them also he felt the same community, as
    though more rarely and in a way not to be spoken except by
    putting out his hand to touch their bark and leaves.'

73 Fifty Faggots

This poem, untitled, is part of a letter sent to Robert Frost from London, dated 15 May 1915: 'This is the end of I hope my last week's reading for "Marlborough" . . . One of my reliefs in this week's work was to write these lines founded on carrying up 50 bunts (short faggots of thin and thick brushwood mixed) and putting them against our hedge.' After the poem, Thomas asks, 'Are they [the lines] *north* of Boston only?' *North of Boston* was the second volume of Frost's poetry published in England and favourably reviewed by Thomas (see *GB*, p. 233). The phrase 'north of Boston' occurs frequently in his letters to Frost: it is short-hand for poems based on rural incidents presented in simulated colloquial language.

15   Thomas included Webster's 'Dirge' ('Call for the robin-redbreast and the wren') in *TE*, p. 74.

74 Sedge-Warblers [Cancelled version]

In a letter to Robert Frost, dated 23 May 1915, Thomas wrote: 'It seemed I had dried up, owing to Marlborough, but I have done a thing today. I shall send [it] if I find time to copy it. It came of a Sunday with no work but a cycle ride with Bronwen [his elder daughter]. It is devilish like habit, but I am all rules and evasions.' Earlier in the letter Thomas wrote: 'But it has been pleasant walking up and down, too [i.e. from Steep village to his study up on Wick Green]. Such a lovely May it is, hot and with a bustling wind.' He added a postscript the next day: 'There are a good many moments when I feel there is hardly anybody that matters except God in Gloucestershire or any other county. I have been very impatient with people lately and yet sorry they have drifted off.'

See *Berg FNB* 80:

> *23 May 1915*: beyond Warnford . . .

> Water crowfoot and marigolds iris leaf and clear swift combing water but no nymph only the sedge warblers in millions more continuous than earth and clearer than sweetest voice singing

sweetest *words* I know, tho' often grating or shrill and always
jerky and spasmodic with nice sweet gentle iterations and 3 or 4
together or in fours.

Long ago it would have borne a nymph
　　– cloudless clear sail
Now it reflects the chestnut petals from the distant park
She could
Love all day long and never hate or tire
the best of May
Buttercups brighter than brass
　　– soft.

77 Words

During June 1915, after finishing *Marlborough*, Thomas had spent
some time re-reading Frost's *North of Boston* while he was writing
his article on Rupert Brooke. He then set off on a cycling tour and
spent three days with W. J. Haines 'cycling about and talking of you
[Frost]'. Before leaving Steep, Thomas had written a long letter to
Frost about his own verse. 'Words' and 'The Word' (Poem 78)
should be seen in the context of this period of stock-taking which
ended with his enlistment a fortnight later.

78 The Word

See Berg, *FNB* 80, undated, after 2 June 1915:

　　　Things forgotten–
　I have forgotten the names of the stars, the big above the little
　and to one side – and dates of wars etc.
　　　But I remember
　Those little copses of blackbird and nettles. bramble where
　a man might hide For ever dead or alive.

See Berg *FNB* 61: '28 January 1913. Story of man remembering little
sweet woodbird he only heard once as a child.'

79 Under the Wood

See *Berg FNB* 80, undated, after 2 June 1915: 'Lazy keeper in col
under woods [above ~~wood hanger~~] – smokes and has one green
shrivelled stoat, he killed ages ago when trees were young – never
shoots now.' This sentence is in the middle of prose notes used for
Poem 80.

80 Haymaking

Thomas devotes four pages of notes to this poem in *Berg FNB* 80,
undated, but after 2 June 1915:

> [p. 11]
> Park mead of thin grass mown by white priest or grove of low
> squat oaks and long grass and men under – a solitary yew – also
> on the slopes – wych hazel and flowering elder – a rick in
> midfield – tosser idle – men lean on rakes – old fashioned as
> Crome or Constable.
>
>   How old it is. I seem to see it now as some one long years
> hence will see it in a picture.
>
>   Hot air has a kernel of cold
>
> [~~The hot air has a kernel sweet of cold~~]
>
> [p. 12]
> The hunchbacked woman that roots daisies up in Salisbury
>   Close.
> honeysuckle and white musk rose in lanes of Sherfield English
> by the mill.
> Water racing white and tossing at foot of mill fall in Compton
> Chamberlain, happier in sun than any crowd of children
> pouring out of school.
>
>   clearer, no
> Old tracks down the Downs no ⌃ straighter, than wind strikes on
> the sea.
> Lazy keeper . . . never shoots now. [See Note to Poem 79.]

[p. 13]
hawthorn and ivy intertwined – and inseparable in Forest of
    Dean,
with low bracken and tall foxglove between.
the thunder sky's dark blue maw
Clean Cotswolds with dark winds and pink stone towns and
    villages steep.
The fluster of the blood adown her throat
The little house in the great trees

After thunder and night rain, glorious hot bright fresh morning
with clouds like gods bathing in the sea before they made the
world.

(Words light as gossamer, Honey sweet, precious as gold and
strong as steel.
As the hills are old.) [See Poem 76, 'Words'.]

In thunderstorm when we hurry home the ducks set out for a
    walk
in a line along the road to reach the hollow that will be pools.
The little fine antennae of the hollies
The fallen fir cones stand up in the heat.

[p. 14]
[This page is cancelled with a diagonal line]:

The fiery air had a kernel sweet of cold
After the thunder far away had ~~rolled~~ stopped
And in the quietness (guileless) the clouds overhead
Like the first gods before they made the world
And joyous bathed in Homer's sea
A lighter wind in the silent grass said Yes.

With the autumn of the hollies that falls in June
The perfect smooth white empty road was strewn
And fir cones standing up stiff on their head
The – fir stood close under great elms

———

The millpond water racing white and tossing
Crystal rejoiced [*above* ~~with happiness~~] more in the sun than
any crowd
Of children running out of school aloud

———

And in the little copses where a sleeper
Alive or dead might
Might lie for ever lost the nettle creeper
And garden warblers sang unceasingly
What never then ~~in their~~ shrieked in the fierce glee
The swifts.

[p. 151]
Older than Clare and work was the Moreland [*sic*] and Crome.

There follow twelve lines of a first sketch of Poem 81, 'A Dream',
and then:

          bathing in stormless sea
In beauty and in divine ~~happiness~~ Beauty.

81 A Dream

See Thomas's letter to Frost from 13 Rusham Rd., Balham, dated
22 July 1915. After giving some reasons for his enlistment on 14 July,
Thomas wrote: 'A month or two [ago] I dreamt we were walking
near Ledington but we lost one another in a strange place and I
woke saying to myself "Somehow someday I shall be here again"
which I made the last lines of some verses.'

Berg FNB 80, undated, after 2 June 1915, has two draft versions of
this poem; the second version is very close to the printed text
except for alternative versions of l. 14:

Saying 'Someday, somehow, I shall be here again
Saying 'I shall be here, someday, somehow, again.

Thomas recorded many dreams in his various notebooks, all
carefully worked over as if for publication, often with clear
indications of their source in waking experience. When this poem
was written Thomas was gradually reaching a decision not to

follow Frost and settle in New Hampshire. On his own admission,
the dream firmly recalls his long visit to Frost in August 1914. After
that visit Thomas went to South Wales. *Berg MS 64B9046* contains
Penderyn, a holograph essay, dated 6 Sept. 1914 by Thomas, which
includes a careful description of the underground river course and
the waterfalls at Ystradfellte seen during a long walk from Neath to
Penderyn and the Brecknock Beacons. The following sentence from
the essay suggests ll. 2–7: 'There was now no valley, and not a yard
of level ground between these hills. The river in one place ran black
underground, and in another danced down a quarter mile of
cascades, white as milk.'

Some time between the late autumn of 1914 and his enlistment,
Thomas collected and labelled all his field notebooks, perhaps
while in search of material that resembled the incidents and
encounters in Frost's poems *North of Boston*. The essay *Penderyn* is
in the usual penultimate stage prior to publication; opposite the
title and original date, Thomas has added 'not copied yet, March
1915'.

In *Berg FNB* 80, on the page after one dated 23 May 1915,
Thomas gives a numbered list of topics:

(1) She came then, but she never came again
(2) The first peacock
(3) See back [i.e. the last pages of the notebook with a series of
    brief entries dated from 1 Jan. 1915 to 2 May 1915. The final
    entry, while he was a soldier training in London, is dated
    7 Sept. 1915.]
(4) The stone the carthorse kicks against so oft. [See Poem 82]
(5) Sometimes someday I shall be here again (waking from
dream of deep pool. Full of [?inn]
[?white] water revolving and plunging – dream of Frost too and
a walk to this.) I woke with this line of farewell to the place.
(6) [The first entry referred to in Note to Poem 82.]

82 The Brook

The child in the poem is the poet's younger daughter, Myfanwy.
The day after writing it, Sunday, 11 June 1915, Thomas wrote to

Frost about his decision to visit London on Wednesday for a
medical examination prior to enlisting in The Artists' Rifles.

See *Berg FNB* 80 for three relevant entries:

(1) Undated, between 23 May and 2 June 1915:

> Not since ~~the horse~~
> The horseman and the horse in silver shoes
> That lie now in the Bramdean tumulus
> Ceased riding on the Downs
> That sleep within [*above* lie within] the barrow ~~by the Dean~~
> on the heath

> past rode
> Ceased riding on the Downs.

(2) Page 9, dated 2 June 1915:

> The smell like honeycomb of
> mugwort dull

(3) Page 10, undated, after 2 June 1915:

> Nobody's been here before says Baba [Myfanwy] paddling
> in sandy brook – so she thinks.

> Mellow the blackbird, tart the thrush
> The bat hangs head down in the barn

> And this heavy elder scent like a rose
> And the rose scent like a memory
> Where the dark water bursts straight out into the world

> The rodent flycatcher grey on the fence.

83 Aspens

See Thomas's letter to Eleanor Farjeon (*TLFY*, pp. 152–3), dated 21
July 1915: 'About "Aspens" you missed just the turn that I thought
essential. *I* was the aspen. "We" meant the trees and I with my
dejected shyness. Does that clear it up, or do you think in rereading
it that I have not emphasised it enough?'

22   See note to Poem 30, p. 388.

84 The Mill-Water

See *Berg FNB* 80, undated, after 2 June 1915: 'Mill full sound –
heard by those alone who are thinking and stop suddenly – and by
those who watch long – so that they seem to feel with all who ever
listened to it when mill was there.'

85 For these [Prayer]

Thomas began this poem on the day before he was passed
medically fit for enlistment, and finished it the next day. It is
referred to as 'the prayer' in his letter to Eleanor Farjeon, dated
15 July 1915 – whence the new editorial title.

   See *Berg FNB* 80, undated, after 2 June 1915, for a cancelled early
approach to this poem:

> I don't wish for an acre of land
> But for content and something to be contented with or else
> If I could live long enough to get content with what I have
>   the hills
> An acre of land between ~~Cutts~~ and the sea and near them both
> or some hilltop
> A station for the herald Mercury
> Garden whose sunflowers every one
> Was fit to be the sign of the rising sun.
>
> I do not wish for them, but not too late
> And not too little, for content but
> Something to be contented with perhaps.

86 Digging [2]

This was the first poem after his enlistment and was written at his
parents' home in Balham while he was off-duty with a strained
tendon. See the letter to Eleanor Farjeon (dated 21 July 1915 in
TLFY, pp. 153–4) which contains the first draft of the poem: '. . . I
have been perspiring these six hours over ten lines which perhaps
are not right yet. But if you would type them for me I could see
them better.'

4   These references follow directly from his recently completed *Life of the Duke of Marlborough*.

See *Berg FNB* 80, undated, but before 25 Mar. 1915, immediately after brief entries about Poems 21 and 27 and before entry on Poem 45:

> Finding an old pipe and one of mine in garden. Someone will assuredly find mine when I am not.
> He created the elephant.

89 October

This was the first poem written since Thomas's first week as a soldier. His training was mainly in London (where he was billeted on his parents), with musketry practice at High Beech, Essex, where he later moved his family (see *TLFY*, pp. 164–72). After Eleanor Farjeon had typed some copies of 'October' he replied in an undated letter (*TLFY*, p. 169):

> I expect you are right about the rhymes, most of them. The original version was in blank verse, but quite different. Hasn't Bronwen taught you tormentil, the tiny yellow flower in short hill grass, a flat buttercup or avens with rather separate petals. Tormentilla it is. The accent is on the second syllable which doesn't (as I see it) affect the merit of the line whatever it may be; I mean doesn't tell against it. I suppose the influence of High Beech and the Artists ought to be clearer. I am going to slightly better conditions, but don't expect to write till I am disabled again. The knee is now well.

See first entry in *Berg FNB* 80, dated 1 Jan. 1915, after a series of nature notes: 'A mood long blackened and obscured by the name of melancholy.'

90 There's nothing like the sun

See *Berg FNB* 80, 1 Nov. 1915: 'Sweet as last damsons on spangled tree when November starling imitates the swallow in sunny interval between rain and all is still and dripping.' And 16 Nov. 1915: 'There's nothing like the sun in January –.'

91 The Thrush

The poem was probably written after reading Gordon Bottomley's poem 'Eager Spring' in *TE* (which appeared in late 1915). See *GB*, pp. 255–7, especially Letter 160: 'In case you can attend to an anthology I am sending mine with your thrush in it. It comes with love to you and Emily.'

See three scattered references to thrush song among many in the notebooks:

(1) *Berg FNB* 64: '8 July 1913. Rusham Road [Balham]: 6–7.15 a.m. one thrush hammering away at one triple cry, message or whatever anyone else likes.'

(2) *Berg FNB* 80: on the right-hand side: '1 February 1915: How I noticed the one thrush near the tip of poplar 250 yards beyond Nightingale Lane in opening of Rusham Road – he was singing, the only one.'

On the left-hand side:

I hear you alone and see
You alone at the end of the lane
Near the bare poplar's tip
Singing continuously.

(3) *Berg FNB* 80; after an entry dated 26 Nov. 1915:

Thrush
When winter's ahead
What can you see in November
That you see in April
When Winter's dead,

92 Liberty

The Keatsian echoes in the poem could be amplified by reading Thomas's comments on Keats's Odes (see his *Keats*, pp. 53–8) and character (especially *Keats*, pp. 74–5). 'Liberty' is referred to in his letter to Robert Frost dated 6 Dec. 1915: 'I don't want to read anything. On the other hand as soon as I get really free with

nothing else before me to do I incline to write. I have written two
things here [Hare Hall Camp] or rather three, but one was just
rhyming on. – I am always just a little more outside things than
most of the others, without being made to feel so at all acutely.
They aren't surprised, whether I come in or stay out of a group.'
(The third poem, 'rhyming on', probably refers to 'The Thrush'.)

See *Berg FNB* 80, undated entry, after 7 Sept. and before 1 Nov.
1915:

> The moonlight lies on the grass as white as frost beyond
> the brink of the tall elm shadow.
>
> The worst of all is
>
> ~~When nothing matters~~
> The worst of all is doing nothing when There's nothing to do and
> you are only free For what you do not like and you like nothing.
> (See later) [Thomas]
>
> The moonless night died to a sunless day
> a light
> A little light that for hours you can see nothing but itself

See also an undated entry, after 1 Nov. and before 16 Nov. 1915:

> If I could have all such hours in a pile and dip in and take a
> handful and be rich or sweep all away for ever I should be rich
> to be so poor.

6   93 'This is no case of petty right or wrong'

See Thomas's letter to Eleanor Farjeon, dated 7 Jan. 1916 (*TLFY*,
p. 180): 'I am not sure that "love true" [l. 6] is a mistake, but
perhaps "love I will not" is, and I suggest

> Philosophers
> ~~Can see~~ I hate not Germans, nor grow hot
> With love of English, to please newspapers.

But perhaps it won't do. I am so busy now.'

Although *Bod* gives the place and date of composition as Steep,
26 Dec. 1915, the letter quoted above to Eleanor Farjeon continues:

'I did write the couplets [ll. 20–6] at Steep, but the others some weeks ago here [Hare Hall Camp]. Helen won't like them a bit and I kept them by me undecided. I hope you are right.' Actually Helen liked the poem when she saw it and urged him to send it to editors.

The mood behind the poem – almost a justification of his decision to enlist – is reflected in a later letter to Gordon Bottomley (*GB*, no. 161, dated 11 Feb. 1916). But it is even more explicit in the following extracts from a letter sent to Robert Frost, dated 2 Jan. 1916:

> Yesterday I got up to London (it being Saturday) for the day and saw Monro and Davies . . . In town I saw my father too, and he made me very sick. . . . Nothing much happened. We argued about the war and he showed that his real feeling when he is not trying to be nice and comfortable is one of contempt. I know what contempt is and partly what I suffered was from the reminder that I had probably made Helen feel exactly the same. I came more readily back to camp than ever before. I shall recover; but it makes a difference.

The conscious literary echoes and tone of the poem reflect his choice of extracts for Section VI ('Great Ones') of *TE*, pp. 133–54. Thomas had made similar points in his 1914 article, 'England', reprinted in *The Last Sheaf*, especially p. 111:

> I believe the man who thought it a 'quaint' idea to love England would feel very much as I do about these passages and about Walton altogether. I believe that England means something like this to most of us; that all ideas of England are developed, spun out, from such a centre into something large or infinite, solid or aëry, according to each man's nature and capacity; that England is a system of vast circumferences circling round the minute neighbouring points of home.

See *Berg FNB* 77: '26 August 1914. Wet day – with a third moon bright and almost orange low down clear of cloud and I thought of men eastward seeing it at the same moment. It seems foolish to have loved England up to now without knowing it could perhaps be ravaged and I could and perhaps *would* do nothing to prevent it.'

Two Christmas letters to his Californian aunt also illustrate Thomas's long wrestle with himself about the war:

(1) dated 23 Nov. 1914:

The war must probably last many months, more than a year, longer . . . I can't imagine that as men are at present, and as I imagine they will long remain, a nation is much use that is not capable of this violent folly, when the body and whatever of the mind can work with the body prevails and boasts itself. But I should like to avoid too much of this strain because it is not the strain of the men who are fighting or going to fight, but rather of morbid people in whom their balance and fusion of mind and body is impossible, and who admire frantically what is impossible to themselves.

(2) dated 21 Nov. 1915:

The men about me never talk of the war for more than a moment or two at a time, though most of them will be in it before long. I really hope my turn will come and that I shall see what it really is and come out of it with my head and most of my limbs. Then I may yet go to America and begin afresh and this time will not have been wasted.

There are three earlier relevant entries in *Berg FNB* 79 (dated by Thomas 'from October–December 1914'):

The war national but as yet dark and chaotic in brain – e.g. no good war poems early in Napoleonic Wars. Some writers can go on with old work but no reason why they should at once be able to admit war into their subject matter. Poetry excepting cheapest kind shows this dark chaotic character.

People expressing all sorts of views and trumping up old canting catchwords, but not yet the compact essential real truth to this occasion alone.

Statesman may say 'No price too high when honour and freedom are at stake' etc. But can't be translated into poetry.

England
Where a woman and child can cross safe.
The kernel is yourself and your country the nut – her life depends on the nut.

War. 31 October 1914 – morning after Turkey's declaration of
War. The young don't feel their responsibility and are afraid of
their skins (said Salter the Post-man).
(I know what I was like at their age.)

Finally, see *Berg FNB* 80, dated 26 Nov. 1915:

This is no case of little right or wrong
That statesman and philosopher
Can see. For it involves our love. I do not know and
hardly more I care
But do know that bone of her bone [I am?]

rain that smokes along the wind athwart the wood

Cry God save England else we too will sink

live with
And shall be [clothed and?] and fed like animals.

94 Rain

For an earlier, and deceptively similar, prose account of Thomas's
response to the rain, composed at Steep during August and
September 1911, see *The Icknield Way*, pp. 280–3:

I lay awake listening to the rain, and at first it was as pleasant
to my ear and my mind as it had long been desired; but before I
fell asleep it had become a majestic and finally a terrible thing,
instead of a sweet sound and symbol. It was accusing and trying
me and passing judgment. Long I lay still under the sentence,
listening to the rain, and then at last listening to words which
seemed to be spoken by a ghostly double beside me. He was
muttering: The all-night rain puts out summer like a torch. In
the heavy, black rain falling straight from invisible, dark sky to
invisible, dark earth the heat of summer is annihilated, the
splendour is dead, the summer is gone. The midnight rain buries
it away where it has buried all sound but its own. I am alone in
the dark still night, and my ear listens to the rain piping in the
gutters and roaring softly in the trees of the world. Even so will
the rain fall darkly upon the grass over the grave when my ears

can hear it no more. I have been glad of the sound of rain, and wildly sad of it in the past; but that is all over as if it had never been; my eye is dull and my heart beating evenly and quietly; I stir neither foot nor hand; I shall not be quieter when I lie under the wet grass and the rain falls, and I of less account than the grass. The summer is gone, and never can it return. There will never be any summer any more, and I am weary of everything. I stay because I am too weak to go. I crawl on because it is easier than to stop. I put my face to the window. There is nothing out there but the blackness and sound of rain. Neither when I shut my eyes can I see anything. I am alone. Once I heard through the rain a bird's questioning watery cry – once only and suddenly. It seemed content, and the solitary note brought up against me the order of nature, all its beauty, exuberance, and everlastingness like an accusation. I am not a part of nature. I am alone. There is nothing else in my world but my dead heart and brain within me and the rain without. Once there was summer, and a great heat and splendour over the earth terrified me and asked me what I could show that was worthy of such an earth. It smote and humiliated me, yet I had eyes to behold it, and I prostrated myself, and by adoration made myself worthy of the splendour. Was I not once blind to the splendour because there was something within me equal to itself? What was it? Love . . . a name! . . . a word! . . . less than the watery question of the bird out in the rain. The rain has drowned the splendour. Everything is drowned and dead, all that was once lovely and alive in the world, all that had once been alive and was memorable though dead is now dung for a future that is infinitely less than the falling dark rain. For a moment the mind's eye and ear pretend to see and hear what the eye and ear themselves once knew with delight. The rain denies. There is nothing to be seen or heard, and there never was. Memory, the last chord of the lute, is broken. The rain has been and will be for ever over the earth. There never was anything but the dark rain. Beauty and strength are as nothing to it. Eyes could not flash in it.

I have been lying dreaming until now, and now I have awakened, and there is still nothing but the rain. I am alone. The unborn is not more weak or more ignorant, and like the unborn

I wait and wait, knowing neither what has been nor what is to come, because of the rain, which is, has been, and must be. The house is still and silent, and those small noises that make me start are only the imagination of the spirit or they are the rain. There is only the rain for it to feed on and to crawl in. The rain swallows it up as the sea does its own foam. I will lie still and stretch out my body and close my eyes. My breath is all that has been spared by the rain, and that comes softly and at long intervals, as if it were trying to hide itself from the rain. I feel that I am so little I have crept away into a corner and been forgotten by the rain. All else has perished except me and the rain. There is no room for anything in the world but the rain. It alone is great and strong. It alone knows joy. It chants monotonous praise of the order of nature, which I have disobeyed or slipped out of. I have done evilly and weakly, and I have left undone. Fool! you never were alive. Lie still. Stretch out yourself like foam on a wave, and think no more of good or evil. There was no good and no evil. There was life and there was death, and you chose. Now there is neither life nor death, but only the rain. Sleep as all things, past, present, and future, lie still and sleep, except the rain, the heavy, black rain falling straight through the air that was once a sea of life. That was a dream only. The truth is that the rain falls for ever and I am melting into it. Black and monotonously sounding is the midnight and solitude of the rain. In a little while or in an age – for it is all one – I shall know the full truth of the words I used to love, I knew not why, in my days of nature, in the days before the rain: 'Blessed are the dead that the rain rains on.'

The stresses undergone by Thomas while composing *The Icknield Way* are fully documented in *GB*, pp. 208–21.

95 Song [2]

As a Lance-Corporal Instructor in map-reading at this time Thomas had fewer weekend leaves at home and more daily responsibilities, but ample leisure to write in Camp at weekends. See his letter to Robert Frost of 16 Jan. 1916: 'Half the men are away this weekend, and the rest are out with friends, and I have had a lot of time to myself – which always tempts me to write and sometimes I do.' And in another letter to Frost of 30 Jan. 1916:

> I got home a week ago for 24 hours. Now this weekend has to be spent in camp with no work to do except look after the hut while my superior is away. These are the worst days. The only real cure is to get quite alone and write. I can sometimes get the hut empty and write. Then I sometimes write in the train going home late. I must send you one or two recent verses. 'Lob' and 'Words' are to appear in a big hotchpotch called 'Form' in March. Otherwise I keep out of print.

See, too, the following extract from a letter to his wife, probably written on 24 Jan. 1916: 'Fancy your thinking I might have someone in view in those verses beginning "The clouds that are so light". Fancy your being pleased at the idea. Well, perhaps you wouldn't be, if there really were someone, in which case I would hardly write verses, I think.'

96 Roads

33   A reference to the Welsh Roman Road called 'Sarn Helen'. See his letter to Eleanor Farjeon, dated 24 Jan. 1916:

> 16 verses I see it makes. Helen is the lady in the Mabinogion, the Welsh lady who married Maxen the Emperor and gave her name to the great old mountain roads – Sarn Helen they are all marked on the maps. Do you remember the 'Dream of Maxen'? She is known to mythologists as one of the travelling goddesses of the dusk. But perhaps I don't convey much in my 16 verses.

Thomas expands the point, too, in the letter to his wife quoted above (Poem 95):

> I like some of it a good deal. That Helen is more real than the lady in the 4 verses [of Song [2]]. Oh, you needn't think of another lady. There would have to be 2 to make a love affair and I am only one. Nobody but you would ever be likely to respond as I wished. I don't like to think anybody but I could respond to

you. If you turned to anybody else I should come to an end immediately.

There are numerous references to roads, and paths, and long walks in the extant Field Note Books. See especially *Berg FNB* 53, containing notes of a series of cycle journeys with his son, Merfyn; the notebook is headed 'Marlboro', Pewsey, Amesbury, Salisbury, Tisbury' and dated 1 May 1911:

> *11 May, Avebury*. I never saw such a village for paths etc. round about, all over a space of about a mile – a good book might be written of these paths alone, a very good book. The crosses might have been made on purpose to exorcise the Druid's ghosts. Children of 8 or 9 (girls) gathering cowslips silently, bending, and unbending, in field just before I entered Avebury and they reminded me of the children in Chaucer's Prioress' Tale (p. 86. ll. 1688–9) for one sang a hymn like a song.

This was one of the notebooks used for *The Icknield Way* (1913).

98 February Afternoon

The mood of this poem is to some extent explained in two letters. One is to Frost, dated 21 Feb. 1916: 'I have had a bit of a holiday lately. I took a chill somewhat and had to take to bed in my father's house.' The other, dated 6 Feb. 1916, is to his wife: 'Well I can't write more. I am only fit to lie and listen to Mother reading Revelations.'

See *Berg FNB* 80: '*4 February 1915*. Sometimes dozens of starlings – separately in hedge and in oaks of meadow behind are talking at same time – the sweetest sound, democratic crowd imaginable. The sweetest democracy imaginable. Thrushes sing till after 5.15.'

99 'I may come near loving you'

The relationship between father and son was a difficult one but not as implacable as this poem suggests. (See *Edward Thomas* (*Writers of Wales*), p. 58.) During his first seven or eight months as a soldier training in and around London, Thomas spent a great deal of time at his parents' home. This poem was written there when the poet was sick with a chill (see note to Poem 98); a little earlier he had

decided to avoid his father for a time because of their opposed
attitudes to the war (see note to Poem 93) and, I suspect, 'Thomas's
refusal to take a commission. This temporary breach was probably
exacerbated by the father's attitude to his son's poetry. The poet's
nephew (Mr. E. E. Thomas), the elder son of Julian Thomas, has
kindly allowed me to quote the following extract from a notebook
diary kept by his father during 1914–18: 'Tuesday, 23 March 1915 . . .
I read out a score of Edwy's poetry to Mother and Maud [J. T.'s
wife] the other night. Father calls them pure piffle and says no one
will publish them. He may be right as to the last part of the
sentence.' Julian was very close to his eldest brother and at a Fabian
Summer School in late 1918 he read his brother's poems to a group
that included G. B. Shaw and C. E. M. Joad. Many of P. H.
Thomas's grandchildren and one grand-nephew have told me that
they regard this picture as a partial and incomplete one.

100 'These things that poets said'

Thomas's *The Tenth Muse* (a slightly modified form of Chapter 8
from his *Feminine Influence on the Poets*) was reissued in 1916 and a
re-reading of its introductory paragraph may have prompted this
poem. See *The Tenth Muse*, p. 8: 'Their [women's] chief direct
influence has been exerted by the stimulation of desire – desire to
possess not only them but other known and unknown things
deemed necessary to that perfection of beauty and happiness
which love proposes. It is a desire of impossible things which the
poet alternately assuages and arouses again by poetry, in himself
and in us.' The relationship between love and poetry is developed
more fully on p. 2 of the abandoned typescript of *Ecstasy* in *Berg*
73B6771 (fourteen typescript pages left unfinished in September
1913).

101 'No one so much as you'

This poem about Thomas's mother, a companion piece to Poem
99, was written at the end of a short illness spent at his parents'
home. (See R. P. Eckert, *Edward Thomas*, pp. 248–9, and *Edward
Thomas (Writers of Wales)*, pp. 58–9.) The close relationship
between mother and son is borne out by Thomas's letter to Robert

Frost from 13 Rusham Road, Balham, after his enlistment (dated 22 July 1915): 'There is no one to keep me here [England] except my mother. She might come too. But I couldn't in this present mess pack up and get born again in New Hampshire. I couldn't have before I took the king's shilling.'

An earlier picture of his mother (probably written between 1913 and 1914) emerges from the poet's fragment of autobiography, *The Childhood of Edward Thomas*:

> My mother I can hardly see save as she is now while I am writing. I cannot see her but I can summon up her presence. She is plainest to me not quite dressed, in white bodice and petticoat, her arms and shoulders rounded and creamy smooth. My affection for her was leavened with lesser likings and with admiration. I liked the scent of her fresh warm skin and supposed it unique. Her straight nose and chin made a profile that for years formed my standard. No hair was so beautiful to me as hers was, light golden brown hair, long and rippling. Her singing at fall of night, especially if we were alone together, soothed and fascinated me, as though it had been divine, at once the mightiest and the softest sound in the world. [pp. 18–19]

> But I liked to please my mother and keep undisturbed the love that was between us. I sometimes did little unexpected kind things out of my tenderness for her, and was always glad to be the one to take up tea for her if she was unwell, and so on, or to help her with the housework when she was left servantless. But with her as with everyone I was deceitful and had dread of being caught doing what I ought not to do. It was a great and frequent dread. For I felt that most things a boy liked doing annoyed some elder or another; that to annoy an elder was the essence of wrong. My solution was to try not to annoy at the same time that I was doing almost as I liked. Deceit and dread increased rapidly. [p. 76]

102 The Unknown

For Edward Thomas's lifelong concern with the ideals of 'love' and 'beauty' – which he shared with Gordon Bottomley – see 'The

Fountain' in his collection of stories, *Rest and Unrest* (1910),
pp. 143–4:

> As a boy it was of such a being that I used to think – though my
> imagination was not energetic enough to body it forth quite
> clearly – when I felt, in loneliest places among the woods or
> clouds, that my foot-falls had scared something shy, beautiful,
> and divine. And more than so, she was akin to the spirit abroad
> on many days that had awed or harassed me with loveliness – to
> the spirit on the dewy clovers, in the last star that hung like a
> bird of light scattering gold and silver from her wings in the cold
> blue and gloomy rose of the dawn; to the spirit in mountain or
> forest waters, in many unstained rivers, in all places where
> Nature had stung me with a sense of her own pure force, pure
> and without pity . . .
>
> These were the fancies of the moment. She was in sight for
> less than a minute as I went up from the sea over the moor, and
> when I turned in one of its hollows she had disappeared and I
> saw nothing but sea and sky, which were as one.

These ideas are further explored in Poem 103.

103 Celandine

This poem was written after Thomas had received a letter from
Frost on his birthday, 3 Mar. 1916. See his reply to Frost, dated 5
Mar. 1916:

> I have been restless lately. Partly the annoyance of my promotion
> [to Corporal] being delayed. Partly the rain and the long hours
> indoors. Partly my 10 days chill. Then there has been measles in
> the camp for 6 weeks and now we have it and are isolated and
> denied our leave this week, which includes my birthday when I
> meant to be at Steep . . . This should only improve what you
> condemn as my fastidious taste in souls. Yet soul is a word I feel
> I can't have used for years and years. Anyhow here I have to like
> people because they are more my sort than the others, although
> I realise at certain times they are not my sort at all and will
> vanish away after the war. What almost completes the illusion is
> that I can't help talking to them as if they were friends.

Partly what made me restless was the desire to write, without the power. It lasted 5 or 6 weeks till yesterday I rhymed some. Your talking of epic and play rather stirred me. I shall be careful not to *indulge* in a spring run of lyrics, I had better try again to make other people speak. I suppose I take it easily, especially now when it is partly an indulgence. – I wish you would send some of yours without bargaining.

104 'Home' [3]

The background to this poem is filled out by Thomas's letter to Frost (dated 21 May 1916) about his visit to the theatre to see Bottomley's play, *Wife of King Lear*:

Bottomley and his wife I just had a word with. I was with a young artist named Paul Nash who has just joined us as a map reader. He is a change from the two schoolmasters I see most of. He is wonderful at finding birds' nests. There is another artist, too, aged 24, a Welshman, absolutely a perfect Welshman, kind, simple, yet all extremes, and rather unreal and incredible except in his admirations – he admires his wife and Rembrandt, for example. I am really lucky to have such a crowd of people always round and these two or three nearer! You might guess from 'Home' how much nearer.

See also note to Poem 103.

106–9 Household Poems

For these four poems about his family see Thomas's letters to Bottomley: (1) Letter 166, dated 16 Apr. 1916: 'I am sending a set of 4 I did lately, not because I think you will want to use them but because they are rather different in kind.' (2) Letter 167, dated 24 Apr. 1916: 'The household poems ought perhaps to appear as a bunch.'

The poems were not selected by Bottomley for inclusion in *AANP* but I assume Thomas used the typescript sent to Bottomley (or a copy of it) for his own selection for *EE*.

106 [1 Bronwen]

Bronwen was born on 29 Oct. 1902 and died on 29 Mar. 1975.
Originally trained as a dress designer, she frequently acted as
companion to older friends of her parents. Her first two husbands
died tragically – one after an illness subsequent to a motor cycle
accident, the other of a brain tumour. In between marriages and
long illnesses she lived with her mother in Hampstead or Sheldon.
While her third husband was in the R.A.F. during the last war she
was a matron at Charterhouse. Subsequently, she and her husband
retired to Eastbury where she spent her last years. She is survived
by one son and three grandchildren.

   See *TLFY*, pp. 193–4, which explains Thomas's love of the Essex
place-names used in his poem. Thomas used local Ordnance
Survey maps as a map-reading instructor at Hare Hall Camp.

107 [2 Merfyn]

Merfyn was born on 15 Jan. 1900 and died on 2 Aug. 1965, six
months after his retirement as technical editor (from 1946 to 1965)
of the journal *Bus and Coach* (and *Motor Transport*) which he
joined in 1923 after qualifying as a draughtsman with A.E.C. and
London General Omnibus Co. A founder member of the Institute
of Road Transport Engineers. Served in England with a Kent Rifle
Regiment in 1918; commissioned in 1940, he was evacuated from
Calais and served with R.E.M.E. Corps in the Middle East 1941–6,
attaining the rank of Major. A highly esteemed technical journalist
whose articles were published in many countries. He is survived by
his widow, one son, and two grandchildren.

14–17   Thomas's children have recalled for me his informal lessons in
natural history interlarded with fanciful tales of proverbs, folk
stories, and songs of all kinds. As his letters to Frost show, Thomas
was unhappily disappointed about Merfyn's adolescent interests, so
unlike his own. Here are extracts from an unpublished memoir of
his father recorded by Merfyn in 1952 for Rowland Watson:

I did not understand him nor he me, and while I did not
appreciate his point of view he could not or he would not see
mine. . . . I have the most happy memories of our life together,
of his gentle kindness, of his knowledge and appreciation of the
countryside and the simple things of life which he instilled into
me and which I retain today. . . . There were happy days walking
across country when I learnt from him about trees and flowers
and about birds and animals.

Some of Thomas's tales about proverbs appeared in *Four-and-
Twenty Blackbirds* (1915).

108 [3 Myfanwy]

Myfanwy, born on 16 Aug. 1910, was educated in Sevenoaks and
Tonbridge during her mother's long illness and spent the weekdays
with her aunt. Trained as a secretary, she held various posts with
her uncle, with the B.B.C., with Henry Williamson, with Batsford's
the publishers, and at Malvern College, before qualifying as a
teacher. She settled with her mother at Eastbury and taught at a
local school from 1954 to 1975. At one time sub-editor of the
Adelphi magazine and a reviewer of children's books for *The
Listener*, she organized the fund for the Memorial Window at
Eastbury where she still lives and is the literary executrix of her
parents' estates. She has one daughter and four grandchildren.

Thomas's letters to Robert Frost at this time contain many
references to his financial situation and his plans to improve it by
joining Frost in New Hampshire if the war were to end in 1916. The
poet's determination to give all his children a country upbringing
is best seen in his comments on 'Nature-teaching in schools' in *The
South Country* (1909), pp. 141–6. The following extract concludes
his argument (pp. 145–6):

Yet Nature-study is not designed to produce naturalists, any
more than music is taught in order to make musicians. If you
produce nothing but naturalists you fail, and you will produce
very few. The aim of study is to widen the culture of child and
man, to do systematically what Mark Pattison tells us in his dry
way he did for himself, by walking and outdoor sports, then – at

the late age of seventeen – by collecting and reading such books
as *The Natural History of Selborne*, and finally by a slow process
of transition from natural history into 'the more abstract poetic
emotion . . . a conscious and declared poetical sentiment and a
devoted reading of the poets.' Geology did not come for another
ten years, 'to complete the cycle of thought, and to give that
intellectual foundation which is required to make the testimony
of the eye, roaming over an undulating surface, fruitful and
satisfying. When I came in after years to read *The Prelude* I
recognized, as if it were my own history which was being told,
the steps by which the love of the country boy for his hills and
moors grew into poetical susceptibility for all imaginative
presentations of beauty in every direction.' The botany, etc.,
would naturally be related to the neighbourhood of school or
home; for there is no parish or district of which it might not be
said, as Jefferies and Thoreau each said of his own, that it is a
microcosm. By this means the natural history may easily be
linked to a preliminary study of hill and valley and stream, the
positions of houses, mills and villages, and the reasons for them,
and the food supply, and so on, and this in turn leads on to –
nay, involves – all that is most real in geography and history. The
landscape retains the most permanent marks of the past, and a
wise examination of it should evoke the beginnings of the
majestic sentiment of our oneness with the future and the past,
just as natural history should help to give the child a sense of
oneness with all forms of life. To put it at its lowest, some such
cycle of knowledge is needed if a generation that insists more
and more on living in the country, or spending many weeks
there, is not to be bored or to be compelled to entrench itself
behind the imported amusements of the town.

109 [4 Helen]

Helen, born on 11 July 1877, died on 12 Apr. 1967. She lived at Forge
House, Otford, Kent, after Edward's death, suffering increasingly
for many years from delayed shock and nervous exhaustion,
despite the conflicting remedies of various specialists. On their
advice she returned intermittently to live in London and, in 1926,

settled at 5, The Gables, Hampstead which was her principal home until March 1939. *As It Was*, a desperate attempt at psychotherapy, was begun at Otford and, like its sequel *World Without End*, completed in Hampstead. From about 1932 she spent more and more time at Starwell Farm, Sheldon, Chippenham, and finally settled there until 1954 when she joined her youngest daughter at Bridge Cottage, Eastbury, Berkshire. Despite failing eyesight she remained an active broadcaster, gardener, and countrywoman until her very last year. A memorial window to Edward and Helen Thomas, executed by Laurence Whistler and supported by public subscription, was dedicated in Eastbury Church on 16 Oct. 1971.

For some amplification of this intimate poem to his wife, see 'Edward Thomas: A Memorial Tribute' in *English*, vol. xxi, No. 109, pp. 18–21.

112 When we two walked

1   A reference to a long walk taken by the poet and his wife before Easter 1914.

115 'I never saw that land before'

For a discussion of the place of an imaginary land in Thomas's writings see *Edward Thomas (Writers of Wales)*, pp. 67–74.

119 The sun used to shine

The occasion of this poem – recalling the holiday spent by Thomas and his family with Frost's family in Herefordshire during August 1914 – was probably the receipt of a letter from Frost on 21 May 1916 after a long silence. (Thomas's previous letter to Frost is dated 16 Mar. 1916 and was in answer to the letter that had arrived on his birthday, 3 Mar.)

121 As the team's head brass

This poem reflects the poet's maturing decision to abandon his job as a mapreading instructor and to apply for a commission with the possibility of a posting to France. His chief concern was the

financial plight of his family. He was hoping for a Civil List
Pension to relieve family needs and in June 1916 he was granted a
£300 lump sum instead. See especially the following letters:

(1) to Eleanor Farjeon, 28 May 1916:

> We are only free in the evenings nowadays. They won't let us
> alone. We have to do the usual duties. Every N.C.O. is to be
> made universally competent. No doubt it is very good for us as
> well as for the country and I really am determined not to mind
> much. The new hours [i.e. the introduction of British Summer
> Time] give us a longer evening, so that we can still walk a little. I
> have even written several things which I send you.

(2) to Robert Frost, 10 June 1916:

> Now the Government instead of a pension is going to give me
> £300 in a lump. This will simplify some things. Mervyn's case,
> for example, especially as my engineer brother [Theodore] has
> promised to get him into a big motor works on September 1st
> and this is being settled. Also I am rather expecting I may get a
> commission before very long as an officer in the Anti-Aircraft
> Corps . . . I am accumulating such a mass of verse and I have an
> affection for so many.

(3) to Frost, 28 July 1916:

> A new step I have taken makes a good moment for writing. I
> offered myself for Artillery and today I was accepted, which
> means I shall go very soon to an Artillery School and be out in
> France or who knows where in a few months. After months of
> panic and uncertainty I feel much happier again except that I
> don't take easily to the trigonometry needed for artillery
> calculations. I have done very nearly all that I could do here in
> the way of teaching, lecturing, and taking charge of men in and
> out of doors. My old acquaintances were mostly moving out.
> The speeding up of things left no chance of enjoying the walks
> we used to have. So I had to go . . . Of course I can't write any
> more verses just now and have not done for a month or so. The
> last I did were during a 3 days' walk that Helen and I took at the

end of June when I had a few days leave due to me. We had fine
bright weather and saw [Vivian Locke] Ellis and a few others in
Sussex and Kent. It was too short. I can only be content now in
regular almost continuous work when I have no time for
comparisons.

124 'Early one morning in May I set out'

The composition of this poem – a reflection of the poet's lifelong
interest in folk-songs (see his *The Pocket Book of Poems and Songs
for the Open Air* (1907)) – caused him a great deal of trouble, as his
letters to Eleanor Farjeon of 19 and 24 June 1916 (*TLFY*, pp.
199–200), and the three manuscript drafts in M_2, show. Behind the
poem, too – especially the reference to burning his letters in line 6
– was the upheaval caused by the loss of his hill-top study and the
final move from Steep to Essex (see *GB*, Letter 169).

127 'There was a time when this poor frame was whole'

This poem was composed during 'three days sick and confined to
the camp, practically to the hut and this [i.e. Poems 125–7] is the
result' (*TLFY*, p. 200). For the poet's attitude to the poem – which
reflects his decision to apply for a commission – see a letter to
Eleanor Farjeon dated 29 June 1916: 'I wish you could shut your
eyes to many big things as I do without trying. If they do prey on
me I don't know it. But then I wasn't in a bad mood when I wrote
those lines you thought sick – I think you meant the longest of
those three. I thought it was more than a shade heroic.'

128 The Green Roads

See Thomas's letter to Eleanor Farjeon, 29 June 1916 (*TLFY*, p. 202):
'This is the latest. A wet warm free afternoon. The forest is a
fragment left 6 miles from here [Gidea Park, Romford, Essex], the
best of all this country. I go there every time I can. There is a
cottage not far off where you might like to stay some day. The
people have been there 53 years. You can't imagine a wilder quieter
place.'

129 When first

13   *The twelfth*: although Thomas did not move to Berryfield Cottage, Ashford (near Steep), until November 1906, he and Helen had been looking for a house there, near Bedales School, the previous year. Parts of his *The Heart of England* (1906), written in 1905, suggest a knowledge of this district.

130 The Gallows

Selsfield House, East Grinstead was the home of Vivian Locke Ellis where Thomas had spent some time as a paying guest in the winter of 1912 and in the early spring of 1914. He and Helen spent the last four days of his week's leave (30 June-6 July 1916) at Selsfield visiting friends, including Harry Hooton (in Coulsden) and Eleanor Farjeon (in London).

In spite of its grim undertones of front line warfare, this poem illustrates Thomas's close involvement with his children during his many Army leaves. See especially a letter to Eleanor Farjeon dated 7 July 1916 (*TLFY*, p. 202): 'At Ellises I could not help writing these four verses on the theme of some stories I used to tell Baba [Myfanwy] there. The other 3 [the three verses of "The Dark Forest" (Poem 131)] I believe are no good, the forest is perhaps a too obvious metaphor.' A recently found *Helen* manuscript is headed 'For Baba'.

131 'Dark is the forest and deep, and overhead'

A final stanza – the last entry in M_2 – probably reflects the poet's feelings after the London visit to his parents. Soon afterwards his mother had an eye operation. See *GB*, Letter 172, dated 2 Oct. 1916: 'my Mother in London. I must see as often as possible . . . She is very lonely with us all away. Not that she complains.' See too the note to Poem 130. By removing this final personal stanza Thomas makes the 'metaphor' of the forest less obvious:

> beloved and lover or child and
> Not even ⌃ ~~mother and child or sister and brother~~,
> One from within, one from
> Without the forest could recognize each other,
> Since they have changed their home.

132 When he should laugh

See Thomas's letter to Robert Frost, dated 28 July 1916, announcing his decision to accept a commission in the Artillery: 'No news. My Mother has lately been operated on for cataract and is in a nursing home waiting to see again. She is not happy over my new chance of going out as an officer – I ought to be an officer in less than a few months. Nor is Helen. She is not often happy now. She is tired and anxious.'

133 The Swifts

See three letters to Eleanor Farjeon:

(1) (Postmark) 11 Aug. 1916, 'Hospital – Thursday': 'I entered this place on Tuesday morning [with a swollen arm after vaccination] and ever since have been too bored to do anything but wish myself out. I can't read. This afternoon I had to write something. I wrote these 2 verses, which I am afraid may simply make you think them perfectly true.'

(2) From Steep, 20 Aug. 1916: 'Don't you worry about typing those 2 verses, in which I have changed "August blue" to "harvest blue". I was glad to have them to write anyway – shall be lucky to do more till the swifts are back again.'

(3) From R.A. School, Handel Street, W.C.3 (*TLFY*, p. 213): 'By the way, you misread the poem you didn't so much like – about the swifts – missing the point that year after year I see them, *realising it is the last time*, i.e. just before they go away for the winter (early in August). Perhaps it is too much natural history.' This last point echoes the letter to his aunt about a re-telling of the Mabinogian stories (14 Feb. 1915): 'As they stand the old stories are works of art in which, as in every work of art, the writer accepts many things he could not explain and feels no need of explanation. If he did feel that need he would make a work of philosophy or natural history, and not a work of art.'

See also *Berg FNB* 80, undated, after 2 June 1915, between entries for Poems 80 and 82: 'Swift with tail and wings so sharp and? It seems the bow has flown off with the arrow.'

134 Blenheim Oranges

See letters to Eleanor Farjeon:

(1) dated 27 Aug. 1916: 'I have been resting yesterday and today at Rusham Road. We get practically every weekend. The result is I got tired of logarithms and wrote 8 verses which you see before you. When I come I should like to borrow about the last 12 things I have written. I want to send them to the prospective publisher I told you about [Roger Ingpen], with these if they are good enough.'

(2) Dated 19 Sept. 1916: 'In case I don't [see you] could you send me a copy of those last verses – the Blenheim Oranges – of mine? I can't find one or the original. You will see I have written some more too – if you *can* see the faint type. Perhaps one of them is better than the others.'

17–24   These lines recall Thomas's early and continued affection for the old London houses of his youth which play such a significant part in his novel *The Happy-Go-Lucky Morgans* (1913). (Cf. E. M. Forster's description of one such local house, 'Battersea Rise' in his *Abinger Harvest* (Part III – 'The Past').) See *GB*, Letter 66, dated 27 Mar. 1907:

> Then I do want to arrange my chiefly pathetic memories of the Suburbs – their grave charming old Annes now tumbling down at the feet of the villa-builders – their little bits of waste ground – my own special memories – a little girl, the first whose sex I dimly knew (when I was 7 or 8) – the quite new houses so difficult to like and yet to be liked. But of course not 100 people want such a book.

135 'That girl's clear eyes utterly concealed all'

There is no hard evidence to explain this poem, which seems like a response to a portrait in the Royal Artillery School, Handel St., where the poet was studying as an Officer Cadet. If so, 'Seventeen Thirty-Nine' (l. 14) is the date of the painting. But the poem may be an echo of a minor eighteenth-century poem unidentifiable. See letter to Frost on 11 Sept. 1916 about Frost's suggestion that he and

Thomas should collaborate on an anthology of love poems, 'The Old Cloak', perhaps suggested by Thomas's 'Words' (Poem 77):

> I don't believe I can do much yet at 'The Old Cloak'. You can't imagine the degree of my disinclination for books. Sometimes I say I will read Shakespeare's sonnets again and I do, or half do, but never more than that. I should love to do it with you. I thought of what love poems could go in – could Burns's 'Whistle and I'll come to ye, my lad'? There are the songs in the very earliest Elizabethan dramatists. There's a deal of Chaucer, Shakespeare, Cowper, Wordsworth and the ballads: some Crabbe: one poem apiece out of Prior and several minor 18th century people: a few of Blake's. But I don't begin to look at books: I must keep all my *conscious attention* for my work.

136 'What will they do when I am gone? It is plain'

The initial note of regret with which the poem begins presumably reflects the poet's last visit to Steep before he moved his family to High Beech, near Loughton, Essex. His cottage in Steep village was already let to the poet John Freeman, with whom Thomas's younger daughter was staying: his elder daughter was living with her aunt in London; his son, now an engineering apprentice, was lodging in Walthamstow. Helen was on a walking tour of the Lake District with her sister Irene – who had recently lost her husband after a long illness – and Thomas was left to arrange the final move from Steep, which he visited once more during his final training at Codford.

137 The Trumpet

Thomas was eager to begin his field training as an officer-cadet, after the (for him) exacting mathematical training at Handel St., London. He was now an experienced N.C.O. with considerable knowledge of camp life. The trumpeters at the Trowbridge Barracks attracted his attention from the first. See two letters to Eleanor Farjeon:

(1) 24 Sept. 1916: 'We are in tents and so we see the night sky. The trumpet blows for everything and I like that too, though the

trumpeter is not excellent. We have had our costume criticised a good deal and have had to buy gloves and so on. But it is not so bad as it was painted . . . I hope you liked some of the verses.'

(2) Wednesday, n.d. (Eleanor Farjeon has the sequence of letters wrong here, I believe. She thinks 'The Trumpet' belongs to November. See *TLFY*, p. 218): 'However you can see I have some ease, because I have written some verses suggested by the trumpet calls which go all day. They are not well done and the trumpet is cracked, but the Reveille pleases me (more than it does most sleepers). Here is the result. You see I have written it with only capitals to mark lines, because people are all around me and I don't want them to know.'

138 'He rolls in the orchard: he is stained with moss'

Some background to this poem is expanded in the poet's letters:

(1) To Eleanor Farjeon on 2 Nov. 1916: 'also to send you some verses I managed to write before the end of my leave'.

(2) On 6 Nov. 1916: 'Thank you for typing the verses. I see that "At the age of six" [l. 20] is a rather rough way of explaining who speaks. But he did tell me he was six too and seemed to realise he had a long way to go.'

(3) To Robert Frost from Trowbridge, on 4 Nov. 1916: 'One day when the sun was warm we bathed in the Frome. This is the country I came to when I wrote my "Swinburne" [May–June 1912]. It has two good little rivers, one in a shallow level valley, the other in a steepsided narrow one. There is a castle and many fine old houses near, and Salisbury Plain just too far off for our short afternoons, but its old White Horse plainly visible all day.'

(4) To Frost, during a weekend leave at High Beech, near Loughton, Essex, on 19 Oct. 1916: 'I have just written the second thing since I left London a month ago. If I can type the two you shall see them. I am wondering if any of these last few sets of verses have pleased you at all.'

139 Lights Out

For the use of the 'forest as metaphor', see Notes to Poems 130 and 131 above.

Two letters to Eleanor Farjeon are relevant:

(1) From Trowbridge on 6 Nov. 1916: 'Now I have actually done still another piece which I call "Lights Out". It sums up what I have often thought at that call. I wish it were as brief – 2 pairs of long notes. I wonder is it nearly as good as it might be.'

(2) On 11 Nov. 1916: 'Oh, Granville Barker is in my room now, but is just being shunted off to a School for Coast Defence. I suppose his friends have urged his country not to risk his life. I hope I shall always be as eager to risk mine as I have been these last few months.'

140 The long small room

In his letter to Eleanor Farjeon of 13 Nov. Thomas writes: 'I am worried about the impression the willow made on you. As a matter of fact I started with the last line as what I was working to. I am only fearing it has a sort of Japanesy suddenness of ending. But it is true, whether or not it is a legitimate switch to make. I will think of it as much like somebody else as possible.' (For this reference to Japanese verse see Thomas's interest in the work of Yone Noguchi in *GB*, and, more particularly, his *Lafcadio Hearn*, pp. 71–82.)

141 The Sheiling

Gordon Bottomley – Thomas's friend and correspondent over thirteen years – lived at The Sheiling, Silverdale, near Carnforth. Thomas spent three days from his long post-OCTU leave to visit Bottomley. The poem is a crystallization of their friendship and recalls the attraction of Bottomley's cultured, restful invalid existence for Thomas. (See the introduction to *GB*, pp. 2–7, C. C. Abbott's *Gordon Bottomley, Poems and Plays* (1953), and *Poet and Painter: Being the correspondence between G. B. and Paul Nash 1940–1946*, ed. C. C. Abbott and Anthony Bertram (1953).)

In some ways this poem is a late reply to Bottomley's poem to Thomas which precedes Bottomley's *Riding to Lithend* (1907). Both poets were interested in Old Icelandic literature and, because Thomas's comment on the 'Japanesy ending' to 'The long small room' (Poem 140) suggests a mood of retrospective survey at this time, it is not over-fanciful to detect an echo of scaldic alliteration and assonance – as available then in English translations – in some of these stanzas.

11 In the *Bod* manuscript Thomas alters 'Soft' to 'Safe', possibly in deference to Bottomley's ill health and inability to take up any form of national service.

16 *maker*: a pun on the Scottish word for poet, as well as a tribute to Emily Bottomley's gifts as a home-maker.

142 'Some day, I think, there will be people enough'

This poem is written on a loose leaf inserted into the book in which *Bod* is written. At the bottom of the leaf is a note by Helen Thomas: 'Sent from Codford', where Thomas was awaiting embarkation. In a letter to Helen from Codford, dated 22 Jan. 1917, he wrote: 'You never mentioned receiving those verses about Green Lane, Froxfield [near Steep]. Did you get them? They were written in December and suggested by our last walk there in September.' Perhaps these are the verses referred to in his letter to Eleanor Farjeon from Trowbridge on 2 Nov. 1916: 'I did something else too coming down in the train on a long dark journey when people were talking and I wasn't, but I have got it still to finish.' If the poem was written in two stages, this may explain the discontinuity suggested by the dots after l. 8.

143 'Out in the dark, over the snow'

Thomas liked his new home at High Beech. See:

(1) His letter to Elinor Frost on 27 Nov. 1916: 'Except on Saturdays and Sundays and holidays we see nothing only aeroplanes and deer in the forest. Baba [Myfanwy] has no companions. She goes about

telling herself stories . . . The forest is beautiful, oaks, hornbeams, beeches, bracken, hollies, and some heather. But it is really High Beach, not Beech, on account of the pebbly soil. There are 7 or 8 miles of forest, by 1 or 2 miles wide, all in the high ground, with many tiny ponds and long wide glades.'

(2) A letter to Eleanor Farjeon from R.A. Mess, Tin Town, Lydd, on 27 Dec. 1916: 'I am going to send you in exchange some verses I made on Sunday. It is really Baba who speaks, not I. Something she felt put me on to it. But I am afraid I am meddling now. A real poem would include and imply all these things I am writing, or so I fancy. . . . It is curious how I feel no anxiety or trouble as soon as I am back here, though I was so very glad to be at home.'

(3) A letter to Robert Frost (headed 'High Beech' but sent from Lydd) on 31 Dec. 1916:

I was home for Christmas by an unexpected piece of luck. We were very happy with housework and wood gathering in the forest and a few walks. We had some snow and sunshine on Christmas day. Mervyn's holiday coincided with mine. Some of the time I spent at my Mother's house and in London buying the remainder of my things for the front. . . . I wonder have you had your duplicate of the Ms. which I sent over a month ago? It looks now as if I should not see the proofs [of *EE*]. Bottomley or John Freeman will do it for me. . . . When I am alone – as I am during the evening just now because the officer who shares my room is away – I hardly know what to do. I can't write now and still less can I read. I have rhymed but I have burnt my rhymes and feel proud of it.

144 'The sorrow of true love'

This poem is on the last page of the diary kept by Thomas during his last three months as a soldier. The diary was in the possession of his son, Merfyn, until his death in 1965, and was rediscovered by Merfyn's son (Edward) in the summer of 1970. It was first printed along with the diary and a foreword in *The Anglo-Welsh Review* (Autumn, 1971); the diary is now reprinted here (pp. 137–72). The poem was written on 13 Jan. 1917, at Lydd, two days after the poet's last leave when he said good-bye to his family. See diary entry for 11 Jan. and especially the entry for 13 Jan. 1917: 'Cold drizzle. Horton [his C.O.] and the battery left early for Codford. Even wrote verses. Early to bed.' There is an identical copy of the first five lines in Helen's hand dated 13 Feb. 1917.

Appendix 1

Verse published before *Collected Poems* (1920)

Reference to all poems in this table is to their chronological number in the present edition. The titles in brackets are the titles used in the various publications in which the poems first appeared.

(Unless stated otherwise all the poems were attributed to 'Edward Eastaway'.)

1915 Poems 8 ('Interval') and 33 ('House and Man') in *Root and Branch* [*RB*], vol. i, No. 4, edited and published by James Guthrie, The Pear Tree Press, 1913–15.
Poems 80 ('Haymaking') and 11 ('The Manor Farm') in *This England, An Anthology from her Writers* [*TE*], compiled by Edward Thomas, Oxford University Press.

1916 Poems 56 ('Lob') and 77 ('Words') in *Form*, edited by Austin O. Spare and Francis Marsden, vol. i, No. 1, April.
Six Poems [*SP*], by Edward Eastaway, printed by James Guthrie at The Pear Tree Press.
[Contents: Poems 75 ('Sedge-Warblers'), 93 ('This is no case'), 83 ('Aspens'), 19 ('A Private'), 88 ('Cock-Crow'), and 30 ('Beauty').]

1917 Poems 4 ('Old Man'), 102 ('The Unknown'), and 78 ('The Word') in *Poetry*, vol. ix, October 1916-March 1917.
An Annual of New Poetry [*AANP*], Constable & Co., March.
[Contents: Poems 4 ('Old Man'), 20 ('Snow'), 25 ('The Cuckoo'), 44 ('The New House'), 54 ('Wind and Mist'), 102 ('The Unknown'), 78 ('The Word'), 7 ('After Rain'), 83 ('Aspens'), 19 ('A Private'), 74 ('Sedge-Warblers'), 85 ('For These'), 96 ('Roads'), 17 ('The Source'), 58 ('Lovers'), 30 ('Beauty'), 82 ('The Brook'), and 65 ('Song').]
Poems 41 ('The Bridge'), 134 ('Gone, gone again'), 21 ('Adlestrop'), and 73 ('Fifty Faggots') in the *New Statesman* [*NS*], 28 April, p. 87.

Poems [*EE*], by Edward Thomas ('Edward Eastaway'), Selwyn &
Blount, London, October. Reprinted November.[1]
[Contents: Poems 137 ('The Trumpet'), 5 ('The Sign-post'),
22 ('Tears'), 48 ('Two Pewits'), 11 ('The Manor Farm'),
39 ('The Owl'), 26 ('Swedes'), 49 ('Will you come?'), 121 ('As the
team's head-brass'), 105 ('Thaw'), 8 ('Interval'), 111 ('Like the touch
of rain'), 50 ('The Path'), 14 ('The Combe'), 106 ('If I should ever
by chance'), 108 ('What shall I give?'), 107 ('If I were to own'),
109 ('And you, Helen'), 129 ('When first'), 60 ('Head and Bottle'),
122 ('After you speak'), 46 ('Sowing'), 112 ('When we two walked'),
59 ('In Memoriam'), 73 ('Fifty Faggots'), 126 ('Women he liked'),
124 ('Early one morning'), 116 ('Cherry Trees'), 117 ('It rains'),
63 ('The Huxter'), 55 ('A Gentleman'), 41 ('The Bridge'), 56 ('Lob'),
123 ('Bright Clouds'), 95 ('The clouds that are so light'), 118 ('Some
eyes condemn'), 36 ('May 23'), 70 ('The Glory'), 67 ('Melancholy'),
21 ('Adlestrop'), 128 ('The Green Roads'), 28 ('The Mill-pond'),
125 ('It was upon'), 113 ('Tall Nettles'), 80 ('Haymaking'),
133 ('How at once'), 134 ('Gone, gone again'), 119 ('The sun used to
shine'), 89 ('October'), 140 ('The long small room'), 92 ('Liberty'),
2 ('November'), 141 ('The Sheiling'), 130 ('The Gallows'),
9 ('Birds' Nests'), 94 ('Rain'), 104 (' "Home" '), 90 ('There's nothing
like the sun'), 132 ('When he should laugh'), 13 ('An Old Song'),
18 ('The Penny Whistle'), 139 ('Lights Out'), 88 ('Cock-crow'), and
77 ('Words').]
Also two proof copies printed for Selwyn & Blount before July, but
not seen by the poet.
This identical volume was published by Henry Holt & Co.,
New York, in January 1918 from sheets sent over by Roger Ingpen.
Poem 24 ('The Lofty Sky') by Edward Eastaway in *Root and Branch*,
vol. ii, No. 2, December.

1918   Poems 27 ('The Unknown Bird') and 61 ('Home') by Edward
        Eastaway in *Root and Branch*, vol. ii, No. 4, June.

1 Prepared from Thomas's typescript. The duplicate set, for Frost, was lost
at sea. Proofs were not seen by the poet.

Last Poems [*LP*], by Edward Thomas, Selwyn & Blount, London, December.[2]

[Contents: Poems 115 ('I never saw that Land before'), 131 ('The Dark Forest'), 103 ('Celandine'), 97 ('The Ash Grove'), 4 ('Old Man'), 91 ('The Thrush'), 76 ('I built myself a House of Glass'), 98 ('February Afternoon'), 86 ('Digging'), 87 ('Two Houses'), 84 ('The Mill-water'), 81 ('A Dream'), 75 ('Sedge-Warblers'), 79 ('Under the Woods'), 136 ('What will they do?'), 68 ('Tonight'), 66 ('A Cat'), 102 ('The Unknown'), 65 ('Song'), 64 ('She dotes'), 85 ('For These'), 47 ('March the Third'), 44 ('The New House'), 3 ('March'), 25 ('The Cuckoo'), 23 ('Over the Hills'), 61 ('Home'), 15 ('The Hollow Wood'), 54 ('Wind and Mist'), 27 ('The Unknown Bird'), 24 ('The Lofty Sky'), 7 ('After Rain'), 57 ('Digging'), 43 ('But these things also'), 69 ('April'), 37 ('The Barn'), 45 ('The Barn and the Down'), 40 ('The Child on the Cliffs'), 42 ('Good-night'), 51 ('The Wasp Trap'), 71 ('July'), 52 ('A Tale'), 34 ('Parting'), 58 ('Lovers'), 135 ('That Girl's Clear Eyes'), 138 ('The Child in the Orchard'), 17 ('The Source'), 10 ('The Mountain Chapel'), 35 ('First known when lost'), 78 ('The Word'), 100 ('These things that Poets said'), 38 ('Home'), 83 ('Aspens'), 12 ('An Old Song'), 127 ('There was a Time'), 32 ('Ambition'), 120 ('No one cares less than I'), 96 ('Roads'), 93 ('This is no case of petty Right or Wrong'), 72 ('The Chalk-Pit'), 62 ('Health'), 30 ('Beauty'), 20 ('Snow'), 16 ('The New Year'), 82 ('The Brook'), 6 ('The Other'), 33 ('House and Man'), 31 ('The Gypsy'), 29 ('Man and Dog'), 19 ('A Private'), and 143 ('Out in the Dark').]
Twelve Poets, A Miscellany of New Verse [*TP*], Selwyn & Blount. Presumably published at the same time as *Last Poems*, and containing ten poems by Thomas from that volume in this order: Poems 131, 91, 68, 47, 15, 42, 10, 97, 100, 143.

2 Selwyn Blount's 'Announcements for Autumn 1918', included in the volume, describes the contents: 'In this volume are collected those poems of the late Edward Thomas that were not included in the volume of POEMS published last year, which revealed to its readers a hitherto unexpected gift of the author. Here are many pieces printed from the Poet's manuscripts as well as some that have appeared in Constable's Anthology and in periodicals.'

1919   Poem 1 ('Up in the Wind') in *In Memoriam: Edward Thomas: Being Number Two of The Green Pasture Series* [*IM*], The Morland Press, July.

Collected Poems [*CP*]. Significant additions between 1920 and 1949

Collected Poems, by Edward Thomas, with a foreword by Walter de la Mare, Selwyn & Blount Ltd., 1920.
[Contents: Sixty-four poems in the same order as *Poems* [*EE*], followed by Poem 1 (mistitled 'Up The Wind' in the list of contents and in the text) and the seventy-one poems of *Last Poems* [*LP*].]

Collected Poems, by Edward Thomas, New Edition, Ingpen & Grant, 1928.
Four additional poems included after the penultimate poem of the previous edition, viz., Poems 142 ('The Lane'), 114 ('The Watchers'), 101 ('No One So Much As You'), and 110 ('The Wind's Song').

This edition was reset and issued by Faber & Faber Ltd., September 1936, with a new edition (third impression) in February 1944. Poem 99 was added after 'The Wind's Song' in the fifth impression in June 1949. (See letter from Julian Thomas to R. P. Eckert, dated 22 March 1938: 'I expect you have seen Faber's edition of Edward's Poems, the first to be free from misprints unless my vigilance and Walter de la Mare's has been in vain.')

Appendix 2

Just as she is turning in to the [~~cott~~] house [~~door~~] or leaving it, the baby [Myfanwy Thomas] plucks a feather of old man's beard. [~~Its~~] The bush grows [~~beside the~~] just across the path from the door. Sometimes she stands by it squeezing off tip after tip from the [~~bush~~] branches and shrivelling them between her fingers on to the path in grey-green shreds. So the bush is still [~~no taller than~~] only half as tall as she is, though it is the same age. She never talks of it, but I wonder how much of the garden she will remember, the hedge with the old damson trees topping it, the vegetable rows, the path bending [~~to~~] round the house corner, the old man's beard opposite the door, and me sometimes forbidding her to touch it, if she lives to my years. As for myself I cannot remember when I first smelt that green bitterness. I, too, often gather a sprig from the bush and sniff it, and roll it between my fingers and sniff again and think, trying to [~~remember~~] discover what it is that I am remembering. [~~but in vain.~~] I do not wholly like the smell, yet [~~per?~~] would rather lose many meaningless sweeter ones than this bitter [~~unintelligible~~] one of which I have mislaid the key. As I hold the sprig to my nose and slowly withdraw it, I think of nothing, I see, I hear nothing, yet I seem too to be listening, [~~as I hold the sprig to my nose, and withdraw it~~], lying in wait for whatever it is I ought to remember but never do. No garden comes back to me, no hedge or path, no grey green bush called old man's beard or lad's love, no figure of mother or father or [~~chil~~] playmate, only [~~an~~] a [~~endless~~] dark avenue without an end.

Appendix 3

FOREWORD BY WALTER DE LA MARE
TO THE 1ST EDITION (1920) OF *Collected Poems*

All that Edward Thomas was as a friend lies only half-concealed in his poems. He wrote many books. A few of them – 'Light and Twilight', 'The Happy-Go-Lucky Morgans', 'Richard Jefferies', for instance – were of his own choice and after his own heart. Many of the others were in the nature of obligations thrust upon him. For in order to be able to write not merely for a living, but in happy obedience to the life within, task work, against the grain, may be inevitable.

His complete freedom of mind, his fine sense of literature, his love of truth, his delicate yet vigorous intuition are never absent even in his merest journey-work. But there cannot but be a vital difference between this and what is done for pure love of it. He toiled on, 'Happy sometimes, sometimes suffering a heavy body and a heavy heart' under the grimmest disciplinarian a man can have – himself.

Nevertheless his rarer qualities were obviously not such as can please a wide public; nor was he possessed of some of the admirable faculties that can and do. He was not a *born* story-teller; nor that chameleonic creature, a dramatist. He had less invention than fantasy. He detested mere cleverness; and compromise was alien to his nature. He could delight in 'a poor man of any sort down to a king'; but the range intended here is obviously exclusive and graduated. He was not therefore possessed of that happy and dangerous facility of being all things to *all* men. Faithful and solitary lover of 'the lovely that is not beloved' – not by most of us at much expense, he could not, then, as have other men of genius simultaneously woo fame and win fortune. His chief desire was to express himself and his own truth – and therefore life and humanity; and compared with a true artist's conscience, Tamerlane is tender-hearted. That

                              right hand
Crawling crab-like over the clean white page,
Resting awhile each morning on the pillow,
Then once more starting to crawl on towards age . . .

His poems were a release from this bondage.

Late in his life, when he seemed to have given up hope of it, there came to him this sudden creative impulse, the incentive of a new form into which he could pour his thoughts, feelings and memories with ease and freedom and delight. Utterly unforeseen also may have been the discovery that he was born to live and die a soldier. Yet in those last years, however desperate at times the distaste and disquiet, however sharp the sacrifice, he found an unusual serenity and satisfaction. His comradeship, his humour blossomed over. He plunged back from books into life, and wrote only for sheer joy in writing. To read 'The Trumpet', 'Tears', or 'This is no Case of Petty Right or Wrong' is to realize the brave spirit that compelled him to fling away the safety which without the least loss of honour he might have accepted, and to go back to his men, and his guns, and death. These poems reveal, too, that he was doubly homesick, for this and for another world, no less clearly than they show how intense a happiness to him was the fruition of his lifelong hope and desire to prove himself a poet. On the one side his 'Words':

Out of us all
That make rhymes,
Will you choose
Sometimes–
As the winds use
A crack in a wall
Or a drain,
Their joy or their pain
To whistle through–
Choose me,
You English words?

I know you:
You are light as dreams,

Tough as oak,
Precious as gold,
As poppies and corn,
Or an old cloak;
Sweet as our birds
To the ear,
As the burnet rose
In the heat
Of Midsummer . . .

Make me content
With some sweetness
From Wales
Whose nightingales
Have no wings,–
From Wiltshire and Kent
And Herefordshire,
And the villages there,–
From the names, and the things
No less.
Let me sometimes dance
With you,
Or climb
Or stand perchance
In ecstasy,
Fixed and free
In a rhyme,
As poets do.

And on the other side, one of the loveliest and most perfect in form of all his poems, 'Lights Out':

I have come to the borders of sleep,
The unfathomable deep
Forest where all must lose
Their way, however straight,
Or winding, soon or late;
They cannot choose . . .

> Here love ends,
> Despair, ambition ends,
> All pleasure and all trouble,
> Although most sweet or bitter,
> Here ends in sleep that is sweeter
> Than tasks most noble . . .

This intensity of solitude, this impassioned, almost trance-like delight in things natural, simple, 'short-lived and happy-seeming', 'lovely of motion, shape and hue', is expressed – even when the clouds of melancholy and of self-distrust lour darkest – on every page of this book. A light shines in it, like that of 'cowslips wet with the dew of their birth'. If one word could tell of his all, that word would be England. 'The Manor Farm', 'The Mill-Water', 'Adlestrop', 'Roads', 'The Gallows', 'Lob', 'If I should ever by Chance', 'The Mountain Chapel', 'An Old Song' – it is foolish to catalogue – but *their* word is England; and if music and natural magic are not the very essence of such poems as 'The Unknown Bird', 'The Child on the Cliffs', 'The Word', 'Beauty', 'Snow', 'The Brook', 'Out in the Dark', then I have never even guessed the meaning of the phrase.

When, indeed, Edward Thomas was killed in Flanders, a mirror of England was shattered of so pure and true a crystal that a clearer and tenderer reflection of it can be found no other where than in these poems; neither in 'Clare and Cobbett, Morland and Crome', nor among the living, to whom he was devoted – in Hardy, Hudson, Doughty. England's roads and heaths and woods, its secret haunts and solitudes, its houses, its people – themselves resembling its thorns and juniper – its very flints and dust, were his freedom and his peace. He pierced to their being, not through dreams, or rhapsodies, not by the strange light of fantasy, rarely with the vision that makes of them a transient veil of the unseen. They were to him 'lovelier than any mysteries'. 'To say "God bless it", was all that I could do.'

There is nothing precious, elaborate, brilliant, esoteric, obscure in his work. The feeling is never 'fine', the thought never curious, or the word far-fetched. Loose-woven, monotonous, unrelieved, the verse, as verse, may appear to a careless reader accustomed to the customary. It must be read slowly, as naturally as if it were talk, without much emphasis; it will then surrender himself, his beautiful world, his compassionate and suffering heart, his fine, lucid, grave and sensitive mind. This is not a poetry that will drug or intoxicate, civicize or edify – in the usual meaning of the word, though it rebuilds reality. It ennobles by simplification. Above all, it will reveal what a friend this man was to the friendless and to them of small report, though not always his own serenest friend – to the greening stoat on the gamekeeper's shed, the weed by the wayside, the wanderer, 'soldiers and poor unable to rejoice'. 'If we could see all, all might seem good.'

These poems, moreover, differ from most poems, not only because they usually share so quiet a self-communion. They tell also, not so much of rare, exalted, chosen moments, of fleeting inexplicable intuitions, but of Thomas's daily and, one might say, common experience. They proceed from a saturation, like that of Gideon's fleece; from contemplation rather than from sheer energy of insight. They are not drops of attar in a crystal vase, inestimably precious though such drops and vessels may be. Long-looking, long-desiring, long-loving these win at last to the inmost being of a thing. So it was with Edward Thomas. Like every other individual writer, he had unlearned all literary influences. The anxious and long-suffering labourer was worthy of his belated hire, and this volume is a crockful of the purest waters of his life.

Reading it, every friend Thomas had must be conscious – though none more desperately than I – of an inexpressible regret that so much more was his to give if richer opportunity had been taken and a more selfless receptivity had been that friend's to offer. Every remembrance of him brings back his company to me with a gladness never untinged by this remorse. For to be alone with him was a touchstone of everything artificial and shallow, of everything sweet and natural in the world in which we lived. One could learn and learn from him not the mere knowledge of the living things and scenes around us which were as familiar to him as his own handwriting, but of their life in himself. He never contemned any man's ignorance unless it was pompous or prosperous, and mine, I can vouch, gave him ample opportunity.

We met for the first time – one still, blue, darkening summer evening – in a place curiously uncharacteristic of him, one of the back streets of the City of London, to him far rather the astonishing 'wen' than the hub of God's universe. The streets were already deserted. I was first at the tryst, and presently out of a neighbouring court echoed that peculiarly leisurely footfall, and his figure appeared in the twilight. Gulliver himself could hardly have looked a stranger phenomenon in Lilliput than he appeared in Real-Turtle-Soup-Land – his clothes, his gait, his face, his bearing. We sat and talked, the dams down, in a stale underground city café, until the tactful waitresses piled chairs on the marble-topped tables around us as a tacit hint that we should soon be outstaying our welcome.

No set portrait was ever made of him, I think, by any artist less indifferent than the camera. But how vivid are his features in remembrance! His face was fair, long and rather narrow, and in its customary gravity wore an expression rather distant and detached. There was a glint of gold in his sun-baked hair. The eyes, long-lashed and stooping a little beneath the full rounded lids, were of a clear dark blue:

> Some eyes condemn the earth they gaze upon
> Some wait patiently till they know far more
> Than earth can tell them . . .

The lips were finely lined and wide, the chin square. His shoes were to his stature; the hands that had cradled so many wild birds' eggs, and were familiar with every flower in the Southern counties, were powerful and bony; the gestures few; the frame vigorous:

> 'You had a garden
> Of flint and clay, too?' 'True; that was real enough.
> The flint was the one crop that never failed.
> The clay first broke my heart, and then my back;
> And the back heals not . . .'

His smile could be whimsical, stealthy, shy, ardent, mocking, or drily ironical; he seldom laughed. 'When he should laugh the wise man knows full well. For he knows what is truly laughable.' His voice was low and gentle, but musical, with a curious sweetness and hollowness when he sang his old Welsh songs to his children. I have never heard English used so fastidiously and yet so unaffectedly as in his talk. *Style* in talk, indeed, is a rare charm; and it was his. You could listen to it for its own sake, just as for its style solely you can read a book. He must have thought like that; like that he felt. There were things and people, blind, callous, indifferent, veneered, destructive he hated, because he loved life, loved to talk about it, rare and racy, old and charactered. He might avoid, did avoid, what intimidated, chilled, or made him self-conscious; he never condescended. So children and the aged, the unfriended and the free were as natural and welcome to him as swallows under the eaves.

His learning was of men and things at first hand rather than of facts at second or third; of books in his kind rather than of indoor arts and 'literature'. What he gave to a friend in his company was not only himself, but that friend's self made infinitely less clumsy and shallow than usual, and at ease. To be with him in the country was to be in one's own native place, and even a Cockney's starven roots may thirst for the soil. Nobody in this world closely resembling him have I ever had the happiness to meet: others of his friends have said the same thing. So, when he died, a ghost of one's self went away with him; though it need be no mere deceit of one's consciousness that makes the dead more real and clear in their isolation, and in that loving remembrance which, as time goes on in our experience of the world, must number them, not among the few, but among the many.

The only justification for this preface to his poems is its attempt, however slight and partial, to portray their writer as he was to one who knew him in his personal life. Close criticism of them – of their art and craftsmanship – would be as superfluous here as the full appreciation it would be so difficult a delight to try to express. But when it is considered how long and diligently, and at what expense of spirit, Edward Thomas worked as a man of letters; how many books he wrote; how much of his best writing is practically lost in the newspapers that so swiftly seduce the dead past into burying its dead; then it is little less than tragic to think how comparatively unheeded in any public sense was his coming and going. Nevertheless, it is a pious duty to have confidence in the children of this and of succeeding generations. Thomas has true lovers today;

but when the noise of the present is silenced – and the drums and tramplings of the war in which he died – his voice will be heard far more clearly; the words of a heart and mind devoted throughout his life to all that can make the world a decent and natural home for the meek and the lovely, the true, the rare, the patient, the independent and the oppressed.

'. . . And I rose up, and knew that I was tired, and continued my journey . . .'

Appendix 4

GENERAL INTRODUCTION BY R. GEORGE THOMAS
TO *The Collected Poems* (1978)

An understanding of Edward Thomas's poetry is strengthened considerably when the poems are read in the order in which they were composed against the background of his day-to-day life. The close bond between the man and his poetry has been recalled by Walter de la Mare in the Foreword to the *Collected Poems* which first appeared in 1920. Forswearing close criticism of their art and craftsmanship, de la Mare makes a prophecy about their future: 'When the noise of the present is silenced . . . his voice will be heard far more clearly; the words of a heart and mind devoted throughout his life to all that can make the world a decent and natural home for the meek and the lovely, the true, the rare, the patient, the independent and the oppressed.' The elegiac note is coloured by an acute sense of the lost promise of a much-neglected writer. The poems as now presented support de la Mare's claim and, with the aid of quotations in the notes, emphasize a consistent element in Thomas's life as a writer – the search for an understanding of his own nature.[1]

Hints at the intensity with which Thomas conducted this quest are scattered throughout his prose writings. His prose was varied and prolific. Between 1896 and 1915 he wrote nature studies, topographical books, regular reviews, literary criticism, biographies, a series of stories, sketches, and reflections, a semi-autobiographical novel, and a fragment of autobiography. There are many more perceptive comments on the nature and practice of poetry in his prose articles and reviews than those usually quoted from his letters to friends. An anthology of these opinions would show conclusively that Thomas owed little intellectually to Robert Frost when he named him as the 'onlie begetter' of his verse. Although Frost gave

1 For a fuller but incomplete analysis of the poems in chronological order see my *Edward Thomas (Writers of Wales)* (1972), pp. 36–66.

him the necessary spur and confidence to attempt verse writing, Thomas had noted fifteen years earlier (in a long, unsigned article on 'The Frontiers of English Prose' in *Literature*, 23 September 1899) the 'apparent destruction of the boundaries between poetry and prose, and between verse and prose. The point is that not only do most writers use verse and prose, but they treat also in both styles the same subjects, or objects, the same class.' The article is very much an undergraduate essay, but Thomas consistently followed the logic of its argument and devoted much care to the 'prose-poems' which he frequently inserted into his reviews, sketches, and topographical works. This consistency was partly responsible for the declining market for Thomas's personal prose and explains his growing realization of the need both to find a wider audience for poetry and to bring all writing (in prose and verse) closer to the natural springs of colloquial usage.[2] An anthology of his critical comments on poetry would reveal the intellectual firmness of Thomas who is too often presented as a wavering character. The iron dependability of his life as a soldier in France was not the sudden development of a civilian-soldier aged thirty-nine; Thomas's personality, cursed with bouts of melancholic introspection from late adolescence, had a hard centre. This seems to have been concealed from his numerous literary friends, but it is present in the wry ironic comments that conclude the many self-portraits scattered throughout his prose writings. In an article on 'How I Began', commissioned by Holbrook Jackson for *T. P.'s Weekly*, 31 January 1913, Thomas stated clearly his life-long search for an adequate means of expression. He had contributed articles on other poets to *T. P.'s Weekly* during these doldrum twenty-one months, before friendship with Frost, the

2 Before he had met Frost, he argues the case in *The Country* and (at great length) in his *Walter Pater: A Critical Study* (especially on pp. 69, 73, 97–109, and 219–20). His thesis begins: 'For the last hundred years ideas and the material for ideas have come to the reading classes mainly through books and bookish conversation. Their ideas are in advance of their experience, their vocabulary in advance of their ideas, and their eyelids "are a little weary" ' (p. 69). And it leads to his final dissatisfaction with Pater's prose: 'What Pater has attained is an exquisite unnaturalness' (p. 220). This was an unpopular opinion in 1913 when his *Pater* appeared.

apparent loss of livelihood because of the onset of war, and a newly found confidence in himself led to his experiments with verse writing. Some of these articles were later included in *A Literary Pilgrim in England*, published, posthumously in 1917 but completed, as his verse 'began to run', alongside his short critical biography of Keats (1916).[3] Thomas referred derisively to his brief studies of writers in their native surroundings as *'Omes and 'Aunts* – an indication of his attitude to the demands of some publishers' lists.

His views on three contemporary writers (W. H. Hudson, Hardy, and Meredith) anticipate the direction his own poetry would take and the principles he would follow:[4]

In Mr Hudson curiosity is a passion, or rather, it is part of the greater passion of love. He loves what things are . . . What he reverences and loves is the earth, and the earth he knows is, humanly speaking, everlasting.

The general effect [in a Hardy poem] is to aid reality by suggestions of gross and humble simplicity. . . . In a recurring line, like the following, the name gives even a kind of magic reality. . . . Sometimes the place is given, it appears, out of pure fidelity to the fact. He writes no poetry that could suffer by names and dates. . . . For Mr Hardy has really done something to quicken and stouten the sense of past time and generations.

. . . the incidents of walking, as a pleasure, as a joy, as a medicine . . . And the joy of the limbs, the senses, and the brain, during country walks – in certain isolated days – are expressed by Meredith once and for all, with a kind of braced hedonistic Puritanism. But though he loved what he saw and heard and touched, his poetry was never purely sensuous, and it became less and less so. Like Shelley, he felt the moral qualities of Nature. . . . When he spoke of Earth, he meant more than most mean who speak of God. He meant that power which in the open air, in

3 For the use of his *Keats* as a guide to Thomas's conception of the poetic temperament, see my *Edward Thomas*, pp. 20–2, 35.

4 See *A Literary Pilgrim in England*, especially pp. 44–52 (for Meredith), pp. 144–54 (for Hardy), and pp. 190–9 (for Hudson).

poetry, in the company of noble men and women, prompted, strengthened, and could fulfil, the desire of a man to make himself, not a transitory member of a parochial species, but a citizen of the Earth. . . . He seeks a superb health. Nature has inspired him to the search. Nature alone can satisfy it. She seems to him to offer sanity, true perspective.

These enduring themes in Thomas's eighteen years as a writer recur in all his intimate correspondence;[5] they survive intact in his best verse and in the laconic records of his war diary. They inspired one possible title for his selection of poems for Roger Ingpen – *Lob and other Poems* – and they explain the qualified nature of an apparently 'patriotic' alternative title – *The Trumpet and Other Poems*.[6] 'Lob' and 'The Trumpet'; enduring countryside and voluntary response to self-sacrifice; solitary walking and alert acceptance of birds at the Observation Post in No Man's Land; a determined grip on ideals of 'Love' and 'Beauty' with an ironic, almost Puritanical, recognition of lust: these are the antinomies that provide the tension-releasing energy of his best verse.

The double vision extends to his admiration for the deceptive quality of Hudson's style – 'It is in fact, a combination, as curious as it is ripe and profound, of the eloquent and the colloquial, now the one, now the other' – and appears in his ironic comment in *The Country*: 'When a poet writes, I believe he is often only putting into words what such another old man puzzled out among the sheep in a long lifetime'. It enabled this London-bred nature poet to detect that 'The sonnet on Westminster Bridge is not a local poem, but

5 And in the recollections of his friends who tried to set down imperfect records of his talk around 1937 and which I have been able to consult privately. Many of these themes were fully developed in his *Richard Jefferies. His Life and Work* (1909), but the theme of 'Thomas as War Poet' needs full-scale treatment. It is a complex subject, closely integrated with Thomas's rediscovery of self-confidence as a writer of poetry and – because of the tightening of family bonds as a consequence of the war – his reappraisal of the nature of love for his wife, his children, and his parents.
6 Subsequently adopted by Faber and Faber for their Second War selection of his verse in 1940. Evidence for Thomas's attitude to the war is given in the notes to most of his verse. See also my *Edward Thomas*, pp. 23–35.

proves that Wordsworth on a great occasion made no distinction between God-made country and man-made town' and, in an aside on Hilaire Belloc's love of Sussex, to reveal one of the sources of his own newly discovered self-confidence in 1914: 'Well, many a man has made less of things he loves by not being able to make much of himself, the lover.' The uneven quality of some of his verse – particularly before he enlisted in July 1915, and occasionally during his long spell as a map-reading instructor at Hare Hall Camp, Romford – reflects the fierce honesty with which he used verse-writing to uncover the doubts as well as the certainties in his make-up. Yet the tenacious craftsman's exploration of the flexibility of this new medium of expression eventually gave greater depth to his best poems.[7] The jottings of his war diary should prove, if proof were needed, that he continued this self-exploration to the day before his death.

His lifelong struggle as a writer centred around the need to come to terms with his own rifted personality. Particularly after 1910 when he seemed more and more determined to spend less time as a reviewer in order to devote more energy to the writing of sketches, narratives, tales, and natural observations based on his absorbing interest in human life lived in natural surroundings, Thomas appeared to lose touch with the taste of the growing popular audience which was so necessary for commercial success. His letters reveal his distaste for editors and publishers who urged him to become a specialist 'country writer'. He compromised by accepting commissioned topographical books in which, occasionally, he gave

7 See his letter to his American aunt (in the *Eckert Coll.* Eng. lett. d. 281), dated 26 March 1914, complaining about his 'still unsolved problem of being virtually unemployed' and asking for some notes on the *Bhagavadgita*: 'Your letter on the subject of the will was a very interesting as well as a very kind one but I am afraid I am too loose and unstable, also too aimless and lacking in a sense of the whole or of human life outside my own, to profit by any teaching except accidental personal influence. Even ambition would be a help. But I do not possess it. I should like to excel, and I have frittered away much time in various attempts to [~~improve~~] express myself accurately. Stronger than this is my self-obsession and its consequence the [~~satisfaction~~] indulgence in easy simple ever-unsatisfying pleasures.'

hints of those intense moments of perception of the timelessness behind the observed world about which he wished to write. His preserved notebooks indicate that his private writing was as much concerned with people he met in out-of-the-way places as with his own almost Turneresque response to the effects of light and of clouds in his many recorded landscapes. The life of vagabonds – an instructive contrast to the life of a study-bound writer – attracted him throughout his adult life; an extension of this interest partially explains his new-found success as a soldier, once he had learned to conceal his shyness with strangers.

Alongside this fascination with the apparently free life, went a strong habit of analytical introspection that pervades his prose and verse. His was an ironic cast of mind. He refused to be taken in by the idealized picturesque, or the social cosiness of London literary circles, or the popular praise for decadent literary pastiche. Reviewing was a staple source of his income, and his friends refer to most of his criticism as hack drudgery. I prefer to believe that literary criticism was congenial to the side of his temperament that pruned the floweriness of his early prose style, that rejected the fashion for Swinburne and Pater, and continued to advocate the value of Yeats, Masefield, Pound, and Frost against the taste of his friends. And so the wheel came full circle. The despiser of easy, newspaper patriotic verse lived to write about an idealized 'This England', and championed the purity of English words and rhythms in a new, personal, and revivifying manner.

His poetry is much less an expression of one man's attitude to the Great War – although it is precisely that – than a directly phrased *summa* of a lifetime's experience. Little is extenuated in this concern with the quality of life, removed from, but not rejecting, the strains of an urban existence. Without the techniques of modern psychology, Thomas explores the significance of personal relationships and the difficulties that confront any artist who seeks to respond directly to experience when his humanistic faith is minimal because he has no faith in religious or political millennia.

Although he suffered at least three severe bouts of acute depression during his adult life – with little relief from a variety of doctors – Edward Thomas was supported by a trained historical perspective that encouraged him to search the past (of man and nature) for certitudes and parallels, even when his divided self demanded a faith in the future. So, in no simple sense, the onset of war (and his ultimate decision first to enlist and, later, to volunteer for service in France) merged into the discovery of himself as a poet. This writer, who apparently had tried to escape so often from humdrum tasks in search of an ideal world of natural and human beauty, was able to reconcile soldiering and poetry as long as he remained in touch with the secure bases of his most profound affections. This is the special quality of his verse. It is about Steep, about Wales, about the long-lived-in Heart of England, about the lost ideal world. As Walter de la Mare divined, it is personal to an intense degree. At its best, with little self-pity and without self-absorption, it is both a remarkable response to war and a veiled act of self-discovery. In 1913 Edward Thomas had abandoned the manuscript of a book on *Ecstasy* because, one suspects, his intellectual detachment shied away from the unidentified unknown. In his verse he balanced acceptance and affirmation against defiance and defeat; while exploring the complementary drives of desire and love, he balanced a tense self-discipline against fears of the morrow.

Index of First Lines